CHINNAMASTĀ

BUDDHIST TRADITION SERIES

VOLUME 22

Chinnamastā

The Aweful Buddhist and Hindu Tantric Goddess

ELISABETH ANNE BENARD

MOTILAL BANARSIDASS PUBLISHERS
PRIVATE LIMITED • DELHI

*4th Reprint: **Delhi, 2017***
First Indian Edition: Delhi, 1994

ISBN: 978-81-208-1065-5 (Cloth)
ISBN: 978-81-208-1748-7 (Paper)

MOTILAL BANARSIDASS
41 U.A. Bungalow Road, Jawahar Nagar, Delhi 110 007
8 Mahalaxmi Chamber, 22 Bhulabhai Desai Road, Mumbai 400 026
203 Royapettah High Road, Mylapore, Chennai 600 004
236, 9th Main III Block, Jayanagar, Bengaluru 560 011
8 Camac Street, Kolkata 700 017
Ashok Rajpath, Patna 800 004
Chowk, Varanasi 221 001

Printed in India

by RP Jain at NAB Printing Unit,
A-44, Naraina Industrial Area, Phase I, New Delhi–110028
and published by JP Jain for Motilal Banarsidass Publishers (P) Ltd,
41 U.A. Bungalow Road, Jawahar Nagar, Delhi-110007

Foreword

Elisabeth Benard's work on the Hindu-Buddhist goddess Chinnamastā is a product of indefatigable energy, not overlooking any lead from Sanskrit and Tibetan texts or from knowledgeable informants. So to cast light on a goddess that was strangely obscure and yet implicates any Indian goddess properly to be called wondrous or arousing of awe.

Although completed in the United States, her treatise does not follow a History of Religions approach with a baggage of technical terms. Besides, Dr. Benard avoids the guessing and speculations that characterized some previous references to this goddess. Throughout she employs a direct communication with the reader while soberly basing her conclusions on stated sources.

One welcome feature of Benard's book is the translation of much material from the *Śākta Pramoda*. Another fine feature is the treatment of the goddess's names, both the 108 and 1,000 list. Her classification of the names by the *rasas* of Hindu drama is probably unique.

This work is a solid contribution to the theories of the Hindu and Buddhist Tantras and their symbolism, in particular as related to the goddess.

New York — ALEX WAYMAN

Contents

List of Illustrations

Preface

When I tell a Buddhist or Hindu scholar that I am writing on Chinnamastā, many scholars shrug their shoulders and say, "I am sorry but I never heard of her." Others know her name but no more. Then I show them an illustration of Chinnamastā. Some of them gasp but others are intrigued. A very small group of scholars exclaim, "Tell me what you have found out; I have been trying to understand her for years." When I first saw Chinnamastā, I was mystified and somewhat horrified. I asked myself, "Who is this goddess who is decapitated, holds a severed head, and drinks blood gushing from her neck?" Eager to forget this vision, I tried to find a category in which I could file her. No category was appropriate; she was not a mother goddess, a goddess of prosperity, or even a wrathful manifestation of the Great Goddess. She defied classification. Unable to 'file her away', I tried to rationalize her unique appearance. Who did she represent or what message was she expressing? No logical explanation became evident. By this time, my horror was transformed into fascination and I kept thinking about Chinnamastā. Everyday I asked myself, "Who is Chinnamastā; why is she depicted in this way?"

Unable to penetrate her mysterious message, I began to look for books or articles about her. Realizing that only a few articles were written about her, I decided to attempt a comprehensive study on Chinnamastā. Moreover, I realized that this research could only be done in India in order to find the necessary texts and to meet scholars who would discuss her.

I would like to thank the American Institute of Indian Studies for providing a doctoral research grant 1986-87 to study in Varanasi and Sarnath, India. Many of the manuscripts and books which discussed Chinnamastā could only be found in India or Nepal. Most of the texts are *sādhanas* and many of the *sādhanas* are from the 'Dhīḥ Project' established by the late Jagannāth Upādhyāya and the Director of the Central Institute of Higher Tibetan Studies, Samdong Rimpoche, in Sarnath. They graciously permitted me to copy all their manuscripts on Chinnamastā and Pandit Vraj Vallabh Dwivedī, present Director of the 'Dhīḥ Project', spent many months discussing these manuscripts and the 'Chinnamastātantra' of the *Śākta Pramoda*. I would like to thank everyone in the 'Dhīḥ Project' for all their invaluable help and insightful discussions. Also I would like to thank Hemendra Chakravorty of Varanasi for commenting on numerous *sādhanas* and ritual texts on Chinnamastā, as well as lending me books from his private library. This work could not have been done without the help of numerous people in North America, Europe, India, Nepal, and Tibet; I thank everyone for their help. I especially thank two *kalyāṇamitras*, Diana Cutler and Karma Lekshe Tsomo. Also I appreciate the financial support for publication from the Center of Arts and Humanities and the University Research Council at the University of Hawaii at Manoa. I thank Mary Slusser for permission to reproduce the detail of Chinnamuṇḍā from the Vajravārāhī painting (plate 3).

My greatest gratitude is to four people who encouraged, inspired, and guided me through all these tumultuous years of trying to understand Chinnamastā. I thank my husband, Nima Dorjee, who applies his wonderful qualities of the wise old person and the playful child at the appropriate times. I thank His Holiness Sakya Trizin, whose vast wisdom coupled with compassion elucidates the subtlety of Tibetan Buddhism, and the late Dezhung Rimpoche, the epitome of Avalokiteśvara. To one who can be as enigmatic, yet as profound as Chinnamastā—Alex Wayman—I thank you for your creativity, uncanny perceptions, love for a good debate, exactness, kindness and passion for the arcane and the subtle.

Honolulu, Hawaii
September 1991

ELISABETH ANNE BENARD

Introduction

Chinnamastā/Chinnamuṇḍā, the uncanny Buddhist-Hindu Goddess, explodes one's limited understanding of the phenomenal world in order to reveal unconditioned reality. Both her names mean the "one with the severed-head" because she holds *her own* head in her hand. The *sādhana* in the *Sādhanamālā* describes Chinnamuṇḍā as one "who is of yellow colour, who holds in her left hand her own severed head which she severed with her own scimitar (*kartṛ*) held in her right hand . . . . She is nude . . . streams of blood issuing from the severed body fall into the mouth of her severed head and into the mouths of the two Yoginīs on either side of her." This paradoxical goddess, overwhelms and initially frightens. She pushes one beyond dualities into the realm of the unconditioned and unconditional—a spiritual experience eagerly sought but frightening and repelling when actually experienced. One is reminded of Arjuna's vision of Kṛṣṇa as God in the *Bhagavad Gītā*, Arjuna exclaims:

> Having seen what was never seen before, I am astonished, and my heart is shaken with fear. Show me, O God, that same form of Yours (as before)! Be merciful, Lord of Gods, Refuge of the World! (11:45)

Arjuna's ordinary reality is exploded into a million parts which destroyed the 'human-constructed' limits. This experience of unconditioned reality is both marvellous and frightening; later in this book Chinnamastā's hundred and eight names and one thousand names will illustrate this paradoxical and awe-inspiring combination of the marvellous and furious. Rudolf Otto described the nature of unconditioned reality as that which makes a person stand in awe (*tremendum*) and simultaneously fascinates one (*fascinas*). Chinnamastā is an aweful goddess in this sense.

She is also a paradoxical one who non-verbally indicates unconditioned reality. Practitioners apply this teaching to become liberated from cyclic existence. Unfortunately, one primarily finds Chinnamastā in sensational 'Tantric art' books which portray Tantra as exotic sexual practices or degenerate perversions. In these books explanations of Chinnamastā are brief and superficial. In reality, however, Chinnamastā indicates a transcendence of the ordinary or portrays the ordinary as extraordinary.

There is a famous story about the Buddha who once taught in an enigmatic way, by holding a flower. Everyone waited patiently for the teaching to begin; only Mahākāśyapa smiled. The Buddha smiled with him. The teaching was concluded. An ordinary flower evoked the experience of understanding the non-duality of ordinary/extraordinary. Chinnamastā uses her ordinary body in an extraordinary manner; she is able to function with a severed head.

Chinnamastā, this 'aweful' goddess, is a Tantric goddess *par excellence.* A single definition of Tantra is very difficult because of the variety of Tantric traditions existing in the world—from Kashmir Śaivism and Hindu Śākta, etc. in India to a variety of Buddhist Tantras in Nepal, Tibet, and Japan. Many contemporary Hindu ascetics define Tantra as action done with the body (*tanū*) for the purpose of protecting/bringing about release (*tra*). One etymology of Tantra divides the word into two roots, *tan* to stretch or expand and *tra* to save or protect. By combining these two roots, Tantra means the increase of methods available in order to liberate oneself from cyclic existence. Ideally, these methods should be efficacious and expedient. Furthermore, in researching about Tantra, one realizes the importance of the human body as the principal instrument for liberation rather than an impediment as propounded in other traditions.

The body consists of numerous levels of subtlety and all Tantric traditions agree that a subtle body is composed of subtle channels (*nāḍīs*) and winds (*prāṇa*), which circulate in the subtle channels. Furthermore they agree on the existence of three principal subtle channels, two ancillary ones which crisscross around a central channel. The subtle winds course through the two ancillary channels but in most people the subtle wind cannot enter the central channel because the two ancillary ones form knots at the points where they crisscross it. As long as the subtle winds cannot enter the central one, one experiences the duality of ordinary reality. By yogic methods one learns to untie these 'knots' thereby opening the central channel. When the subtle winds course through the central channel, the dichotomy of conditioned and unconditioned disappears. I would argue that Chinnamastā anthropomorphically represents this central channel, her two attendants represent the two ancillary subtle channels; their feet are intertwined with Chinnamastā's thereby replicating the two ancillary channels which are intertwined with the central channel near the navel. Moreover, there are three bloodstreams and if correctly depicted the right bloodstream enters the right attendant's mouth, the left bloodstream the left attendant's mouth, and the central one is drunk by Chinnamastā. Since the attendants drink only from the right or left respectively, this indicates that they do not know the yogic process of manipulating the winds into the central channel. They experience the duality of ordinary reality. In contrast Chinnamastā, a great yoginī, drinks her own blood from the central channel, thereby experiencing the collapse of duality. Thus Chinnamastā is the Tantric goddess *par excellence* because she represents the essential instrument and method of achieving liberation through the Tantric-yogic process of the manipulation of the subtle winds coursing through the subtle channels.

Who is she? Her legends are few but consistencies are apparent throughout the diverse material ranging from the Mahāsiddha and Tantric tradition to the Purāṇas. Among the Hindu legends, Chinnamastā is Śiva's consort and in the *Śākta Mahābhāgvata Purāṇa*, she is one of the Daśa Mahāvidyas (ten great knowledge goddesses). In the Buddhist tradition she is connected with the Mahāsiddha tradition, especially the female Mahāsiddhas, Mekhalā, Kanakhalā, and most importantly, Lakṣmīṅkarā. Many of Chinnamuṇḍā *sādhanas* included Lakṣmīṅkarā in their transmission lineages. In both the traditions she is an unusual emanation of a popular goddess: in Hinduism Durgā; and in Buddhism Vajravārāhī-Vajrayoginī.

Various scholars assert a different origin for her. Some scholars, such as B. Bhattacharyya, hold that she is originally a Buddhist creation and is incorporated by the Hindus. Some Hindu scholars do not even consider the possibility for a non-Hindu origin, such as Shankaranarayanan who claim a Vedic antecedent. Since Chinnamastā is a rare form of a popular goddess, few know much about her. When I visited a Hindu temple dedicated to Chinnamastā, the ritual priests, whose family have been the priests for centuries, were surprised and delighted that Chinnamastā was worshipped in Nepal, Tibet, and Mongolia. Likewise, the Tibetan Buddhist practitioners wanted to know more about the Hindu Chinnamastā. Both Buddhism and Hinduism have Tantric traditions and the nascence of Tantra is obscure. Extant Buddhist texts of Chinnamuṇḍā indicate an earlier origin than the Hindu ones; however, oral teachings must have preceded the texts. With these difficulties of overlapping between the two traditions and the uncertainty of the birth of Tantra, a definitive Hindu or Buddhist origin of Chinnamastā cannot be asserted.

This is the first monograph which examines Chinnamastā's rituals, her names and forms (*nāmarūpa*) and their symbolism by comparing and contrasting her *sādhanas* (spiritual practices) in Hinduism and Buddhism. The entire Hindu 'Chinnamastātantra' section from the *Śākta Pramoda*, the Buddhist 'Chinnamuṇḍā Vajravārāhī sādhana' and 'Trikāyavajrayoginī stuti' are translated for the first time into English. Since Chinnamastā is a rare goddess, her texts were not popularized or made 'fashionable' according to the dictates of a particular group at a particular time. The earliest extant texts date from the ninth and tenth centuries—a time when Hindu and Buddhist Tantras were developing under common influences and in the same places in India. Having such texts about Chinnamastā/Chinnamuṇḍā from these centuries, one can begin to understand the mutuality of a general Tantric tradition and the exclusivity of a particular Hindu or Buddhist Tantric tradition. Hence the study, not only examines Chinnamastā, but also attempts to understand what is a Tantric tradition.

Invocation

Homage to Goddess Chinnamastā

Yajñarūpaṃ yajñadātrīṃ yajñagrahaṇākāriṇīm /
mokṣadām sarvasattvebhyaśchinnamastāṃ namāmyaham //

I pay homage to Chinnamastā who is the sacrifice; the sacrificer, and the recipient of the sacrifice. May she liberate all beings.

Homage to Chinnamuṇḍā

rDo rje phag mo dbu bchad mai' /
sgrub thabs 'bri klog byed pai' dges /
ma gyur sems can thams cad kyis /
'khor gsum mi dmigs rtogs par shog //

Homage to Chinnamuṇḍā Vajravārāhī . May she help all sentient beings to realize that the offerer, the offering, and the recipient of the offering do not ultimately exist.

Chapter 1

Legends and Origin of Chinnamastā/ Chinnamuṇḍā

The study of Chinnamastā's legends and origin is a fine example of the fluidity of the Hindu and Buddhist Tantric traditions. In the Hindu tradition Chinnamastā is associated with the popular goddess Durgā, as one of her ten manifestations known as the Daśa Mahāvidyās.[1] The Sanskrit word *mahāvidyā* is a combination of the adjective *mahā* meaning great or supreme and the noun *vidyā* which is from the verbal root *vid* meaning to know, to learn, to ascertain, to experience. (*Vid* is a direct cognate with the English verb 'to wit'.) By combining *mahā* with *vidyā*, one can translate the word *mahāvidyā* as supreme knowledge.[2] From the Hindu perspective supreme knowledge is soteriological, i.e. knowledge which reveals the way of releasing oneself from the bonds of cyclic existence or *saṃsāra*. The ultimate goal of all Hindus is to achieve *mokṣa* or liberation from the snares of *saṃsāra*. Thus as a Mahāvidyā, Chinnamastā embodying this essential knowledge, helps beings in achieving *mokṣa*.

MAHĀBHĀGAVATA PURĀṆA

In chapter eight of the tenth-century Śākta *Mahābhāgavata Purāṇa* we find the earliest account of the Daśa Mahāvidyās.[3] In the *Mahābhāgavata Purāṇa* the popular Hindu God Śiva extolls the glory of the Hindu Goddess Durgā in her multiple manifestations to Sage Nārada.[4] Chapter four through chapter twelve relate Durgā's manifestation as Satī, daughter of Prajāpati Dakṣa. In chapter four she weds Śiva and in chapter eight Śiva recounts to Sage Nārada Satī's insistence on attending the great sacrifice (*yajña*) performed by her father. Though this legend of Dakṣa's great sacrifice is well known from the fourth century, in this version the Devī (the great Goddess) eclipses Śiva's greatness as the more potent force. In the beginning of chapter eight Satī is portrayed as a dutiful Hindu wife asking her husband's permission to attend her father's sacrifice. Since they were not invited by Dakṣa, Śiva insisted that she should not go. However, Satī insisted that they did not need an invitation because she was Dakṣa's daughter. Since all entreaties failed, Satī decided to remind Śiva that she was no ordinary woman but a powerful being with awesome aspects. Śiva narrated the confrontation to Sage Nārada as follows:[5]

> Instantly her eyes reddened with anger. Satī thought (to herself), "Śiva had received me as his wife by my choice but today he censured and slighted me. I will show him my power." Seeing the goddess with her lips trembling with anger and her eyes blazing like the conflagration at the end of an aeon, Śiva closed his eyes. Suddenly she displayed her terrible teeth in her fierce mouth and laughed. Observing this, Śiva became very afraid and trembled with an averted face. With much difficulty, he reopened his eyes and beheld a terrible form. Abandoning her golden clothes, Satī's skin became discolored. She was nude with dishevelled hair, a lolling tongue and four arms; her black body was covered with sweat. Decorated with a garland of skulls, she was exceedingly fierce and had a frightful roar. On her head was a crescent moon and a crown as luminous as the rising sun. In this terrific form blazing with her own effulgence, she roared and stood in all her glory before Śiva. Bewildered with fright, Śiva forsook her and trembling with an averted face, he fled in all directions as if deluded. With a terrific laugh, Satī roared and said to him, "Don't be afraid." Hearing these sounds, terrified Śiva swiftly fled in all directions. Seeing her husband overpowered by fear, Satī became merciful and having only the desire to restrain him, she appeared in a transcendent form in each of the ten directions. In whichever direction Śiva fled, she was there. Seeing one terrible form, Śiva ran in another direction in order to escape but he was always confronted by another one. Śiva remained still and shut his eyes. When he reopened them, he saw before him the Dark One (Śyāmā which is another name for Kālī), whose smiling face was like a fully-opened lotus. Nude with large breasts, with fierce, wide eyes, dishevelled hair and four arms, she blazed like ten million suns as she stood in the southern direction. Seeing Śyāmā, Śiva overcome with fear asked, "Who are you, O Dark One? Where is my beloved Satī?"
>
> Satī replied, "Śiva, do you not see that I am Satī who is before you. Kālī, Tārā, Lokeśikamalā, Bhuvaneśvarī, Chinnamastā, Ṣoḍaśī, Tripurasundarī, Bagalāmukhī, Dhūmavatī, and Mātaṅgī are my forms."[6]
>
> Śiva spoke, "If you are satisfied with me, O Supportress of the World (Jagaddhātrī), please tell me clearly which form is whose?"
>
> Satī replied, "The black one with the fierce eyes who is in front of you is Kālī. In the zenith is the dark green Mahāvidyā Tārā whose nature is Mahākāla (the great Black One). To your right (in the east) the very frightening goddess with the severed head is Chinnamastā, O Magnanimous One. To your left (in the west) is Bhuvaneśvarī. The one behind you (in the north) is the destroyer of foes, Bagalā(mukhī). In the southeast

> corner in the widow's form is Mahāvidyā Dhūmavatī, O Maheśvara; and in the southwest is Tripurasundarī. In the northwest corner is the Mahāvidyā Mātaṅgī, in the northeast is the Mahāvidyā Ṣoḍaśī, and at the nadir is Bhairavī. O Śiva, do not be afraid; these are my supreme forms and pervade within all my other forms.[7]

The chapter continues with the proper mode of worshipping them with *mantra* (mystical syllables), *yantra* (mystical diagrams), *pūjā* (ritual worship), *homa* (fire offering ritual), *puraścaraṇa* (repetition of the name with fire offerings), *stotra* (praises), and *kavaca* (protection syllables).[8] Whoever worships in this fashion will attain the special abilities to destroy (enemies), to expel, to agitate, to bewilder, to put to flight, to stupefy, and to create enmity.[9] The chapter concludes:

> I am your dearest and you are my dear husband. I shall go to my father's sacrifice in order to destroy his pride. Even if you do not go, you should give me your permission. This is my greatest desire. Whether you give me permission or not, I shall go and destroy the sacrifice of my father Prajāpati Dakṣa.
>
> Śiva spoke to Sage Nārada, "Hearing her words, I was paralyzed with fear and said to fierce-eyed Kālī, 'I know that you are Parameśvarī (Supreme Goddess), the best and complete Prakṛti. Please forgive me for what I uttered in delusion. You are the primordial, supreme knowledge which exists in everything. You are abiding in every particle, autonomous and you are the supreme power (*śakti*). You are beyond all correct and incorrect actions. If you wish to go, O Satī, in order to destroy the sacrifice, what power do I have to prevent you! In delusion, whatever I said as a husband, please forgive me. O Satī, do what pleases you.' "
>
> Satī, the mother of the universe, with a slight smile spoke. "O Lord, you stay here with your attendants. I am going to my father's sacrifice." Having said this, the form of Mahāvidyā Tārā in the zenith and all other eight forms merged into the form of Kālī. Then Satī in the form of Kālī went in a bejewelled chariot drawn by 10,000 lions to her father's sacrifice.[10]

This episode in the *Mahābhāgavata Purāṇa* states that the Daśa Mahāvidyās are Durgā's supreme forms and pervade all other forms.[11] Mahāvidyā Chinnamastā, who is in the east, is described as a frightening goddess holding her own severed head. In Hinduism, the eastern direction is an auspicious one in contrast to the southeast direction which is inauspicious because of its connection with the realm of the dead. The eastern direction symbolizes regeneration or a renewal, such as a new day beginning in the eastern direction. Chinnamastā has similar connotations of renewal and being beyond death. Just as Uṣas, the Vedic goddess of dawn "is young, being born again and again, though ancient; shining with a uniform hue, she wastes away the life of mortals" (*Ṛgveda* 1.92.10) and "as she has shone in former days, so she shines now and will shine in the future, never ageing, immortal" (1.113:13-15),[12] similarly Chinnamastā has this potential for renewal and the quality of being beyond death.

Chinnamastā does not have Vedic antecedents; however, these praises to the Vedic Uṣas illustrate how the eastern direction is associated with auspiciousness and renewal. Furthermore, by this association with the east, Chinnamastā represents the aspects of the goddess symbolizing transition and cyclic renewal—the continuous process of creation, preservation, destruction, and re-creation. As Uṣas does not age nor decay, Chinnamastā, even with a decapitated head, remains perpetually an optimum sixteen-year-old unaffected by her unusual circumstances. Though decapitated she defies death and remains a potent force in the universe. Seeing one aspect of the sun at dawn, we see one aspect of the Goddess as Chinnamastā. Thus Chinnamastā's association with the east indicates auspicious renewal of the process of life and death.

THE ŚĀKTA PĪṬHAS

In the *Śākta Pīṭhas* Sircar states that this story of Satī and her death has been retold and elaborated in the Indian literature, such as in Kālīdāsa's *Kumārasaṁbhava* (I, 21), the *Devībhāgavata Purāṇa* (VII, chap.30), and *Kālīkā Purāṇa* (chap.18) wherein inconsolable Śiva slung Satī's body over his shoulder and danced the wild destructive Tāṇḍava dance.[13] The gods, fearing the destruction of the world, asked Viṣṇu to intervene and pleaded with Śiva to stop this dance of grief. Overcome by sadness, Śiva did not stop. Viṣṇu with his discus cut off parts of Satī's body. As Śiva danced, the place where each part of the Satī's body fell in India, is known as a *śākta pīṭha*, a holy seat of the goddess. In Sircar's extensive list of *śātka pīṭhas*, Chinnamastā is not included.[14] However, at a temple dedicated to Chinnamastā in Cintapūrṇī, Himachal Pradesh, the ritual priests (*pujārī*) stated that this temple is indeed the *pīṭha* where Satī's forehead (Skt. *mastaka*) fell. Though no textual proof can confirm this, the devotees, who come to this temple, do believe that this is the *śākta pīṭha* of the goddess's forehead (*mastaka*). While the date of establishing this Cintapūṃī temple is unclear, currently it is an important Devī temple among the Devī worshippers who make pilgrimages to Himachal Pradesh.[15] Thus, Chinnamastā or Chinnamastakā, which literally means "the severed head or foreheaded one", is identified with the Great Goddess as part of Satī, as well as one of the Daśa Mahāvidyās.

In the *Śākta Pīṭhas* there is the interesting correspondence of the Daśa Mahāvidyās with the ten avatars of Viṣṇu. Sircar states that the Daśa

Mahāvidyās are a "late medieval Śākta adaptation of the Daśāvatāra conception",[16] and he cites the *Guhyātiguhya Tantra* as giving the correspondence between the ten avatars of Viṣṇu and the ten Mahāvidyās:

> Kṛṣṇa and Kālī, Rāma and Tārā, Narasiṃha and Chinnamastā, Vāmana and Bhuvaneśvarī, Paraśurāma and Sundarī, Matsya and Dhūmavātī, Kūrma and Bagalā, Balarāma and Bhairavī, Buddha and Mahālakṣmī, Kālki and Durgā.[17]

This *Guhyātiguhya Tantra* list does not seem to be a traditional list; the boar incarnation is omitted and both Kṛṣṇa and Balarāma are included. Since the boar avatar is one of the oldest avatars, and the legend is mentioned in the *Taittirīya Saṃhitā* and the *Śatapatha Brāhmaṇa*, it is surprising that he is omitted here.[18] Moreover, the uncommon inclusion of both Kṛṣṇa and Balarāma (not to be confused with Rāma or Paraśurāma) on the same list and the omission of two of the usual Daśa Mahāvidyās, Kamalā and Mātaṅgī, are surprising. A more traditional list can be found in the *Muṇḍamālā*:

> Kṛṣṇa and Kālī, Rāma and Tāriṇī, Varāha and Bhuvanā, Narasiṃha and Bhairavī, Vāmana and Dhūmavātī, Bhṛgukula and Chinnā, Matsya and Kamalā, Kūrma and Bagalāmukhī, Buddha and Mātaṅgī, Kālikā and Ṣoḍaśī.[19]

The Tantric texts containing a correspondence between the ten avatars of Viṣṇu and the ten Mahāvidyās are few and are not well known texts.[20] Kinsley disagrees with Sircar, saying, "The ten Mahāvidāys, however, are more than a Śākta version of the Vaiṣṇava ten avatars, or at least the Mahāvidyās differ significantly from the avatars in appearance and function."[21]

Neither the *Guhyātiguhya Tantra* nor the *Muṇḍamālā Tantra* explains this correspondence of the Daśa Mahāvidyās and the Viṣṇu's avatars. However, one may speculate why there is a correspondence of Narasiṃha and Chinnamastā in the *Guhyātiguhya Tantra*. In Narasiṃha legend, Narasiṃha had to defeat the leader of the *asuras* (rivals to the gods), Hiraṇyakaśipu, who had received a boon which made him almost invincible. His boon provided that he was never to be killed by "the striking and throwing of weapons of my enemies, thunderbolts . . . by water or fire . . . free from the threats of gods, *daitya*, seers, *siddha*, and whatever other beings you have created . . . not be slain in heaven, on earth, in the daytime, at night, from neither above nor below. In order to kill Hiraṇyakaśipu, Viṣṇu became neither man nor beast but a combination of the two, a man-lion, and killed him with his claws at sunset which was neither day nor night.

Examining this myth, one sees the importance of the liminal quality which is "neither this or that". Viṣṇu became neither a man nor a lion, killing at sunset which was neither day nor night. This ambiguous combination of the best of both the human and animal realms enhanced Viṣṇu's supreme power, rather than diminished it. Chinnamastā epitomizes this ambiguity by her arresting form in which she is alive, yet decapitated. She has the power of being invulnerable to death. Being beyond the cycle of birth and death, she can help others surmount cyclic existence. As Narasiṃha is a form of Viṣṇu who defies categorization and is more potent for being beyond categorization, so is Chinnamastā who challenges classification by her liminal quality of transcending birth and death.[22]

The correspondence between Chinnamastā and Paraśurāma (Bhṛgukula) from the *Muṇḍamālā*'s list is an interesting one. Paraśurāma is the son of Reṇukā who is equated by some to be another name for the Goddess Chinnamastā.[23] In the *Mahābhārata* (3.117.5-19), Reṇukā, the wife of Jamadagni, observed the king of celestial musicians, Citraratha, in lustful enjoyment with the heavenly *apsarā*. Having the desire to enjoy her husband in a similar fashion, she lost her normal brilliance emanating from her virtuous feelings. Jamadagni, seeing this loss of brilliance and learning of its cause through his meditation, ordered his eldest son to kill his mother, but the son refused. Of Jamadagni's five-sons only the youngest, Paraśurāma, consented to kill his mother on the condition that she would be reborn purified. He performed the deed and, not remembering what had occurred, Reṇukā returned to life pure and resplendent. In this episode Reṇukā is considered a *chinnamastā*, one with a severed head. We note, however, that in this instance Reṇukā was a passive recipient of the beheading and not the Goddess Chinnamastā who actively and consciously severed her own head.

In *Kalyāṇa*, Vasudeva Agrawala interpreted esoterically the Reṇukā myth.[24] *Reṇu* or *Reṇukā* means 'semen'. Her five sons are the five *cakras* of the body and Paraśurāma represents the smallest *cakra*, the *viśuddha* (lit. very pure) *cakra*, located at the throat.[25] The forest where Citraratha and his nymphs played symbolizes the mind as an abode of lust. A mind stimulated by sexual energy prevents a yogi from establishing mastery over himself. The only way to gain control is by burning the lust and bringing the semen up to the fifth *cakra*, the *viśuddha cakra*. This association of Paraśurāma with the *viśuddha cakra* helps one in understanding an esoteric significance of Chinnamastā's severed throat. It is exactly at this *cakra* that one can gain mastery over oneself, unaffected by lust. Chinnamastā depicted as standing over a couple in sexual union symbolizes her invulnerability to the sway of sexual passion and thereby she is capable of bringing the 'blood' up to her *viśuddha cakra*. This ability signifies that Chinnamastā is a masterful *yogin*. Thus in these two Tantras, Chinnamastā's association with Narasiṃha or with Paraśurāma is an esoteric one on many levels.

In the *Prāṇatoṣiṇītantra*, a compilation of the Tantric texts,[26] there is a story of the origin of Chinnamastā from the *Nārada Pañcarātra*:

> One day Pārvatī went to bathe in the Mandākinī river (above Haridvar, U.P.) with her attendants Jayā and Vijayā. After bathing, the great goddess' colour became black because she was sexually aroused. After some time, her two attendants asked her, "Give us some food. We are hungry." She replied, "I shall give you food but please wait." After a while, again they asked her. She replied, "Please wait, I am thinking about some matters." Waiting a while, they implored her, "You are the mother of the universe. A child asks everything from her mother. The mother gives her children not only food but also coverings for the body. So that is why we are praying to you for food. You are known for your mercy; please give us food." Hearing this, the consort of Śiva told them that she would give them anything when they reached home. But again her two attendants, Ḍākinī and Varṇinī begged her, "We are overpowered with hunger, O Mother of the Universe! Give us food so we may be satisfied, O Merciful One, Bestower of Boons and Fulfiller of Desires."[27]

Hearing this true statement, the merciful goddess smiled and severed her head with her fingernails.[28] As soon as she severed her head, her head fell on the palm of her left hand. Three bloodstreams emerged from her throat; the left and right fell respectively into the mouths of her flanking attendants and the central fell into her mouth. After performing this, all were satisfied and later returned home. (From this act) Pārvatī became known as Chinnamastā.[29]

Also in the *Prāṇatoṣiṇītantra*, one finds a similar story of Chinnamastā's origin from the *Svatantratantra*. Śiva narrates:

> I shall tell you of the emergence of Chinnamastā, Tārā, and Kālīkā. In the Kṛta Yuga on Mt. Kailāsa, the best of mountains, Mahāmāyā was engaged in Mahāvrata with me. At the time of my seminal emission, she appeared fierce and from her body two *śaktīs* emerged who became her two attendants known as Ḍākinī and Varṇinī. One day Caṇḍanāyikā with her two attendants went to the bank of the Puṣpabhadrā river [Bengal?]. When it was noon, her hungry attendants asked Caṇḍikā, "Please give us food." Hearing this, the smiling and auspicious Caṇḍikā looked in all directions and severed her head. With the left bloodstream, she satisfied

> Ḍākinī, with the right one, she satisfied Varṇinī and from the central one, she drank her own blood. After playing in this way, she replaced her head on her body and assumed her original form. At dusk, they returned home. When I saw her pale appearanee, I suspected that she was abused by another. This infuriated me. From this anger a portion of me arose and became known as Krodha Bhairava. This happened on the day of Virarātri. Thus Chinnamastā was born on Virarātri.[30]

These two similar stories explain the emergence of Chinnamastā as a form of Śiva's consort. The *Nārada Pañcarātra* story emphasizes the greatness of Chinnamastā eulogized by her two attendants: "O Mother of the Universe, O Merciful One, Bestower of Boons and Fulfiller of Desires . . . ." This story stresses Chinnamastā's mercy and power in feeding her two attendants with her own blood. The *Svatantratantra* story, which is also centered on the theme of feeding her attendants, includes many ancillary details which are lacking in the *Nārada Pañcarātra* story. The *Nārada Pañcarātra* story states that Pārvatī became black through sexual arousal but there is no specific explanation why she became sexually aroused or any continuation of this idea in this story, whereas the *Svatantratantra* story begins and ends with this idea. Moreover, the *Svatantratantra* story explains the emergence of Chinnamastā's two attendants, the Krodha Bhairava form of Śiva, and Śiva's consort form as Chinnamastā, as well as explaining that all this occurred on the night of Virarātri. A third important detail is that the *Svatantratantra* story states, "After playing in this way . . . ." In Hinduism, this concept of *līlā* which can be understood as divine play, ease, or 'child's play', appearance, charm and pretence.[31] Also she looked in all directions and continued to smile as she severed her head. This indicates a sense of spatial and temporal pervasiveness or power which transcends space and time. In this suspended moment destruction and creation occur simultaneously because she decapitates herself and feeds her attendants and herself. Mircea Eliade referred to such an event as *coincidentia oppositorum* and as a special feature of divinity. Eliade stated that "the actual structure of the divinity . . . transcends all attributes and reconciles all contraries."[32] Chinnamastā displays her divinity by such act, and demonstrates that she was 'playing' and was unaffected except for a temporary paleness. Thus, the *Svatantratantra* story presupposes that the readers are familiar with the story of Chinnamastā's origin but includes other details which are less familiar, whereas, the *Nārada Pañcarātra* story aims at extolling and praising the greatness of Chinnamastā.

Both H. Bhattacharya in *Hinduder Devdevī* and P. Pal in *Hindu Religion and Iconology* theorize about the *Nārada Pañcarātra* story in the *Prāṇatoṣiṇītantra*. H. Bhattacharya states that Chinnamastā symbolizes the incomplete Dakṣa sacrifice where Dakṣa was beheaded by Śiva's attendants. Since Śiva destroyed the sacrifice, the consort of Śiva, who is the nature of the *yajña* (sacrifice), also has a severed head (*chinnamastā*).[33] P. Pal does not accept Bhattacharya's theory and presents his explanation as follows:

> The obvious implication here is of primal sacrifice and renewal of creation. The goddess sacrifices herself, and her blood, drunk by her attendants, renews or resuscitates the universe . . . . Therefore beheading her own head is a temporary expedient to provide food and appears to be a more sanguinary manifestation of the goddess as Śākambharī and Annapūrṇā.[34]

Both Bhattacharya and Pal interpret the theme of the story as a sacrifice. The Hindu pantheon abounds with munificent goddesses, such as Lakṣmī, Annapūrṇā, and the more recent Santoṣīmā, who are expected to fulfil their promises or meet the demands made by their worshippers, just as Ḍākinī and Varṇinī expected Pārvatī to feed them. But I am unaware of any other goddess who decapitates herself in order to feed her attendants and herself and then replaces her head on her body after the act is completed. This is a unique feature of Chinnamastā. In the *Bṛhadāraṇyaka Upaniṣad* (1.4.6.) it states, "The whole (world) is just food and the eater of food. (*Etāvad vā idaṃ sarvaṃ annaṃ caivānnādaś ca.*)" In these legends of Chinnamastā, one sees both aspects of food and the eater of food in both dualistic and singular ways. In the dualistic way Chinnamastā is the food for her two attendants and they are the eaters of food. In the singular way Chinnamastā is both the food and the eater of food, thereby symbolizing the whole world by this act of being devoured and the devourer. The dichotomy of receiver and giver or object and subject collapses into one. Chinnamastā is not only the giver and the receiver, but also the given—she is the sacrificer, the sacrificed, and the recipient of the sacrifice. She is the sacrificer by decapitating herself, the sacrificed by the act of beheading, and the recipient of the sacrifice by drinking the blood. Thus Chinnamastā embodies the complete sacrificial process which symbolizes the entire world through its process of creation, destruction, and re-creation.

"CUT OFF YOUR HEADS"

In Buddhist tradition Chinnamuṇḍā is the severed-head form of Vajravārāhī or Vajrayoginī.[35] In Tāranātha's *Historical Works* we find the *Kahna pa'i rnam thar* (biography of the Mahāsiddha Kṛṣṇācārya).[36] Kṛṣṇācārya's biography contains excerpts of his disciples' biographies, including those of the two Mahāsiddhā sisters, Mekhalā and Kanakhalā. It states:

> When Kṛṣṇācārya arrived in the south in Mahārāṣṭra, two sisters lived there—the eldest was called Mekhalā and the youngest Kanakhalā. When they were ten and eight years old respectively, they were betrothed to two Brahmin youths, but both the youths were too young to marry. Some years later when the two sisters had still not become brides, the local people became very critical of them, but it was said to be due to the power of karma, not to any inherent fault of the girls that they remained unwed. The marriage discussions were broken off.
>
> Later the girls saw the *ācārya* in company with his attendants who were all performing miracles, and they, filled with wonder, said, "We are in great dread of *saṃsāra*. Please show us a means of liberation from it." When they had thus begged the *ācārya*, he saw that they were fit vessels, so empowered them and the very highest wisdom came to them. They practised the teachings and the follow-up teachings and in a short while they also attained the eight ritual gazes and all other powers. Walls, mountains, and waters no longer hindered them, and they attained both intellectual and spiritual powers. They continued to live around the *ācārya*'s assemblage and they held fast to their mental ascetic practices.
>
> Once when both of them were going along a certain road, they met many ordinary yogis, followers of Gorakṣa, who mocked them and said, "You are students of Kṛṣṇapa! Show us some illusions then!" Now, as the abode of those so-called yogis was situated in a particularly beautiful spot, the girls performed a ritual gaze known as "that which leads forth" upon it, and they put the whole place down, unbroken, in a place which was a veritable desert, white in colour and not at all beautiful. The girls said to the yogis, "Now you too will have to perform a trick like this," and they left. Later, when the Gorakṣas begged them for forgiveness, their houses were returned to their previous site.
>
> On another occasion in Bengal, during the reign of King Lalitacandra,[37] when the Mahācārya had seen that the time was right for converting the King, the two girls emerged from a throng of people surrounding the *ācārya*, and paying homage to his feet said, "By the grace of the Guru, we two have attained the very highest and greatest of goals, and now we wish to fly off to the heavens. However, before that we will be happy to do whatever the *ācārya* requests us to do." The *ācārya* replied,"Well then, cut off your heads and offer them to me." The girls drew from their mouths well-tempered swords of wisdom and cutting off their heads without any hindrance at all, offered them into the Guru's hands. Facing backwards, they danced off, rising higher and higher on the heavenly paths, finally disappearing into rainbow light. The goddess Śrījñānā had also previously manifested a miracle similar to this, and even *rākṣasa* and *ḍākinīs* in their ordinary bodily forms started to demonstrate it in considerable numbers. As an antidote to this activity, Vajravārāhī herself appeared in that form, with her head severed, and it is said that this appeared frequently thereafter amongst her *siddhas*.[38]

Also in the *bsTan srung rgya mtsho'i rnam thar*, a collection of biographies of protectors, compiled by SLe lung rje drung bZhad pa'i rdo rje (b.1697) there is a story of a protectoress of Kongpo, Kong btsun de mo.[39] This story is excerpted from *Thugs rje chen po ngan so rang grol* (lit. Mahākāruṇa (=Avalokiteśvara) [in the form called] "self-liberation from the bad realms".) discovered by the *gTer ton*, Orgyan las 'phro gling pa, alias Rig 'zin 'ja' tson snying po.[40] The story states:

> When Padmasambhava conquered the twelve sisters, one of the sisters known as Kong btsun de mo rdo rje bod khams skyong wa (lit. the venerable Kongpo Demo, adamantine protectoress of Tibet) offered her *sādhana*, heart and life to Padmasambhava. She relates her past to him, "Previously in the west in the country of Orgyan, there was a king known as Indrabhūti. He had five sisters of whom the eldest known as Princess Lakṣmīṅkarā became his consort.[41] Her king-father sentenced her to severe punishment. She said, "Father, you do not need to punish me, I will punish myself." Then with a golden razor, she severed her head and white blood flowed from her neck. She walked around the city seven times, astonishing all the citizens who called her the great Chinnamuṇḍā Vārāhī.[42]

The summary of the rest of the story is that after several lifetimes, she was born in Kongpo, Tibet. In that lifetime, she became known as Kong btsun de mo and met Padmasambhava at the Kongpo border. At that time, she promised to protect and assist great saints and dharma practitioners in the future.[43]

In these two Buddhist stories, the origin of the Buddhist Goddess Vajravārāhī in her severed head form, i.e. Chinnamuṇḍā Vajravārāhī, is not explained; however, one finds manifestations of her. The two stories are connected with three female Mahāsiddhās: in Tāranātha's story the two sisters Mekhalā and Kanakhalā are the focus; Orgyan las'phro gling pa's story relates the previous life of Princess Lakṣmīṅkarā, the great Mahāsiddhā. Their own biographies, found in Abhayadatta's account of the eighty-four Mahāsiddhas, do not state that they practised the *sādhana* of the Chinnamuṇḍā form, but in the *Tangyur* these three are authors of the *sādhanas* of Chinnamuṇḍā Vajravārāhī/Vajrayoginī. Since in the few stories which exist about Chinnamuṇḍā Vajravārāhī, the Mahāsiddhas play a principal role, this form of Vajravārāhī, is connected closely with the Buddhist Siddha tradition.[44]

In these Buddhist stories, unlike the Hindu ones, the theme is not of sacrifice. From the outset of Buddhism, blood sacrifice of animals was denounced as inhumane and unnecessary in achieving Nirvāṇa. In the *Kūṭadanta Sutta* (*Dīgha Nikāya*, i, 127) the Buddha relates to the Brahmin Kūṭadanta an incident from one of his previous lives. At that time, when the Buddha was the family priest of a king, he persuaded the king to perform a sacrifice which entailed no killing of oxen, goats, fowls, swine or other living things and no cutting of trees or grass.[45] He thereby encouraged the king that if one performs a sacrifice, one should perform it without a blood sacrifice of animals. Buddha did not condemn all types of sacrifice, because in the *Jātaka Tales* he sacrifices himself to a starving tigress and her cubs.[46] The two Buddhist stories about Chinnamuṇḍā, however, are not discussing blood sacrifice or self-sacrifice; these two stories are demonstrating yogic ability. In the Tāranātha story, the two sisters were able to achieve the state of realization of non-duality as a result of their arduous and devoted practice.

> All inner and outer phenomena perceived as mind,
> Meditating with detachment, all has the same flavour.
> In supreme meditation without effort or striving,
> I found non-dual pure pleasure and perfect Buddhahood.[47]

In the Orgyan las 'phro gling pa story, Lakṣmīṅkarā was to be punished because of her seemingly incestuous relationship with brother. Lakṣmīṅkarā, knowing that her father was misinterpreting her behaviour, displayed her yogic abilities in order that he could realize his ignorance. She wanted to eradicate her father's and the citizens' negative attitudes towards her and to evoke regret in them for criticizing her behaviour. Thus she performed the miracle of walking around the town holding her severed head, revealing to everyone that she was a *siddhā*.[48] Furthermore, in Tibetan Buddhist Tantra when one directly perceives voidness of inherent existence, one attains the path of vision.[49] At this level of direct perception of voidness what ordinarily appears to be solid is no longer seen as solid. Lakṣmīṅkarā is graphically displaying her realization of the voidness of self-nature depicting her non-attachment to self by severing her head. In summation, these two Buddhist stories reflect that the manifestation of Vajravārāhī in her form of Chinnamuṇḍā is connected with adept yogic ability.

ORIGIN OF CHINNAMASTĀ/CHINNAMUṆḌĀ

The best known theory of Chinnamastā's Buddhist or Hindu origin is from B. Bhattacharyya who wrote several articles about the influence of Buddhist Tantrism on Hinduism. Editing various meditation manuals on deities, notably the Buddhist *Sādhanamālā*, he formulated the theory that some Hindu deities must have been originally Buddhist ones, including

Tārā, Chinnamastā and Mañjughoṣa. In regard to Chinnamastā, he compared Buddhist and Hindu meditations on her, *mantras* and iconography from the Buddhist *Sādhanamālā* (dated 1165 C.E.), the Hindu *Chinnamastākalpa* of uncertain origin, and the Hindu Kṛṣṇānanda Āgamavāgīśa's *Tantrasāra* (seventeenth century). He concluded that the Buddhist and Hindu Chinnamastā was the same goddess and 'identical in all details'.[49a] Indeed she is the same goddess but certain details are different. In the Hindu *sādhana* she stands on Rati and Kāma who are in reversed sexual union (*viparīta*) and wears a snake as a sacred cord, but these elements are absent in the Buddhist *sādhanas*.

He compared the *mantras* found in the three above-mentioned texts to establish the Buddhist precedence. The Buddhist *Sādhanamālā* states that the names of the two attendants are prefixed with *vajra* (*i.e.* Vajravairocanī and Vajravarṇanī) and the main goddess' name is Sarvabuddhaḍākinī referring to the severed-head form of Vajrayoginī. The prefix *vajra* is dropped in the *mantra* of the Hindu *Tantrasāra* but the three names, Ḍākinī, Varṇanī, and Vairocanī, remain and *sarvabuddha* (lit., all-awakened) becomes *sarvasiddhi* (lit. all-accomplished). In the Hindu *Chinnamastākalpa sarvabuddha* changes to *sarvabuddhi* (lit. all-enlightened) and the prefix *vajra* reappears. Bhattacharyya does not note this directly but *vajra* is a principal adjective in the Buddhist Tantra, also known as the Vajrayāna—the adamantine path. Hindus typically would not want to use the adjective *vajra* if indeed they incorporated a Buddhist *mantra*. Moreover, *sarvabuddha* which means all Buddhas or Awakened Ones would not be acceptable to Hindus; *buddha* was replaced with *siddhi* or *buddhi*. Bhattacharyya concluded that these words of the *mantra* are decidedly Buddhist. Thus by comparing the iconography, the dates of the manuscripts, and the *mantras*, Bhattacharyya concluded that Chinnamastā is originally Buddhist and this statement has not been disputed by most scholars.[50]

Bhattacharyya claimed that the Buddhist Chinnamastā, usually known as Chinnamuṇḍā Vajrayoginī or Vajravārāhī, was worshipped at least by the seventh century. The *Sādhanamālā* states that Siddha Śabarapa (variant spelling Śabarīpa), disciple of Siddha Nāgārjuna who flourished in the mid-seventh century, is credited with the introduction of a new cult of Vajrayoginī which Bhattacharyya inferred to be that of Chinnamuṇḍā Vajrayoginī.[51] Two Vajrayoginī *sādhanas* are attributed to Siddha Śabara in the Tibetan commentarial canon, *Tangyur*, but neither of these *sādhanas* mention Chinnamuṇḍā Vajrayoginī.[52] Moreover, Mahāsiddha Śabara's sacred biography does not state that he either received or transmitted a meditation of Chinnamuṇḍā Vajrayoginī.

Though the Siddha Śabara connection is not apparent, Chinnamuṇḍā Vajrayoginī is associated with other Mahāsiddhas. The sacred biography of Mahāsiddha Kanhapā (Kṛṣṇācārya) states that seven days prior to his death, he taught his disciples the meditation practice of the severed head Vajravārāhī.[53] Two of Kanhapa's disciples who received teachings on Vajravārāhī from Kanhapa were the Mahāsiddhā sisters, Mekhalā and Kanakhalā. The *Tangyur* has one *sādhana* by these two Mahāsiddhā sisters; it is entitled, "The Practice of Instructions of the Three Swastikas (*Nandyavarta traya mukhagama nāma*)". In this *sādhana* one is told to visualize oneself as dbU bCad Ma Yum, *i.e.*, Chinnamuṇḍā Vajravārāhī, and near the end of the meditation, it is inferred that one visualizes replacing one's head.[54] Thus, the meditational practice of Chinnamuṇḍā Vajravārāhī was transmitted from Mahāsiddha Kanhapa to the two Mahāsiddhā sisters, Mekhalā and Kanakhalā. Unfortunately, I have not been able to trace to whom the sisters transmitted this meditational practice, but it is certain that the teaching came to Tibet since it is in the *Tangyur*.

The Mahāsiddhā, who is the most important in continuing the meditative practice of Chinnamuṇḍā Vajrayoginī which began in India and was transmitted to Nepal and Tibet, is Lakṣmīṅkarā, sister of King Indrabhūti.[55] Though neither the sacred biography of Laksmīṅkāra nor that of her brother, King Indrabhūti, mentions any connection with Chinnamuṇḍā Vajrayoginī, the *Tangyur* has four *sādhanas* on Chinnamuṇḍā Vajrayoginī written by Lakṣmīṅkarā or her disciples. These are the *Vajrayoginī sādhana* by dPal lha lcam Legs smin kara,[56] *Chinnamuṇḍā Vajravārāhī* by Śrīmatī (an epithet for Lakṣmīṅkarā),[57] *Chinnamuṇḍā sādhana nāma* by Birapa (also spelled Birwapa or Virūpa), Lakṣmīṅkarā's disciple,[58] and *Chinnamuṇḍā Vajrayoginī sādhana* by Śāriputra, the disciple of Birapa.[59] *The Blue Annals* (late fifteenth century) states that many Tibetan yogis were initiated and practised the system known as *Phag mo gzhung drug* (the six topics of Vajravārāhī) bestowed by Lakṣmīṅkarā on her disciple Virūpa who in turn conferred it to the great Avadhūtipa, also known as Paiṇḍapātika (T. bSod snyoms pa che ba).[60] The main link in Nepal was the Newari *paṇḍita* Varendraruci, translator of many works in the *Tangyur*, including the *Chinnamuṇḍā Vajravārāhī* by Śrīmatī and the *Chinnamuṇḍā sādhana nāma* by Birapa.[61] In the *Chinnamuṇḍā Vajravārāhī* the translators were Varendraruci and the Tibetan bLo ldan shes rab. *The Blue Annals* states that the translator bLo ldan shes rab (1059-1109) came to Nepal and studied under Hamu dkar po.[62] Though bLo ldan shes rab studied with him, he is not in the transmission lineage, but another of Varendraruci's disciples, dPyal Kun dga' rdo rje, was the key person who introduced the Chinnamuṇḍāsādhana in Tibet. This lineage can be traced from India to Nepal and from there to Tibet during the ninth to eleventh centuries. Many *sādhanas* of Chinnamuṇḍā are extant in the Tibetan Buddhist tradition and the following transmission lineages are some which continue to the present among Tibetan Buddhist practitioners.[63]

TRANSMISSION LINEAGES

Buston in his *Collected Works* stated that the transmission lineage of Chinnamuṇḍā is as follows:

> Vajrayoginī > Legs smin kara (Lakṣmīṅkarā) > Birvapa > Avadhūtipa > bSod snyoms pa che ba > lDong ngar wa bSod snyoms pa chung wa > Bal po Hamu dkar po > dPyal kun dga' rdo rje > Zar ston lo tsa ba > sNar ston hig po > Grags pa tshul khrims > sGrub thabs dkon grags > Yon tan rgya mtsho > Sangs rgyas 'jam rgyal > mKhan po klu sgrub > bKa' bshi pa > dKon mchog gzhon nu bla ma Yan rtse pa > Bu ston rin po che (1290-1364 C.E.).[64]

In the *sGrub thabs kun btus* the lineage is:

> rDo rje 'chang > rGyal yum rdo rje phag mo > lCam Legs smin kara > Bram ze (Brahmin) Birwapa > Avadhūtipa > lDong ngar wa Ting 'dzin rdo rje > bSod snyoms pa chung ba ting 'dzin bzang po > Bal po Bhalendrarusti > dPyal lo tsa ba Kun dga' rdo rje > Zar ston ātsārya > gTsang yang dag rdo rje > dBus pa shes rab rdo rje > lCe mdo sde sengge > and so on.[65]

The *rGyud sde kun btus* only lists Birwapa and his student sTong nyid Ting 'dzin rdo rje for the lineage; the latter is not found in most transmission lineages but he is a contemporary of Hamu Karpo who was the main link between Nepal and Tibet.[66] This text states that Birwapa and sTong nyid Ting 'dzin rdo rje practised many *sādhanas* of Chinnamuṇḍā and received many oral teachings which formed the basis of Mitrayogi's (also spelled Mitra dzo ki) commentary.[67] In Tāranātha's *Yidam rgya mtsho'i sgrub thabs rin chen 'byung gnas* the lineage is Śrī Matī (Lakṣmīṅkarā) and the younger Birwapa; Rab dga discussed their teachings and this formed the basis of Tāranātha's *sādhana*.[68]

One other noteworthy Chinnamuṇḍā lineage is in a Tibetan Buddhist Nyingmapa *gter ma* (rediscovered text) collection on meditational deities.[69] This lineage begins with rDo rje phag mo (Vajravārāhī) to dGa' rab rdo rje to Orgyen yab yum to Khri srong and continues on to Nyang ral

(Nyang ral Nyi ma 'od zer [1124-1192]), and so on. dGa' rab rdo rje is a progenitor of many Nyingmapa lineages ;[70] many begin with him as the first human to receive teachings from a deity. He transmitted this teaching to the great Padmasambhava with consort (Orgyen yab yum) who passed it to the illustrious *dharmarāja* Khri srong lde btsan (755-797?). There is a lapse in the lineage from the late eighth century to the twelfth. Since *gter ma* are buried treasure texts which are later found by a *gter ton*, this text must have remained buried until it was discovered by Nyang ral. Nyang ral is one of the five Great Discoverers (*gter ton*). Since this collection is a *gter ma* and the lineage is a popular Nyingmapa one using it as historical proof is problematic.[71] However if the teaching was transmitted from dGa' rab rdo rje to Padmasambhava, it would be the earliest *sādhana* of *Chinnamuṇḍā Vajrayoginī* (*c.* mid-eighth century).[72] Thus when we examine the various transmission lineages, we find that no lineage included Siddha Śabara but numerous ones have included Mahāsiddhā Lakṣmīṅkarā. Therefore the lineage stems from Mahāsiddhā Lakṣmīṅkarā, not Śabara.

Though many scholars accept the Buddhist origin of Chinnamastā, some scholars disagree that she is originally Buddhist and present arguments for a Hindu origin. In *The Ten Great Cosmic Powers*, S. Shankaranarayanan states:

> Chinnamastā is the thunder clap and the lightning flash. "Shining like a streak of lightning" (*vidyullekheva bhāsvarā*), says the Upanishad. That is why Chinnamastā is known as vajravairocanīyā. She is the force of Virocana, the specially luminous (*viśeṣeṇa rocate'iti virocanaḥ*). Who is this Virocana? It is the Supreme himself, the Primordial Prakāśa. Vajra is her power which he wields. We know the *vajra* is the weapon of Indra . . . in the Veda, the paramount God.[73]

In traditional Hindu fashion, Shankaranarayanan seeks to find Chinnamastā's source in the Vedas and stresses the importance of the word *vajra* in her *mantra* as a connection with the Vedic god, Indra. Admittedly, Indra is a paramount god in the Vedas and he wields his potent *vajra*, but the *sādhanas* about Chinnamastā do not associate her with Indra nor does she hold a *vajra* either in her Hindu or Buddhist form.[74] Also S. Bhattacharji, in her book *The Indian Theogony* stresses that the Vedic Goddess Nirṛti's functions have been replaced by her direct descendents—Kālī, Karalī, Cāmuṇḍā, and Chinnamastā.[75] Both these scholars claim that Chinnamastā is connected to Vedic deities; thereby they imply Vedic antecedents for her.[76]

In the Hindu literature, Chinnamastā is not mentioned until the *upapurāṇas*, such as the *Mahādevībhāgavata Purāṇa* and the *śākta Mahābhāgavata Purāṇa* (*c.* 950 C.E.).[77] This *śākta Mahābhāgavata Purāṇa* seems to be the earliest reference to Chinnamastā in Hindu literature. Judging from the iconographical, mantric, and textual evidences, one can conclude that Chinnamastā/Chinnamuṇḍā is foremost connected with the Tantric traditions in Hinduism and Buddhism. It is difficult to say unequivocally whether she was borrowed from one tradition to the other, but it is clear that she was known and her *sādhanas* were practised by Mahāsiddhās at least from the ninth century in India.

REFERENCES

1. Descriptions of the Daśa Mahāvidyās and their relationship to each other have been discussed in numerous books. See Kinsley, D., *Hindu Goddesses: Visions of the Divine Feminine in the Hindu Religious Tradition*: 161-77. Also Pal, P., *Hindu Iconology*: 57-91.
2. Danielou, A., *Hindu Polytheism*: 268. He states,"The Mahāvidāys are the source of all that is to be known."
3. This is the śākta *Mahābhāgavata Upapurāṇa* (*c*.950 C.E.) and not the celebrated Vaiṣṇava *Mahābhāgavata Purāṇa* . The only two printed editions of this śākta *Mahābhāgavata Purāṇa* are by Gujurati Press, Bombay, 1913 and by Vangavasi Press, Calcutta, 1321 B.S.. I have used primarily the former one and my translation is from this edition. Also see Woodroffe, J., *Principles of Tantra*, Madras, Ganesh and Co., 1986, Vol.1, pp.259-64; his translation is from the latter edition.
4. For a complete synopsis of the *Mahābhāgavata Purāṇa*, see Hazra, R. C., *Studies in the Upapurāṇas*, Vol.2: 320-49. The section on the Daśa Mahāvidyās begins in chapter eight.
5. This is my translation. Please note that all within the parentheses are my insertions.
6. Usually the Daśa Mahāvidyās include Bhairavī but she is not mentioned in verses 62-63. However, when the ten forms are explained in verses 65-71, Bhairavī is included but Lokeśikamalā is omitted.
7. See Vijñānānanada,trans., *The Śrīmad Devī Bhāgavatam*: 1184 for a description of Śrī Devī's residence. Her residence is surrounded by eighteen enclosures and the enclosure adjacent to hers is the residence of the Daśa Mahāvidyās, thereby indicating their supremacy in the hierarchy of emanations of the goddess.
8. All these rituals are discussed in chapter 2.
9. The Sanskrit terms are *māraṇa, ucchāṭana, kṣobhana, mohana, dravana, stambhana*, and *vidveśana* repectively. These are "black magical" powers for controlling one's enemies or influencing favourably beings who have control over oneself. Indeed people have been propitiating deities in order to acquire these powerful forces since time immemorial. However, the Hindu texts condemn these as false goals and stress that one's ultimate goal should be *mokṣa*.
10. *Mahābhāgavata Purāṇa* chapter 8, verses 45-87 (not everything is translated). The Daśa Mahāvidyās are ten forms of Durgā but the chief Mahāvidyā is Kālī. See

Slusser, M., *Nepal Mandala : A Cultural Study of the Kathmandu Valley*, Vol. 1: 322-23 and 330.

11. In the Hindu tradition all the goddesses are manifestations of a Devī, one of her most ubiquitous forms is Durgā. One frequently finds penny posters of Durgā's ten transcendent forms, the Daśa Mahāvidyās, surrounding the central deity, Durgā. See Plate 1 for the Daśa Mahāvidyās.
12. See Macdonell, A.A., *Vedic Mythology*, Delhi, Motilal Banarsidass, rpt. 1981: 47.
13. Sircar, D. C., *The Śākta Pīṭhas* : 5-6.
14. See Sircar for an extensive account of the *pīṭhas* (pp. 80-100).
15. See Bhardwaj, S.M., *Hindu Places of Pilgrimage in India : A Study in Cultural Geography*, Berkeley, University of California Press, 1973:101ff.
16. Sircar: 48.
17. Ibid.: Sircar states that Mahālakṣmī stands for Kamalā and Durgā for Mātangī.
18. *Taittirīya Saṃhitā* (7.1.5) and *Śatapatha Brāhmaṇa* (14.1.2.11).
19. See Rakesa, Visnudatta, *Daśamahāvidyā Mīmāṃsā* : 25. Some of the names are different but they indicate the same deity—Tārinī for Tārā, Bhuvanā for Bhuvaneśvarī, Bhṛgukula for Paraśurāma, and Chinnā for Chinnamastā.
20. I have found only the two—*Guhyātiguhya Tantra* and *Muṇḍamālā*.
21. Kinsley, D., *Hindu Goddesses*: 161-62.
22. Narasiṃha and Chinnamastā are both worshipped on the fourteenth day of the bright fortnight of Vaiśākha month (April-May). See *An Alphabetical List of Feasts and Holidays of the Hindus and Muhammadans* : 62 and *Daśa Mahāvidyā Mīmāṁsā* :16 respectively.
23. Biardeau, M. and Malamoud, C., *Le Sacrifice dans l'Inde Ancienne*, Paris, Presses Universitaires de France, 1976: 151, note 5. Shankaranarayanan, S., *Ten Great Cosmic Powers* :70.
24. See Agrawala, Vasudeva Sarana, "Śiva kā svarūpa", *Kalyāṇa, Śiva aṅka*: 499.
25. This is according to the system of the five *cakras* which are centres of tangible matter (*bhūtas*). The two higher *cakras* which are not centres of tangible matter are not counted in this system.
26. According to D.C. Bhattacharya in *P.K. Gode Commemoration Volume* :27, Ramātosana, seventh lineal descendent of Kṛṣṇānanda, was the author of the *Prāṇatoṣinītantra*. (Cited from Banerji, S.C., *Tantra in Bengal*, Calcutta, Naya Prakash, 1978:78.)
27. There is no indication as to why the attendants' names changed from Jayā and Vijayā to Ḍākinī and Varṇinī.
28. See Wayman, A., *Buddhist Insight* : 375ff, (for a description of a verbal act of truth). Also see W. Norman Brown, "The Basis for the Hindu Act of Truth" in *Review of Religions* (Nov. 1940): 36-45 and "Duty as Truth in Ancient India" in *Proceedings of the American Philosophical Society* 116 no.3 (June 1972): 252-68.
29. *Prāṇatoṣinītantra*, Calcutta, Basumati Sahitya Mandir, 1928:378 (my translation with the help of Hemandra Chakravorty of Varanasi).
30. Ibid.: 379.
31. See Coomaraswamy, A.K., "Līlā", *Journal of the American Oriental Society* 61:2 (1949) p.99.
32. Eliade, M., *Patterns in Comparative Religions*, New York, Sheed and War, 1958:419.
33. Bhattacharya, Hamsanarayana, *Hinduder Devdevī*, Calcutta, 1980, Vol.3:326.
34. Pal, P., *Hindu Religion and Iconology*: 82.
35. All the *sādhanas* in the *Tangyur* give the Sanskrit name as Chinnamuṇḍā, rather

than Chinnamastā, but the two are identified as the same goddess and have the same meaning, "a severed-head one".

36. Tāranātha, *Kahna pa'i rnam thar*, Arunachal Pradesh, Tibetan Nyingmapa Monastery, 1974:319-20. The translation which follows is David Templeton's, published by the Library of Tibetan Works and Archives, Dharamsala, 1989. I thank Jeremy Russell for showing me this before publication. (Tāranātha [1575-1643] was a major proponent of the Tibetan Buddhist *Jo nang pa* school and author of many historical works.
37. King Lalitacandra reigned from late seventh to early eighth century. (See Majumdar, R.C., *History of Ancient Bengal*, Calcutta, G. Bhardwaj and Co., 1974 : 81.)
38. Ibid.: 62-63.
39. The complete title is *Dam can bstan srung rgya mtsho'i rnam par thar pa cha shas tsam brjod pa sngon med legs bshad*: An Account of the Origins and Iconography of the Protective Deities of Tibetan Buddhism, Leh, Tashigang, 1979, Vol.1: 220-22.
40. Orgyan las 'phro gling pa (1585-1656) is a famous *gter ton* (a discover of hidden texts). See Dargyay, E. M., *The Rise of Esoteric Buddhism in Tibet*, Delhi, Motilal Banarsidass, rpt. 1978 : 160-62. For general information about the *gter ma* (hidden texts) tradition in Tibetan Buddhism, especially among the Nyingmapa sect, see Gyatso, J., "Signs, Memory and History: A Tantric Buddhist Theory of Scriptural Transmission", *Journal of International Association of Buddhist Studies*, Vol.9, no.2, pp.7-35.
41. The technical term for this type of consort is *karmamudrā*, indicating she is a consort only for sexual yoga, thereby not committing incest.
42. There is another copy of this story in the *Collected Works* (gsung 'bum) of rTse las rGod tshang pa sna tshogs rang grol (b.1608), New Delhi, 1974, Vol.5, pp.299-302. I thank Cyrus Stearns for this citation. In the aforementioned printed edition of a hand-written text, one important word is different. This text calls her Chinnamuṇḍā Ārya (T. '*phags* = noble or exalted), not Chinnamuṇḍā Vārāhī (T. *phag mo* = sow). These two words are homophones in Tibetan.
43. She is one of the twelve sisters (*bstan ma bchu gnyis*) who protect Buddhism in Tibet.
44. In Tāranātha's story, it is mentioned that the Goddess Śrījñānā previously manifested in this form. This goddess might be simply a form of *jñānaḍākinī*, frequently associated with Vajrayoginī, but this name is probably an epithet for Princess Lakṣmīṅkarā.
45. See Thomas, E.J., *The Life of Buddha as Legend and History*, London, Routledge and Kegan Paul, 1975:175-76.
46. According to popular belief this incident occurred at a place in Nepal presently known as Namo Buddha (or in Tibetan as *sTag mo lus sbyin*, "offering his body to the tigress").
47. Dowman: 317.
48. At this time she bled white blood displaying compassion towards the citizens and her father. (In Tantric Buddhism white liquid symbolizes compassion.)
49. The five paths in ascending order are the equipment, practice, vision, contemplation, and adept. Upon attaining the path of vision, one attains the first stage of the ten-staged Bodhisattva path, the Joyous.

49a. See Bhattacharyya, B., *Introduction to Buddhist Esotericism*: 159.

50. Pal, P., *Hindu Religion and Iconology*: 83; Bhattacharyya, N.N., *History of Śākta Religion*: 96; Banerjea, J.N., *Development of Hindu Iconography*, New Dehli rpt.,

1973: 560

51. Sādhanamālā Vol.2: cxliv ff.
52. Derge *Tangyur*, Vol. 23: 391-92 & 393-97.
53. Dowman, K., *Masters of Mahamudra*: 127. Please note that severed-head Vajrayoginī or Vajravārāhī is the same deity.
54. Derge *Tangyur, rgyud 'grel*, Vol 43 (Zi): 34-35.
55. There are several Lakṣmīṅkarās, the two most important being the sister of King Indrabhūti (late ninth century) and the eleventh century Kashmiri nun Lakṣmīṅkarā, initiator of the fasting ritual (T.*smyung gnas*). Since the nun Lakṣmīṅkarā also was known as being able to severe her head, confusion arises as to which Lakṣmīṅkarā is the author of the *sādhanas*. The *sādhanas* indicate the earlier date because of the transmission lineages, thus I conclude that it is the former Lakṣmīṅkarā who is the author of the *sādhanas*.
56. *Tangyur*, Vol. 23: 390-91.
57. Ibid: 409-11. Note that this *sādhana* is very similar to the one in the *Sādhanamālā* and also similar to a manuscript found in Nepal entitled *Lakṣmisādhana* (which is being studied by the Dhīḥ Project in Sarnath, India).
58. Ibid.: 411-15.
59. Ibid., Vol.82: 14ff.
60. Roerich, G., trans., *The Blue Annals*: 390. This Virūpa and his disciple are from the ninth century and are not the famed eighth-century patriarchs of the Tibetan Buddhist Śakya lineage.
61. Ibid.: 394. He has several names. The name Varendraruci is his title as a scholar (T. mChog tu dbang po gsal ba, lit. "one endowed with clear faculties"). Another is Puṇyākarabhadra (T. bSod nams 'byung gnas bzang po) and still another which is frequently found is Hamu dkar po.
62. Ibid.: 396.
63. Both Choge Trichen Rinpoche and H.H. Sakya Trizin have transmitted the lineage from the *sGrub thabs kun btus* and the *rGyud sde kun btus*.
64. Buston's *Collected Works*, Vol. "La": 20-21. I thank David Jackson for showing me this lineage.
65. *sGrub thabs kun btus* :205-06.
66. Jamyang Loter Wangpo, ed., *rGyud sde kun btus* :412-14. Also see *The Blue Annals*: 392ff. for sTong nyid ting 'dzin rdo rje's biography.
67. Ibid.:414. Also Mitrayogi includes an initiation of Chinnamuṇḍā with twelve deities in his 100 *sādhana* cycle. His biography is in the *The Blue Annals*: 1030ff..
68. Tāranātha, *Yi dam rgya mtsho'i sgrub thabs rin chen 'byung gnas,* Vol.1: 218. Also see *The Blue Annals*: 1087 for Rab dga's biography. Tāranātha said that Rab dga took the essence from the texts of Kuntu dpal mo and younger Birwapa.
69. gTer bdag gling pa with sMin gling lo chen, *sGrubs thabs 'dod 'jo bum bzang,* Vol.1: 27. For general information on the *gter ma* tradition, see Tulku Thondup Rimpoche, *Hidden Teachings of Tibet*, London, Wisdom Publications, 1986, and Gyatso, J., 'Signs, Memory and History: A Tantric Buddhist Theory of Scriptural Transmission', *International Association of Buddhist Studies*, 1986, Vol.9, no.2:7-35.
70. See Dargyay, E. M., *The Rise of Esoteric Buddhism in Tibet*, Delhi, Motilal Banarsidass, 1978: 20ff. Also see Hanson-Barber, A.W., "the Identification of dGa' rab rdo rje", *International Association of Buddhist Studies*, 1986, Vol.9, no.2:55-63. (The author assigns the date 550 C.E. to him but this is suspect.)
71. See Kapstein, M., 'The Purificatory Gem and its Cleaning: A Late Tibetan Polemical Discussion of Apocryphal Texts', *History of Religions*, Feb. 1989,

Vol.28, no.3.: 229ff. Kapstein presents the various positions adopted by the four Tibetan Buddhist sects concerning the authenticity of *gter ma* texts.

72. There are so many different dates assigned to dGa' rab rdo rje and Padmasambhava. The only historical verifiable date is that of the Tibetan king Khri srong lde btsan (755-797?).
73. Shankaranarayanan:70.
74. *Vajra* is a very common word in Buddhist Tantra.
75. Bhattacharji, S., *The Indian Theogony*, Cambridge, Cambridge University Press, 1970 : 85.
76. J.N. Tiwari in his *Goddess Cults in Ancient India* states that Chinnamastā suggests a continuity of ideas with the 'nude squatting goddess'. The only common characteristic is their nudity.
77. It is unfortunate that the Hindu *sādhanas* do not have as extensive transmission lineages as the Buddhist *sādhanas*.

Chapter 2

To Worship a Deity, One Must Become a Deity

Tantra in both Hinduism and Buddhism is foremost a method or practice rather than a specific philosophy; it is primarily concerned with developing and implementing effective methods which enable the practitioner to achieve liberation from cyclic existence. Tantra incorporates theological and philosophical beliefs from 'non-Tantric' Hinduism and Buddhism but its emphasis is actual practice. Concerning Hindu Tantra, Gupta states, "Tantra hardly rejects any form of religious ritualism; it juxtaposes its own particular ritual practices to normative (*smārta*) Hindu rituals."[1] Therefore, Tantric practitioners engage in one or more practices, utilizing Tantric methods to attain *siddhis*, as well as the ultimate goal, liberation. Although the texts and methods are both diverse and vast, Tantric practitioners follow particular texts or methods dictated by their spiritual teacher (*guru*).

HINDU SPIRITUAL PRACTICE

Spiritual practices known as *sādhanas* consist of two broad groups, yoga and ritual worship (*pūjā*). Ritual worship is divided into three kinds: (1) those performed daily (*nitya*), (2) those performed on particular dates (*naimittika*), and (3) those performed for the fulfilment of a special desire or for averting misfortune (*kāmya*).[2] In the Chinnamastā *sādhanas* which will be examined, the main focus is on daily ritual worship but some *naimittika* and *kāmya pūjās* are also included.

In examining the Hindu Tantric practice of Chinnamastā, I shall concentrate on the 'Chinnamastātantra' section of the popular *Śākta Pramoda* which was compiled by King Devānandanasiṃha of Muzaffarpur during the nineteenth century. From the late eighteen hundreds to the present day, the *Śākta Pramoda* has been one of the most popular manuals of Tantric rituals for the practice of each of the ten Mahāvidyās and the five main deities (*pañca devatā*). These five are Kumārī (or Devī), Śiva, Gaṇeśa,

Surya, and Viṣṇu.[3] Another text which will serve as a comparison for the *Śākta Pramoda* is the 'Pracaṇḍacaṇḍikā' section of the *Tantrasāra* written by Kṛṣṇānanda Āgamavāgīśa at the end of the sixteenth century.[4] This text shows remarkable similarities to the *Śākta Pramoda* in the ritual worship (*pūjāvidhiḥ*) section. The final text, the *Śrī Chinnamastā Nityārcana*, composed by Śrī Swamiji Mahārāja, is designed to help practitioners in their daily worship of Chinnamastā.[5] Although *Nityārcana* is similar to the two aforementioned texts, it elaborates on the preliminary practices as well as on the ritual worship section. I shall present the procedure for worshipping Chinnamastā according to the *Śākta Pramoda* with additional material from the *Tantrasāra* and the *Nityārcana*.

DEFINITION OF THE NINE SECTIONS OF RITUAL PRACTICE

In the Chinnamastātantra of the *Śākta Pramoda*, the practice is divided into nine sections: (1) visualized meditation (*dhyāna*); (2) drawing of *yantra*; (3) explication of the *mantra*; (4) ritual worship sequence (*pūjāvidhiḥ*); (5) eulogy (*stotra*); (6) protective 'armour' (*kavaca*); (7) essence (*hṛdaya*); (8) hundred and eight names; and (9) one thousand names.[6] These nine sections will be discussed with special emphasis on the ritual worship sequence, since it is the major section of daily worship.

VISUALIZED MEDITATION

The visualized meditation of Chinnamastā is discussed in depth in chapter 5.

DRAWING OF THE YANTRA

The drawing of the *yantra* is included in the discussion of ritual worship.

EXPLICATION OF THE MANTRA

In Indian civilization the role of sound and word has been investigated from the time of the Vedas to the present. In most Hindu rituals, *mantras* have a prominent part.[7] An etymology for *mantra* is the root *man-* which is associated with thought, will, and intentionality, and the suffix *-tra* which means an 'instrument of that which precedes it', i.e., an instrument of intention. Another meaning is that *man* is related to mind and *-tra* means protection; hence a protection of/for the mind. *Mantra* as an instrument of intention and a protection for the mind is associated with liberation in Hindu rituals. The *Prapañcasāratantra* V, 2, states that "by meditation on the place of ultimate principle (*tattva*) one is saved; thus it is named *mantra*."[8] Each deity has a specific *mantra* and *bīja* (seed syllable) which represent his/her essence. These *mantras* are believed to be of divine origin and are not arbitrarily assigned. By knowing the root *mantra* of a deity, in this case Chinnamastā, one can invoke her and experience her essence which will ultimately bring liberation. Chinnamastā's root *mantra* is composed of nineteen seed syllables, each corresponding to an important deity in the Hindu pantheon. Thus this one-root *mantra* is imbued with the essence of nineteen major deities who will assist the practitioner when requested. Knowledge of the root *mantra* is necessary for practice. Its power is enormous, and it is kept secret to protect it from being misused.

Ritual Worship Procedure (pūjāvidhiḥ)

Ritual worship (*pūjāvidhiḥ*) consists of regular preliminaries, Tantric regular preliminaries, invocation of the deity and the fire ceremony.[9]

Regular preliminaries

1. Regular morning worship

Tantric regular preliminaries

1. *Ācamana* (ablution)
2. Sixfold *Nyāsa* and *Prāṇāyāma*
3. *Mātṛkābījanyāsa*
4. *Ṛsinyāsa*
5. *Karāṅganyāsa*
6. Pervasive *nyāsa*
7. Meditation on the deity (*dhyāna*)
8. Making of *yantra*
9. Meditation of inner *yantra*
   a. by yogis
   b. by householders
10. Conch ritual
11. *Pīṭhapūjā* (seat of the deity)

Invocation of the deity

1. *Āvāhana* (invocation of the deity)
2. *Prāṇapratiṣṭhā*
3. Six-limbed *nyāsa* of the deity
4. *Śākti* worship of the goddess
5. Sacrificial offering (*bali*)

6. Worship of the eight-petalled lotus deities
7. Offering of flowers (*puṣpāñjali*)
8. Worship of the Goddess' attendants (*āvaraṇa*)
9. Valediction of the deity (*visarjana*)

Fire ceremony

Burnt offerings with the repetition of Chinnamastā's *mantras*

Prior to any worship in Hindu practice the place and ritual instruments must be cleaned, purified, and consecrated.[10] Once the place and objects have been consecrated the practitioner must also undergo purification and consecration. *Regular preliminaries* are not mentioned in the *Śākta Pramoda* since it is assumed that a practitioner knows them and will perform them. This includes the remembrance upon awakening of one's guru and chosen deity (*iṣṭadevatā*), bathing (*snāna*), expulsion of mental impurities (*aghamarṣaṇa*), and peace offerings (*tarpaṇa*) to the deities, the seers, the forefathers, lineage of gurus, and one's chosen deity in order to invoke their blessings and establish a spiritual bond with them. One must purify and transform one's body in order to worship because in Hindu practice, all practitioners must become 'divine' before worshipping a deity.[11]

With the completion of the regular preliminaries one begins the *regular Tantric preliminaries* as described in the next section.

Regular Tantric Preliminaries

1. *Ācamana* is the ablution of the body by initially washing one's lips and hands, then with these purified lips saying certain *mantras* as one touches specific parts of the body with purified hands. Vidyārnava states that "*ācamana* is the purification *par excellence*. It is to be performed after every act in which there might be the slightest suspicion of impurity."[12]

2. *Prāṇāyāma and Sixfold Nyāsa* consist of *prāṇāyāma* which is the regulation and control of two of the subtle winds in the body. These winds are *prāṇa*, the upward moving subtle wind and *apāna*, the downward moving subtle wind; together they represent a being's respiration. The winds run through three main subtle channels (*nāḍīs*): the central channel, *suṣumṇā*; the left channel, *iḍā*; and to the right channel, *piṅgalā*. When the two subtle winds flow through the left—*iḍā*, the mind is concentrated and introverted; whereas when the two subtle winds flow through the right, the *piṅgalā*, the mind is scattered and extroverted. Normal breathing is done through one of these channels and does not alternate regularly with each breath between these two channels. *Prāṇāyāma* is a method of regulating the breath so that inhalation (*pūraka*), maintaining the breath (*kumbhaka*), and exhalation (*recaka*) are all equal in length. One inhales through one channel and exhales through the other, then reverses the process. This is done in order to arouse the *kuṇḍalinī*, dormant in the *mūlādhāra cakra*, and causes it to ascend to the *sahasrāra cakra* at the top of the head.[13]

The sixfold *nyāsa* which in general is a process of empowering one's body by touching it and uttering specific *mantras*. By performing this one transforms one's body into a divine body. Since Tantra inherited the Upaniṣadic belief that a person's body is a microcosm of the universe, then by recognizing the correct place on the body a practitioner can activate the cosmic forces latent in one's own body. This sixfold *nyāsa* is the chief of all *nyāsas*. Its performance destroys lesser sins (*upapātaka*) and harmful forces, neutralizes anything inimical towards the practitioner, and makes the eight *siddhis* attainable.[14]

3. *Mātṛkābīja nyāsa* is the placing a different syllable of the alphabet at each part of the body, e.g., "*Aṃ* at the mouth, *Iṃ* at the right eye . . . *Kshaṃ* between the heart and the mouth".[15] By the empowerment of a specific syllable of the Sanskrit alphabet, each part of the body becomes consecrated or 'divine'. This *mātṛkā nyāsa* is both the touching of specific parts of the skin with *mantras* and also the visualizing of letters on each petal of the six *cakras* within the body.[16]

4. *Ṛṣi nyāsa*, like *mātṛkā bīja nyāsa*, involves touching the body in certain places with the appropriate *mantra*. The practitioner is told about the seer who revealed the text, the meter of the text, its deity, its power and the results. In non-Tantric texts this was the criteria for establishing authority, thus it was incorporated in Tantric texts for the same reason of establishing authority of the texts.[17]

5. *Karāṅga nyāsa* is the transmutation and sublimation of the fingers, hands, and limbs through *mantras*. In this section as one touches the right and left small fingers, one repeats a particular *mantra*. One does this progressively with one's ring fingers, middle fingers, index fingers and thumbs; then one puts one's palms together and concludes by touching together the backs of one's hands while saying the appropriate *mantra*. For example, the first *mantra* said while touching the fingers is "*Om Am Kam Kham Gam Gham N Ām Khaḍgāya Hṛdayāya Svāhā*" Though *Śākta Pramoda* gives only one letter of the alphabet with each *mantra*, the *Nityārcana* tells the practitioner that each *mantra* consists of seven letters, e.g., the first short vowel of the Sanskrit alphabet, the first four consonants, nasal, and the first long vowel (*Am, Kam, Khaṃ, Gam, Gham, N, Ām*), then the second short vowel, etc., ending with the semi-vowels, sibilants, and *Kṣam*.[18]

6. *Pervasive nyāsa* protects the whole body once the specific places of the body have been touched from head to feet and in the reverse order three times, concluding with the snapping of fingers around one's head in order to bind the directions (*digbandhana*). This concludes the transformation of the practitioner's body into a divine one and allows the practitioner to begin the meditation on the deity.[19]

7. *Meditation of Chinnamastā* (*dhyāna*) is discussed in chapter 5.

8. *Making the yantra* consists in the drawing of a *yantra* on the ground in front of the practitioner. The word *yantra* is derived from the Sanskrit root *yam* which means 'to sustain', 'to hold', or 'to support the power of a particular object or concept.' In its general sense, a *yantra* is an instrument or a machine, but in its Hindu Tantric sense, it is the abode of the deity.[20] Woodroffe quotes in the *Kaulavaliya Tantra*: 'Mantra is itself the Devatā (the deity) and *yantra* is *mantra* in that it is the body of the Devatā who is the *mantra*."[21]

As with all deities, Chinnamastā has her own specific *yantra*. In order to begin internal or mental worship (*antar pūjā*) of Chinnamastā, a practitioner needs to draw her *yantra* which is an abstract geometrical form. By drawing Chinnamastā's *yantra*, the practitioner is establishing her abode in one's presence. The *yantra* is composed of the outer, middle, and inner sections. The outermost section (*bhūpūra*) encloses everything and prevents anyone or anything from entering the inner sanctum where the deity resides. This *bhūpūra* is protected at its four doors by the field protectors. The middle section consists of an eight-petalled lotus which is associated with different goddesses. The inner section is composed of two inverted triangles with inscribed *mantras* which symbolize the residence of Chinnamastā.[22] Once the practitioner has constructed thc *yantra*, the inner worship of Chinnamastā can begin.

9. *Meditation of inner yantra* refers to the visualized meditation of Chinnamastā and her abode (*yantra*) within the practitioner's body. This is divided into two meditations on Chinnamastā. The first one is for yogis who visualize Chinnamastā with form (*sarūpa*) and the second is for householders, who visualize Chinnamastā in an abstract way. In many Hindu Tantric texts, such as the *Great Liberation*, the yogis are the ones who meditate on the deity without form while the householders meditate on the deity with form; however Chinnamastā's form is such an awesome vision that only yogis can meditate on her with form.[23]

10. *Conch ritual* is an important rite in Hindu Tantric ritual worship. In all forms of Hindu ritual worship there is a general oblation (*samānārghya*) which is a sprinkling of consecrated liquid on the practitioners and offerings in order to purify them. An important Tantric ritual is the preparation of a conch vessel for the special oblation (*viśesārghya*). Since the deity is invited to stay in this vessel during the ritual, it is never moved.

11. *Pīṭhapūjā* is the ritual worship of the sacred seat of the goddess. This sacred seat is a mixture of cosmological places and philosophical concepts. The sacred seat begins with the power of support (*ādhāraśakti*) which is surmounted successively by the Primordial Nature (Prakṛti), by the bluish turtle who holds the universe (*kūrma*), by the King of the Nāgas who also support the world (*ananta*), by the earth (*pṛthivī*) wherein lies the ocean of milk (*kṣīrasamudra*), whereupon is the Jewelled Island (*ratnadvīpa*),[24] from which rises the wish-fulfilling tree (*kalpavṛkṣa*),[25] on top of which is the golden lion seat (*svarṇasiṃhāsana*) wherein is the root of bliss (*ānandakanda*), within this is *Sambilvālaya*, whereupon is the lotus of the nature of all categories of existence (*sarvatattvātmakapadma*),[26] wherein are the three qualities (the three *guṇas*—*sattva*, *rajas*, and *tamas*). The four corners of the seat are the self (*ātman*), inner self (*antarātman*), supreme self (*paramātman*), and wisdom self (*jñānātman*) and in the middle of the lotus lie Rati and Kāma.[27]

11a. *Śaktipūjā* Once the practitioner envisages Chinnamastā's seat, one meditates on Chinnamastā in one's heart and requests her to come.

Invocation of the Deity in Nine Parts

1. *Āvāhana* (invocation of the goddess) is the inviting of Chinnamastā accompanied by her two attendants, Varṇinī and Ḍākinī, to come and be seated on top of the prostrate Rati and Kāma who are in the middle of the lotus at the very centre of her abode (*yantra*). She is asked to come (*āvāhana*), to establish herself (*sthāpana*), to stay fast (*sannirodhana*) and (in most practices but not in this one) to stay face to face (*sammukhīkaraṇa*) with the practitioner.

2. *Prāṇapratiṣṭhā* is the instilling of the vital breath in an image of Chinnamastā or a visualized Chinnamastā. One does this by repeating the *mantra*, "*Am* . . . *hamsah*, let Chinnamastā's vital breath be here; *Am* . . . *hamsah*, let Chinnamastā's self stay here; *Am* . . . *hamsah*, let all of Chinnamastā's senses be here; *Am* . . . *hamsah*, let Chinnamastā's speech, mind, eyes, ears, nose, breath, and feet be here; let the happiness remain for a long time, *Svāhā*."

3. *Six-limbed nyāsa* is the touching of the six major bodily parts of Chinnamastā. Though the Goddess is formless, here she assumes a form in order to be worshipped by the practitioner.

4. *Śaktī worship of Goddess* consists of paying homage to her six main parts which are hypostasized as individual *Śaktīs* (the heart, the top of the head, tuft of hair, shoulders, eye, and 'weapon' goddesses). According to *Nityārcana* one pays homage to the six long vowels which symbolize the six *vidyās* (six knowledge goddesses).

5. *Sacrificial offerings* (*bali*) is a major part of ritual worship because the purpose of this kind of *pūjā* is to serve (*upacāra*) Chinnamastā; whatever is offered to her is termed an *upacāra*. The offerings vary in number; the minimum is five but sixteen offerings are more common. However one can offer ten, thirty-eight, sixty-four, or up to a thousand items.[28] The *Nityārcana* tells the practitioner to offer sixteen items accompanied by *mantras*.[29] When a practitioner offers these items, it is similar to the offerings presented to an honoured guest visiting the household. The sixteen offerings are: (1) water to wash the feet (*pādya*);[30] (2) water to drink (*arghya*); (3) water to wash hands and face (*ācamana*); (4) light food (*madhuparka*)—a mixture of yogurt, clarified butter, and honey; (5) additional water to rinse the mouth (*punar ācamana*); (6) a bath (*snāna*); (7) clothes (*vastra*); (8) ornaments (*bhūṣaṇa*); (9) scent (*gandha*); (10) flowers (*puṣpa*);[31] (11) incense (*dhūpa*); (12) light (*dīpa*); (13) food (*naivedya*); (14) again water to rinse the mouth and hands (*punar ācamana*); (15) betelnut (*tāmbūla*); and (16) peace offerings and salutation (*tarpaṇa* and *namaskāra*).

6. *Worship of eight-petalled lotus deities* is worshipping the Goddess' most intimate attendants; no text elaborates on this step.

7. *Flower offerings* (*puṣpāñjali*) is an offering of five handfuls of flowers. Though not explicitly stated in the texts, the flowers are offered for attaining purity of mind. These symbolize non-deception (*amāyā*), absence of egoism (*anahankāra*), detachment (*arāga*), humility (*amada*), non-delusion (*amoha*), non-deceit (*adambha*), non-hostility (*adveṣa*), imperturbability (*akṣobha*), non-envy (*amātsarya*), non-greed (*alobha*), non-violence (*ahiṃsā*), non-indulgence in the senses (*indriya- nigraha*), benevolence (*dayā*), forgiveness (*kṣamā*), and wisdom (*jñāna*).[32]

8. *Worship of the Goddess' attendants* (*āvaraṇa pūjā*) is performed to honour all Chinnamastā's attendants who reside with her, including those outside of the enclosure, as well as those who reside next to Chinnamastā in the innermost sanctum.

9. *Valediction to Chinnamastā* (*visarjanā*) ceremony begins with the offering of incense, light, and a libation to Chinnamastā. One begs pardon of the Goddess for all one's acts whether virtuous or unvirtuous and offers everything to her. Then taking the consecrated liquid from the conch shell, one sprinkles it on everything and everyone participating in the *pūjā* while entreating the pardon of Chinnamastā for any faults or inappropriate actions. One envisages all her attendants merging into

Chinnamastā and then Chinnamastā disappearing from her *yantra* into one's heart. One mentally worships her there and bids her farewell.

Fire Ceremony

Burnt offerings (*homa*) with the repetition of Chinnamastā's *mantra* is not a daily practice because it involves much time and many offerings. In most temples it is performed regularly but in an individual household it is performed only on a special occasion and usually for a particular reason.[33] Hindu Tantric practitioners perform *homa* with the repetition of *mantras* for either mundane or supramundane reasons. The latter reason is to become liberated but the mundane reasons are numerous. In the *Nārada Purāṇa* (III.87.21ff), the practitioner is told that he/she can attain good fortune, happiness, longevity, be able to make all kings subservient, be free from diseases, attain poetic talents, captivate people, cause death to one's enemies, attain *siddhis*, etc.[34] Each attainment requires particular offerings and a certain amount of time. The *Nārada Purāṇa* (22-23) states:

> Through *mālatī* flowers he attains fluency of speech, through *campaka* flowers, happiness. If one performs a hundred *homas* everyday with the flesh of a goat smeared with *ghee*, and continues it for a month, all kings will be subservient to him.[35]

Other mundane attainments are included in the 'six acts' (*ṣaḍkarman*). These are: the ability to pacify, to remove diseases, or to prevent people from having to undergo terrible consequences (*śānti*), to bewitch beings (*vaśīkaraṇa* or *mohana*), to render a cause or power ineffective (*stambhana*), to create dissension or separation (*vidveṣaṇa*), to compel one's enemies to flee (*uccāṭana*), and to kill (*māraṇa*). Each attainment requires specific offerings, time, and the repetition of *mantras* in a specific order.

In the simplest terms, in front of a fire altar a practitioner presents to Chinnamastā specific offerings with appropriate *mantras*. *Śākta Pramoda* states that one can offer the five *m's*, or honey, sweet milk, etc. The five *m's* are five offerings which begin with *m* —wine (*madya*), meat (*māṃsa*), fish (*matsya*), a consort or parched grain (*mudrā*), and sexual union (*maithuna*). From among the three different kinds of Tantric practitioners, these latter offerings are only recommended for heroic types (*vīra*). Baser types who are 'animal-like' (*paśu*) are forbidden these offerings since they cannot offer them with a pure mind. Indeed it is very difficult even for the heroic types to offer them with a pure mind, but it is a training in controlling the senses and sublimating the power acquired through this restraint. The third type, who are 'divine-like' (*divya*), are neither encouraged nor dissuaded because they do not require external objects to arouse spiritual sentiments. The five offerings can be interpreted literally or they can be understood symbolically, e.g. yogic symbolism.

Since Chinnamastā is a great yoginī, let us look the yogic symbolism as explained in the *Āgamasāra* of the five *m's*. We find the symbolic equivalents of the offerings explained as follows:

1. *Madya* or wine symbolizes introspection and the arousal of the *kuṇḍalinī* to unite with Param Śiva who is at the *Sahasrāra cakra* where the (nectar) *amṛta* is located.

2. *Māṃsa* or meat refers to *ma* the tongue from which words arise. One who feeds on them is a worshipper of *māṃsa*. This person is a yogin who has control over his or her speech or has the power to withdraw from the phenomenal world (*pratyāhāra*).

3. *Matsya* represents two fish (*prāṇa* and *apāna*) who move in the Ganges (*iḍā nāḍī*) and Yamunā (*piṅgalā nāḍī*) and the person who controls them is practising *prāṇāyāma*.

4. *Mudrā* is the soul which resides in the thousand-petalled lotus in the head. One who acquires knowledge of this soul is a worshipper of *mudrā* and practises *dhyāna*.

5. *Maithuna* represents cohabitation which is the root of creation, preservation, and destruction. Its yogic sense is the attainment of *samādhi*.[36]

Stotra (praises)

The section of praises (*stotra*) to Chinnamastā is not an obligatory quotidian practice as the ritual worship (*pūjā*) is; however, the practitioner is encouraged to recite these praises daily upon completion of the ritual worship. In the *stotra* the practitioner eulogizes Chinnamastā's greatness. It is a combination of lauds and descriptions of Chinnamastā and her attendants, Varṇinī and Ḍākinī, but it is not a formal meditation session *per se*. It is foremost a eulogy to Chinnamastā, which is evident by the bracketing of praises to Chinnamastā in the first and last paragraphs. The practitioner is in a good company because the supreme gods, Brahmā, Śiva, and Viṣṇu, as well as yogis pay homage to Chinnamastā in the text. A practitioner professes faith, while affirming loyalty and veneration to her. Moreover, one becomes intimately involved with Chinnamastā by knowing both her form and formless aspects. The *stotra* states, "My obeisance to Mahāmāyā, O Mother, the graceful one, and bestower of knowledge." It is the belief of the practitioner that by extolling Chinnamastā, all efforts and dedication will result in receiving the desired goals—wealth, grain, great knowledge, and the eight *siddhis*.

Kavaca

Kavaca literally means armour or a coat of mail. In the *nyāsa* of the ritual section it refers to crossing one's arms and touching the shoulders (which is also a type of protection). In this section, the practitioner protects the entire body by the recitation of specific *mantras* at designated places of the body, beginning with the head and ending with the feet, and wearing amulets empowered with *mantras*. This practice, unlike the *nāysa* practice which transforms one's body into a divine body, protects the practitioner by requesting deities to guard certain parts of the body. These deities are summoned by the appropriate *mantras* and requested to remain at these parts of the body in order to neutralize negative influences, to propitiate planets, to ward off untimely death, and to provide general protection against all adverse circumstances. By having these deities as protectors, one can neutralize potentially negative forces and has at one's command the great deities, such as Lakṣmī and Saraswatī. The name of this *kavaca*—"victorious over the three worlds"—indicates its potency. The three worlds are: (1) the earth, (2) intermediate space, and (3) the sky. Thus they encompass the entire Hindu conception of the universe.

Hṛdaya (essence)

This section is the 'essence' (*hṛdaya*) of the entire practice. It contains parts of all the important practices, such as *nyāsa*, visualized meditation of Chinnamastā, praises to Chinnamastā, invocation of her as one's protectoress, recitation of her twelve names, and the results obtained by performing this *hṛdaya* practice.

One Hundred and Eight Names; One Thousand Names

These two sections consist in the recitation of Chinnamastā's names. The reasons for and benefits of reciting the names as well as their significances is discussed in chapter 3.

CHINNAMASTĀTANTRA OF ŚĀKTA PRAMODA[37]

The Chinnamastā Meditation (dhyāna)

Chinnamastā is always shown in the *pratyālīḍha* stance, nude holding (her own) severed head and a scimitar (*kartṛ*), and drinking with delight the red nectar stream issuing from her own headless body.[37a] She has fastened her head-jewels with snakes, is three-eyed, and is decorated with a blue lotus at her heart.[38] One should meditate on Chinnamastā as resembling a red hibiscus who is firmly standing on Kāmadeva who is attached to Rati. To her right is Varṇinī who exists in the *rajas guṇa* and who is very white with loose hair, holding a scimitar and skull cup. With her head-jewels fastened with snakes, she drinks with delight the red nectar stream issuing from the Goddess' severed body. Practitioners should meditate on her always as do the gods. (To her left) in the *pratyālīḍha* stance is Ḍākinī delightedly drinking from the red nectar stream which issues from the Goddess' headless body. Existing in the *tamas guṇa*, she is capable of enjoying the entire world even in its state of final dissolution (*pralaya*); (this) goddess is the power *par excellence.* One should always meditate humbly on this Goddess who bestows to her devotees the prosperity desired.

The Method of Drawing the Yantra

Draw an inverted triangle with three (concentric) circles at its centre. Then in the middle of them, draw an inverted triangle. Outside of the largest triangle, draw an eight-petalled lotus surrounded by a *bhūpūra* of three enclosing lines.[39] In the middle of the innermost triangle write *huṃ* and in the corners of the outer triangle write *phaṭ* with *huṃ.*[40]

The Explication of the Mantra

Lakṣmī is in the first syllable (*śrīṃ*); Manobhava is in the Lajjā seed syllable (*hrīṃ*);[41] the goddess who always destroys the five great sins is in the third seed syllable (*klīṃ*),[42] the goddess who has transcended all distinct powers (*guṇātīta*) and bestows liberation and knowledge is in the fourth (*aiṃ*).[43] Varuṇa is in *va*; the sovereign of the gods (Śakra. i.e. Indra) is in *i*.[44] The oblation eater (Agni) is in *ra*; the Lord of the Earth (Vasudhā's or Lakṣmī's consort, i.e. Viṣṇu) is in *va*.[45] Tripuradevī is in *ai*; Tripurasundarī is in *ra*. Goddess Trilokavijayā is always in *o*; Candra is in *ca* and the destroyer of obstacles (Vināyaka, i.e., Gaṇeśa) is in *na*.[46] Kamalā is in *ī*; Sarasvatī is in *ya* [read: *ye*]. In the pair of *hūṃ* the Goddess is always associated with Prakṛti,[47] *phaṭ* is Vaikharī (last stage in speech utterance); *svā* the flower-armed one (Kāmadeva), and *hā* is Rati (who is with Kāmadeva). This is the compilation of the *mantra*.

The entire *mantra* reads as follows:

Śrīṃ Hrīṃ Klīṃ Aim Vajravairocanīye Hūṃ Hūṃ Phaṭ Svāhā.[48]

The Ritual Worship Sequence (Pūjāvidhiḥ)

Regular preliminaries: After completing the regular ritual worship, one should do *mantra ācamana*.

Regular Tantric Preliminaries

1. *Ācamana* (washing with water for purification): (As you sip the water) say *'Śrīṃ, Hrīṃ, Hūṃ'*, as you wipe the water off your lips say *'Aim'*, as you sprinkle your lips say *'Hrīṃ, Hrīṃ'*, while washing your hands say *'Hūṃ'*. Then touching each place with the appropriate *mantra* say "*Śrīṃ, Hrīṃ Hūṃ, Aim Klīṃ, Śrīṃ Hrīṃ Klīṃ Aim, Om, Klīṃ, Im, Krīṃ*" respectively for the face, nose, eyes, ears, navel, heart, head and shoulders.[49] After touching each of these places while reciting the appropriate *mantra*, one becomes an embodiment of Śiva. After performing this *ācamana* for one year, one will see (*darśana*) Chinnamastā.

2. *The six-part nyāsa and prāṇāyāma:* Next do *prāṇāyāma* and the six-part *nyāsa*.[50] (By doing this) one will gain control of the three worlds. Say in order the syllables "*Śrīṃ, Aim, Klīṃ, Sauh, Śrīṃ, Hrīṃ, Klīṃ, Aim, Haum, Om, Krīṃ, Krīṃ, Krīṃ, Im, Hūm, Phaṭ*" and the eighteen-syllable *mantra* of the sixteen knowledge goddesses (*vidyā*).

3. *Mātṛkabīja nyāsa* (*fifty letters of the alphabet*): One should do the *mātṛka nyāsa* (touching each part of the body with the appropriate letter of the alphabet).[51] By doing this one obtains a divine body (lit. *Brahmasvarūpa*) and one's body will become adamantine (*vajradeha*). One will be endowed with absolute supremacy in the world and become a liberated being (*jīvanmukta*) within ten years.

4. *Ṛṣi nyāsa:* Next one should do the *ṛṣi nyāsa*, etc. The seer (*ṛṣi*) is Bhairava, the meter is Samrāṭ, the goddess is Chinnamastā, the seed syllable is *Hūṃ*, the power (*śakti*) is *Svāhā*, and by this application one gains the desired goals. Then as you touch your head, say "*Bhairavāya Ṛṣaye Namaḥ*"; as you touch your mouth, say "*Samrāṭ Chandase Namaḥ*". As you touch your heart, say "*Chinnamastāyai Devatāyai Namaḥ*", as you touch your secret place, say "*Hūṃ Hūṃ Bījāya Namaḥ*", and as you touch your feet, say "*Svāhā Śaktaye Namaḥ*".[52]

5. *Karāṅga nyāsa* (*finger and limbs touching*): Touching the two small fingers together, say "*Om Ām Khaḍgāya Hṛdayāya Svāhā*" (*Om Ām* to the sword and heart *Svāhā*); with the ring fingers together, say "*Om Im Sukhaḍgāya Śirase Svāhā*" (*Om Im* to the good sword and the head *Svāhā*); with the middle fingers together, say "*Om Um Suvajrāya Śikhāyai Svāhā*" (*Om Um* to the good *vajra* and to the tuft of hair *svāhā*); with the index fingers together, say "*Om Aim Pāśāya Kavacāya svāhā*" (*Om Aim* to the noose and the armour [crossed arms] *svāhā*); with the thumbs together, say "*Om Aum Ankuśāya Netratrayāya svāhā*" (*Om Aum* to the hook and the three eyes *svāhā*);[53] with the palms and the backs of the hands together, say "*Om Aḥ surakṣarakṣāsurakṣayāstrāya Phaṭ*"

(*Om·Āḥ* to good protector, protector, good protector and the posterior *śvāhā*).[54]

The *Bhairava Tantra* explains it in this manner. Say "*Ām Khaḍgāya Hṛdyāya Svāhā*" when joining the two small fingers, (then) say "O Goddess with a splendour of ten million moons"; with the two ring fingers joined, say "*Im Sukhaḍgāya Śirase Svāhā*"; with the two middle fingers joined, say "*Um Suvajrāya Śikhāya Svāhā*"; say the twelve syllable *mantra* directed to the Goddess; with the two index fingers joined, say "*Aim Pāśāya Kavacāya Svāhā*"; with two thumbs joined, say "*Aum Aṅkuśāya Netratrayāya Svāhā*"; with the palms and backs of the hands joined, say "*Aḥ Surakṣārakṣāsurakṣāya Phaṭ*". Say these words at the heart, head, tuft of hair, at the shoulders with crossed arms (*kavaca*), and eyes respectively. Then bind the directions (by clicking fingers over one's head in the four cardinal directions and intermediate ones).[55] In the *Triśakti Tantra* Bhairava says that one should precede each phrase of the *nyāsa* with "*Om*".

6. *Pervasive nyāsa (vyāpaka nyāsa)*: One should do the pervasive *nyāsa* by touching the places from one's head to one's feet and from feet to head while repeating the *mantra*. This should be done three times.

7) *Meditation of Chinnamastā (dhyāna)*: One should meditate at one's navel, a half-opened white lotus within its centre is a solar disc as red as a hibiscus and resembling a red *bandhūka* flower. This disc is decorated with a downward pointing (equilateral) triangle consisting of three lines representing the *guṇas—rajas*, *sattva*, and *tamas* (beginning from the left in a clockwise direction). Standing in its centre is Chinnamastā effulgent as ten million suns. In her left hand she holds her own head, her mouth is wide open with the tip of her tongue lolling. She drinks the sanguinary stream issuing from her own throat; her dishevelled hair is decorated with various flowers. In her right hand she holds a scimitar (*kartṛ*), decorated with a skull necklace. She is nude, terrible to behold, and stands in the *pratyālīḍha* stance. Wearing a bone rosary, having full breasts, and having a snake as her sacred thread, she is perpetually sixteen years old. She stands above Rati and Kāma who are in reversed sexual union (i.e., Rati is on top). One should always meditate in this manner with the *mantra*.

She is flanked by Ḍākinī and Varṇinī to her left and right respectively. Varṇinī drinks the sanguinary stream issuing from the Goddess' neck. She is red in colour, has a smiling face, loose hair, and is nude. She holds a skull and scimitar in her left and right hands respectively. Wearing a snake as her sacred thread, she has a fiery splendour. Decorated with various ornaments and a bone rosary, she stands in a *pratyālīḍha* stance. She is perpetually twelve years old.

On Chinnamastā's left side is Ḍākinī whose brilliance equals the fire at the end of an aeon. Her matted hair is as brilliant as lightning. She has three eyes, teeth as white as cranes, protruding canines, and full breasts. She is a large goddess who is excessively fierce with dishevelled hair, nude, and with a lolling tongue. Decorated with a skull rosary, she holds a skull and a scimitar in her left and right hands respectively. Drinking the sanguinary stream issuing from the Goddess' neck, she holds a terrible skull and is exceedingly fierce. A wise practitioner should meditate upon the Goddess attended by these two. In the *Bhairava Tantra* it states that the Goddess drinks the sanguinary stream with her mouth and also she holds her own head with a skull in her left hand. The Tantra states that should someone perform this worship without meditating on Chinnamastā, the Goddess will sever one's head and drink one's blood.

8. *Making the yantra*: The lotus petal should be white in the east, red in the southeast, black in the south, yellow in the southwest, white in the west, red in the northwest, white in the north, black in northeast; and yellow in the centre. In the centre of the lotus is a sun disc with a triangle composed of *rajas*, *sattva*, and *tamas*, coloured red, white, and black respectively.[56] At each corner write "*hrīṃ phaṭ*" and enclose everything in a *bhūpūra*. This *bhūpūra* is coloured red in the east, black in the south, white in the west, and yellow in the north. The four doors are protected by the field protectors (*kṣetrapāla*). Another way is to draw three concentric circles in the middle of a triangle and a triangle in the centre of these circles. In the exterior triangle write "*huṃ phaṭ*" at each corner. Draw an eight-petalled lotus outside the triangle and a *bhūpūra* enclosing everything.

9. *Meditation of inner yantra*: This is the meditation according to the (inner) *yantra*. Śiva spoke, "I shall explain as follows, listen, O Goddess, (meditate) according to this way."[57]

a. *For yogis*: Yogis should meditate like this: in your navel is a lotus surmounted by a sun disc, whereupon is an inverted triangle which is formed of the three *guṇas*. In the middle is the great goddess Chinnamastā blazing as a flame, unequalled and incomparable. She is established in the *yoni mudrā* and her eyes are directed to her heart.[58]

b. *For householders*: Listen, householders, this is the way you should meditate: In your body at the navel is a lotus. The goddess stands there stainless, beyond distinct powers (*guṇa*), subtle, having the lustre of a waxing moon. Comprehensible only through *samādhi*, she is surrounded by the three *guṇas*; incalculable, unqualifiable, she bestows liberation.

10. *Conch ritual*[59] : Before performing the conch ritual one needs to do the *samānārghya* (general oblation). On the ground draw with vermilion sandalwood paste a square, within it a circle, and within it a triangle. Present perfume (*gandha*), unbroken grains of raw rice (*akṣata*), and red flowers (*puṣpa*) while saying "*Om Hrīṃ Ādhāraśaktāye Namaḥ*" (*Om Hrīṃ* homage to the power of support). Perform this ritual worship to empower the oblation, rinse (the conch) with the utterance of "*Phaṭ*". Then say "*Om Samānārghya pātrādhārvāya Namaḥ*" (Homage to the support of the offering vessel of the general oblation). Then presenting these three offerings, say "*Om Samānārghya Pātrāya Namaḥ*" (Homage to the offering vessel of the general oblation). Then pour water into the vessel while saying,"*Hīṃ*". Then address the *tīrthas* (great rivers) with the *aṅkuśa mudrā* (a hooked hand gesture) and the following *mantra*: "*Om Gaṅgā ca Yamunā caiva Godāvarī Sarasvatī Narmadā Sindhu Kāverī Jale'smin Sannidhiṃ Kuru*" (Homage to the Ganges River . . . Kaveri River, please stay in this water.) Then release the perfume, rice grains, and flowers into the water while performing the *dhenu mudrā*.[60] Say the *mantra* ten times beginning with "*Om*".

Special Oblation: Then arrange the conch shell. Draw a square, within it a circle, and within that a triangle.[61] Place the tripod on the triangle and after rinsing the conch shell, while uttering "*Phaṭ*", place it on top of the tripod as one recites, "*Om Maṇ Daśakalātmane Vahnimaṇḍalāya Namaḥ*" (*Om* Homage to the fire whose self consists of ten parts).[62] Then worship all the aforementioned rivers beginning with the Ganges. Say from one's heart, to Chinnamastā who is invited to enter the vessel, "*Śrī Chinnamastā ihāvaha iha tiṣṭha*" (Śrī Chinnamastā, come here, stay here.) Conceal the vessel with a "*Hūṃ*" and do the *gālinī mudrā*. After looking at the water, say "*Vauṣaṭ*" and perform the *sakalīkaraṇa* (giving the deity a finite form by saying the appropriate *mantra* and doing the correct *mudrā*) with the sixteen *mantras*.[63] Perform the ritual worship to Chinnamastā by presenting scent and flowers with a "*Namaḥ*". Then perform the *matsya mudrā*, guard the offering and repeat ten times the root *mantra*. Then say "*Vaṃ*" while performing the *dhenu mudrā* and protect the vessel with a "*Phaṭ*".[64]

11. *Pīṭha pūjā (seat of the deity)*[65]: Perform the worship of the sacred place or seat of the Goddess (*pīṭha pūjā*). Say "*Ādhāraśaktaye Namaḥ, Prakṛtaye Namaḥ, Kūmrāya Namaḥ, Anantāya Namaḥ, Pṛthivyai Namaḥ, Kṣīrasamudrāya Namaḥ, Ratnadvīpāya Namaḥ, Kalpavṛkṣāya Namaḥ*" and top of this "*Svarṇasiṃhāsanāya Namaḥ, Ānandakandāya Namaḥ, Sambilvalāya Namaḥ, Sarvatattvātmakapadmāya Namaḥ, Sam*

Sattvāya Namaḥ, Ram Rajase Namaḥ, Tam Tamase Namaḥ, Ām Ātmane Namaḥ, Ām Antarātmane Namaḥ, Pam Paramātmane Namaḥ, Hrīṃ Jñānātmane Namaḥ" and in the middle of the lotus "*Ratikāmabhyām Namaḥ*". According to the *Bhairava Tantra* one begins with *ādhāraśakti*, followed by *kūrma, nāgarāja, padmanāla, padma, maṇḍala, caturasra, rajas, sattva, tamas*, and Rati with Kāma. This should be done with the *mantra*.

11a. *Śakti pūjā* : Śakti worship is directed to the goddess who stands on Rati and Kāma, i.e., Chinnamastā. Say, *"O Vajravairocanīye, dehi dehi, ehi ehi, gṛhṇa gṛhṇa; mama siddhim dehi dehi, mama śatrūn māraya māraya karālike hūṃ phaṭ svāhā*". (O Vajravairocanī, *give, come, take*; *give* me accomplishments; *kill* my enemies, O Fierce One, *Hūṃ Phaṭ Svāhā*.) Every phrase of the *pītha mantra* begins with "*Om*" and ends with "*Namaḥ*".

Invocation of the Deity

1. *Āvāhana* (invocation of the goddess) : To invoke the Goddess say "*Om sarvasiddhi Varṇinīye, sarvasiddhi Ḍākinīye, Vajravairocanīye, ihāvaha; sarvasiddhi Varṇinīye, sarvasiddhi Ḍākinīye, Vajravairocanīye iha tiṣṭha tiṣṭha, iha sannidehi, iha sanniruddhasva.*" (All-accomplished Varṇinī, all-accomplished Ḍākinī, Vajravairocanī come here; all-accomplished Varṇinī, all-accomplished Ḍākinī, Vajravairocanī, stay here, stay close to here, do not move from here.)

2. *Prāṇapratiṣṭhā* (instilling the vital breath into the image) : Say the *mantra* "*Om Āṃ Hrīṃ Krom Haṃsaḥ*".[66]

3. *The six-limbed nyāsa of Goddess* : Touch the six principal parts of the Goddess (image) saying the appropriate *mantras*.

4. *Śakti worship of the goddess* : Perform the *śakti pūjā*.[67] (From *Nityārcana*) Say, "*Hrāṃ Hṛdayāya Namaḥ/ Hrīṃ Śiraśe Svāhā/ Hrūṃ Śikhāyai Vaṣaṭ / Hraim Kavacāya Hūṃ/ Hraum Netratrayāya Vauṣaṭ/ Hrāḥ Astrāya Phaṭ*". (This is also known as worship of the six long vowels or *vidyās*.)

5. *Sacrificial offering (bali)* : As one offers the *bali* say, "*Vajravairocanī dehi dehi, ehi ehi, gṛhṇa gṛhṇa balim; mama siddhim dehi dehi; mama śatrūn māraya māraya, karālike, Hūm Phaṭ*" (Vajravairocanī *give, come, take* (this) offering; *give* me accomplishment; *kill* my enemies, O Fierce One, *Huṃ Phaṭ*) Say this *mantra* two more times, once to the goddess on the right (preceded by) "*Om Varṇinyai Namaḥ*" and to the goddess on the left (preceded by) "*Om Ḍākinyai Namaḥ*". Again perform the six-limbed *nyāsa* to these two goddesses. Then to the one on the right say "*Om Śaṅkhanidhaye Namaḥ*" and to the one on the left say "*Om Padminidhaye Namaḥ*". (Homage to the conch treasure and to the lotus treasure.)[68]

6. *Worship of eight-petalled lotus deities*: Worship the eight lotus petals, beginning in the east with the cardinal directions (going clockwise), and proceeding to the intermediate directions worship the eight lotus petals thus: Lakṣmī in the east, Kāma in the south, Māyā in the west, Vāṇī in the north, Brahmā in the southeast, Viṣṇu in the southwest, Rudra in the northwest, Īśāna in the northeast, and Sadāśiva in the centre. Each name is preceded by "*Om*" and ends with "*Namaḥ*".

7. *Flower offerings (puṣpāñjali)*: Offer five handfuls of flowers.

8. *Worship the goddess' attendants (āvaraṇa pūjā)*: Begin the worship of the deities of the *bhūpūra*: Agni in southeast, Īśa in northeast, Asura in northwest, Vāyu in southwest.[69] Then repeat the six-limbed *nyāsa*.[70] Now worship the eight heroines (*nāyikās*) beginning in the east, saying "*Om Hrīṃ Kālyai Namaḥ*". Repeat this with Varṇinī, Ḍākinī, Bhairavī, Mahābhairavī, Indrākṣī, Piṅgākṣī, and Saṃhāriṇī. Always begin with "*Om*" and end with "*Namaḥ*". In the centre (of the inner triangle) is "*Hūṃ Phaṭ Namaḥ*" and "*Svāhā Namaḥ*",[71] in the south "*Samrāṭ Chandase Namaḥ*", in the north "*Sarva Varṇebhyo Namaḥ*", and again in the south "*Bīja Śaktibhyām Namaḥ*". Then on the petal tips beginning in the east, worship the eight mother goddesses (*mātṛkās*): Brāhmī, Māheśvarī, (Kumārī),[72] Vaiṣṇavī, Vārāhī, Indrāṇī, Cāmuṇḍā, Mahālakṣmī respectively, beginning with "*Om*" and ending with "*Namaḥ*". Then worship the goddesses at the four doors, beginning in the east: Karālāya, Vikarālāya, Atikarālāya, and Mahākarālāya. Begin with "*Om*" and end with "*Namaḥ*".

9. *Valediction to Chinnamastā (visarjana)*: One offers incense, lamps, and libation to Chinnamastā. Then make the special *saṃhāra mudrā* (showing an open *añjali* [a hand gesture of praying with palms touching and fingers slightly apart as if one is holding a flower]). Then touching the left nostril, you exhale, i.e. bidding the goddess farewell.[73] One visualizes that Chinnamastā (lit., one with the *yoni mudrā*) is a blazing flame which decreases successively as a waning moon until it merges with the sun. Say the *mantra* "*Uttare Śikhare . . .*"[74] (From the *Tantrasāra*): "*Uttare Śikhare Devī*" (O Devi in the north on the mountain peak, i.e., the Himālayas); "*Bhūmyam Parvatavāsinī*" (O Dweller of the mountains), "*Gaccha Devi Mamāntaram*" (O Goddess enter my heart).

Fire Ceremony

***Burnt offerings with repetition of Chinnamastā's mantra*:** Next perform the *puraścaraṇa* presenting burnt offerings (*homa*) with one hundred thousand repetitions of the Chinnamastā's *mantra*.[75] By performing this one acquires *siddhis*. It is stated in the *Bhairava Tantra* that in presenting sacrificial offerings (*bali*) to the goddess, one should give fish, meat, wine, etc. at night or one can offer honey, sweet milk, etc. according to one's means. Present these offerings to Chinnamastā while saying the *mantra*, "*Om sarvasiddhi prade Varṃinīye, sarvasiddhiprade Ḍākinīye, Chinnamastā Devi, ehi ehi, imam balim gṛhṇa gṛhṇa, mama siddhim dehi dehi, Phaṭ Svāhā*". (*Om* bestower of all accomplishments, Varṇinī, bestower of all accomplishments, Ḍākinī, Goddess Chinnamastā, *come*, *take* (these) offerings, *give* me all accomplishments, *Phaṭ Svāhā*.) This is the ritual worship of Sureśvarī (Goddess of the gods).

Stotra (praises)

Īśvara spoke:[76] "With supreme praises I pay homage to Goddess Vairocanī who bestows all auspicious things. Visualize in your navel a white lotus surmounted by a shining solar disc. She is the one and only essence of the world, mother of the three worlds (earth, intermediate space, and sky), and bestower of *dharma*, *kāma*, and *artha*. In the middle of the lotus are three parts which represent the three bodies (i.e. of Chinnamastā, Varṇinī, and Ḍākinī). I pay homage to excellent Chinnamastā, the one with severed head, to the one who removes fear of the god of death (Yama). I pay homage to this *yoginī* with the *yogamudrā*. (1)[77]

"Visualize at the navel a white lotus which is delightfully opened topped by a solar disc as red as a *bandhūka* flower. At its centre is a great inverted triangle (*yoni cakra*). In the middle of this Kāminī and Pradyumna are in reversed sexual embrace and, effulgent as ten million rising suns, the Goddess stands on top of them. (2). . . She holds her own severed head in her left hand and in the other hand a great scimitar (*kartṛ*). Standing in the *pratyālīḍha* stance, she is nude and has loose thick hair. From her severed head she drinks the spurting stream of blood. She is as bright as the ascending sun (i.e., orange red) and her three eyes shine splendidly. (3)

"On her right side is Varṇinī who is drinking[78] the oozing, glistening sanguinary stream from the subtle channel (*nāla*). In her lotus hand she holds a shining scimitar. She is nude, with bone ornaments, a terrific form, red in appearance, and crimson hair. Representing the power of the goddess, she stands in the *pratyālīḍha* stance with thighs and feet extended; she has red eyes and is a *yoginī* who represents *yoganidrām*.[79] (4)

"(On her left is Ḍākinī) who is nude with dishevelled hair, has a violent form like a dense dark cloud at the end of an aeon and has fiercely protruding canines. The tip of her restless tongue is located in the cavity in the middle of her mouth, and her two eyes flash like lightning. This fierce form of blazing Bhoginī is dear to (Chinnamastā's) heart. The blood which has dripped down from Chinnamastā's recently severed head nourishes Ḍākinī. (5)

"Brahmā, Śiva, and Viṣṇu place the Goddess' feet on their heads as do the trustworthy people and great yogis who continuously meditate on her inconceivable form (*nirguṇa* aspect). With my heart I shall meditate on the one essence of *saṃsāra*, mother of the three worlds, excellent Chinnamastā, the cherished one, bestower of wishes, and dispeller of the defilements of the Kaliyuga. (6) She possesses three corporeal forms for the sake of creation, maintenance, and dissolution of the world, and possesses the three *guṇas* whose transformations are represented as Brahmā, Viṣṇu, and Śiva respectively. I shall meditate on the primordial Prakṛti for the purpose of attaining all goals. All people remember (her) by adoring her lotus-like feet. (7)

"I am engaged in the worship of union with another's wife. Also, I desire different things than other people do. I am detached from ordinary people. I am rooted in Bhairavī. I am at the feet of my teacher. I am Bhairava. I am Śiva.[80] (8)

"Previously spoken by Brahmā, this praise has great merit. All accomplishments are fulfilled and it destroys the five great sins. (9) One who recites these praises in the morning, preferably in proximity to the goddess, will achieve the fulfilment of all desires. (10) The goddess bestows desired goals—wealth, grain, children, wife, horses, elephants, and land. The one who recites these praises will certainly obtain great knowledge and the eight *siddhis.* (11)

"I bow to thee who is Mahāmāyā, O Mother, the graceful one and bestower of knowledge; whose hips are wrapped with a tiger skin, who is unusual with a protruding belly and who is multilated, who is of indescribable beauty, decorated with a string of severed heads, and has a sacrificial knife shining white like a jasmine flower (*kunda*). One attains these boons by reciting the praises to Chinnamastā." (12)

The Victorious Over the Three Worlds Kavaca

The glorious Goddess spoke: "Whatever you have told me about these well-guarded knowledges relating to Chinnamastā, I have heard and understood. (1) Now I would like to hear about the 'victorious over the three worlds *kavaca* (armour)' as was previously revealed, O Beloved." (2)

Bhairava replies, "Listen and I shall tell you, O Deveśi,[81] who is worshipped by all the gods. This 'victorious over the three worlds *kavaca*' attracts everyone. (3) With it one can triumph over gods and their rivals;

one can gain mastery over the three worlds by reciting and guarding it. (4) By guarding and reciting this, Brahmā, Viṣṇu, and Śiva become creator, preserver, and destroyer, respectively. (5) This should not be given or taught to false or faithless disciples, but only to devoted ones whom the teacher cherishes more than his own life. (6)

"Bhairava is the seer of the *kavaca*, the metre is Virāṭ, the goddess is Chinnamastā. (7) Its results are victory over the three worlds and liberation.

"*Om Hūṃ*, may Chinnamastā, bestower of strength, protect my head. (8) *Hrīṃ Hrīṃ Aim*, may the nude one protect my forehead and mouth. *Śrīṃ Hrīṃ Huṃ Aim*, may the one who holds a skull and knife protect my eyes. (9) With the goddess' *vidyā* (*mantra*) beginning and ending with "*Om*", may she always protect my ears. *Hūṃ Phaṭ Svāhā*, O Vairocanī, may you protect my eyebrows, etc. (10) *Śrīṃ Hrīṃ Huṃ Aim* ,O Vairocanī, *Hūṃ*, may Chinnamastā holding a skull and scimitar, protect my nose. (11) *Huṃ Phaṭ Svāhā*, the great knowledge goddess who is sixteen years old, has the form of Brahmā, and is flanked by young girls delightedly drinking her blood (i.e., Varṇinī and Ḍākinī). (12) May Chinnamastā, who has her own power (*svaśaktika*), wears a skull garland, is red, and grants the accomplishment of desires, protect my face. (13) Accompanied by Varṇinī and Ḍākinī, may she protect me on all sides. May she who is Ramā (i.e., Lakṣmī); (*Śrīṃ*) protect my tongue. May she who is Lajjā (*Hrīṃ*) protect my throat. (14) May '*Hūṃ*' protect my heart; may Vāgdevī (*Aim*), etc., protect my chest. May 'Ramā' protect my both hands; may Sureśvarī protect both my sides (15). By Māyā (*Hrīṃ*), may Vidyā protect me, may my navel region be protected by the nude one. By '*Hūṃ*', may the Goddess always protect my back. (16) *Aim*, may the one endowed with power, protect my waist and hips. *Hūṃ Aim Vairocaniye Hūṃ Hūṃ Phaṭ Svāhā.* (17) May Mahāvidyā Chinnamastā, effulgent as ten million suns, always protect my thighs. (18) *Hrīṃ Hūṃ* Varṇinī, may you protect my knees; *Srīṃ Hrīṃ Hūṃ Ḍākinī*, may you protect my feet. Repeat the entire *mantra* of Chinnamastā for protection of the whole body. (19)

"In the east is Ekaliṅgā, in the southeast is Yoginī, in the south is Ḍākinī (20), in the southwest is Mahābhairavī, in the west is Bhairavī, in the northwest is Indrāṇī, in the north is Asitāṅgī (21), and in the northeast is Saṃhāriṇī, may they always protect me. May these eight *śaktis* holding scimitar (*kartṛ*) protect in all directions. (22) In the east, *Krīṃ Krīṃ Krīṃ*, protect me; in the southeast, *Hūṃ Hūṃ*, protect me; in the south, *Hrīṃ*, protect me (23); in the southwest, *Krīṃ Krīṃ Krīṃ*, protect me; in the west, *Hrīṃ Hrīṃ*, protect me; in the northwest, *Hrīṃ Hrīṃ*, protect me; in the north, *Svāhā*, protect me (24); in the northeast may Mahākālī with sword in hand protect me. In the zenith, *Srīṃ Hrīṃ Klīṃ Hūṃ Phaṭ* with the great *mantra*, (25) may Tārā holding a sword and scimitar protect me, and in the nadir, *Hrīṃ Śrīṃ Hūṃ Phaṭ*, may Ekajaṭā always protect me. (26) May Mahānīlasarasvatī protect all the intermediate spaces.[82] Now I have told you the sections of the Goddess' *kavaca*. (27)

"One who recites this *kavaca* becomes fierce Bhairava and he becomes lord of gods, rival of the gods, and sages. (28) Those who are wise (recite this *kavaca*). Goddess Madhumatī, herself, comes to the devotee's house; *bhūtinī, yoginī, yakṣiṇī*, and *khecarā* will help devotees.[83] (29) All these will obey one due to the influence of the *kavaca*. These goddesses will approach one and will ask what one desires. This *kavaca* which I have told you is known as Parabrahma (the supreme of ultimate reality). (30) By worshipping the Goddess with scents, etc., by reciting the root *mantra* for one year, one will obtain results. (31)

"By only one who is accomplished in the *mantra*, have the *mantra* written on birch bark, and make this into an amulet. One should wear it on the right arm, at the throat, or anywhere the devotee desires. (32) One will become prosperous and be able to influence the three worlds. Lakṣmī (goddess of wealth) will reside in one's house and Sarasvatī (goddess of eloquence and knowledge) will sit on one's tongue. (33) The Brahamāstra (an indomitable weapon) will become ineffective for one who worships Chinnamastā with the correct *kavaca*. One who worships Chinnamastā without *kavaca* will be killed quickly." (34) This completes the "victorious in the three worlds *kavaca*" which has been told in the *Bhairava Tantra* in the conversation between Bhairava and Bhairavī.

Hṛdaya (essence)

This is the 'essence' (*hṛdaya*) practice. Śrī Pārvatī spoke,[84] "I have heard from you how to worship and so on; now I wish to hear about the *hṛdaya* of Chinnamastā."

Śrī Mahādeva spoke, "O Beloved, I have not told this to anyone, but since you have asked me, I shall tell you, my dear. '*Om*' is Chinnamastā's *hṛdaya*, praise, and *mantra*. Bhairava is the seer, Samrāṭ is the meter, Chinnamastā is the deity, '*Hūṃ*' is the seed syllable, '*Om*' is the power, '*Hrīṃ*' is the *kīla*,[85] and the application is destruction of the enemy.

"This is the way to do the hand *nyāsa*: '*Om Hṛdayāya Namaḥ*' (Om homage to the heart); '*Om Hūṃ Śirase Svāhā*' (*Om Hūṃ* to the head *Svāhā*); '*Om Hrīṃ Śikhāyai Vaṣaṭa*' (*Om Hrīṃ* the sacred hairtuft Vaṣaṭ); '*Om Klīṃ Netratrayāya Vauṣaṭa*' (*Om Klīṃ* to three eyes Vauṣaṭa); '*Om Aim Kavacāya Huṃ*' (*Om Aim* to touching the shoulders by crossing the arms *Hūṃ*); '*Om Hūṃ Astrāya Phaṭ*' (*Om Hūṃ* to the posterior *Phaṭ*).

"Here is the meditation. I shall remember Chinnamastā, destroyer of Māra, who has crimson hair and holds in her lotus-like hand a scimitar. She is very ferocious. She drinks from the copious sanguineous stream from her own severed head. As wind blows away clouds, Chinnamastā casts aside obstacles. By worshipping her, all *siddhis* will be attained. I pay homage to Chinnamastā, the excellent one who holds her own severed head. Though her head is severed, still she is charming and wears silken garments. (1) Always the assembly of gods place their heads to her feet (i.e., worship her); I am honouring her, the bestower of all auspicious things. (2) In every aeon she will be reborn for the continuity of sacrifice (*yajña*). I worship Goddess Chinnamastā who annihilates demons and evil beings. (3) Ṛṣi Vāmadeva spreads the teachings of beautiful Vairocanī effulgent as ten million suns. I pay homage to her whose eyes flash like lightning. (4) Blood gushing continuously from her throat, she satisfies all the *yoginīs* who are devoted at her feet. (5) Concentrate on this and say '*Hūṃ*'. If you recite this *mantra* correctly, your enemies will disappear. (6) If you recite this *mantra* correctly, '*Hūṃ Svāhā*', Chinnamastā will eradicate any afflictions distressing you. Just as the wind blows away clouds, Chinnamastā blows away sufferings. (7) With only her stare, all fierce, cruel, or demonic beings flee to distant places in order to escape her. To her I worship. (8) May there be victory to her who adroitly protects the world, forgives anger, and easily eradicates deception and maliciousness of people. May there be victory to Chinnamastā who imparts indestructible knowledge to kings, transforms demons (into followers), and devours enemies. (9) Armed with a knife, she destroys even the smallest traces of wickedness of the Kaliyuga. As brilliant as the divine blue lotus in the heavenly realms, her effulgence eclipses the sun's radiance. May there be victory to her who frightens the assembly of rivals of gods; may there be victory to the dark forms, Kālī, Chinnamastā, and Karālī. (10) All prosperity of the three worlds is bestowed by her who nurtures the three worlds and increases knowledge by her power. Just as a lotus blossoms with sunshine, may Chinnamastā cause the blossoming of the twice-born's hearts. Chinnamastā is like both Sarasvatī and Pārvatī. (11) O Mother, place a sharp dagger in your hand, whet it very sharply, and swiftly decapitate my enemies. May your fame spread. Please destroy my enemies and wicked ones quickly. Please fulfil my wishes and forgive me of any faults." (12)

"For her devotees, these are the twelve names that Chinnamastā likes to hear: (1) Chinnagrīvā (whose neck is severed), (2) Chinnamastā (whose head is severed), (3) Chinnamuṇḍadharā (one who holds a severed head), (4) Akṣatā (who is whole or uninjured), (5) Kṣodakṣemakarī (who is skillful in causing peace), (6) Svakṣā (who has beautiful eyes), (7) Kṣonīśacchādakṣamā (who protects the kings of the earth) (13), (8) Vairocanī (Indra's wife), (9) Varārohā (lit., fine-thighed one, i.e., beautiful), (10) Balidānapraharṣitā (who delights those who present sacrificial offering), (11) Balipūjātapādābjā (whose lotus feet are honoured with sacrificial offerings), and (12) Vāsudevaprapūjitā (who is worshipped by Vāsudeva, i.e., Kṛṣṇa). (14) These are the twelve names that Chinnamastā likes. By remembering this in the morning when one arises, one's enemies will be destroyed. (15) Who remembers her will have the same wealth as the gods, enemies will be killed, and will be content and peaceful. Her worshippers will have good thoughts. Always they seek refuge in her. This primordial Goddess is worshipped by Śrīśādi (i.e., Viṣṇu, Brahmā, and Śiva); may Chinnamastā, the most auspicious one, help us. (16) One cannot kill one's enemies without knowledge of this *hṛdaya*, O Pārvatī. (17) Anyone who wants to destroy one's enemies quickly, recite this *hṛdaya*. Whatever fruits are desired, Chinnamastā will bestow them happily. (18) Having recited this, merit is acquired and life and health will be bestowed." (19) From the *Śrīnandyāvartta*, this completes Śrī Chinnamastā's *hṛdaya* eulogy in a conversation between Mahādeva and Pārvatī.

REFERENCES

1. Gupta, S.; *Hindu Tantrism*: 121.
2. Ibid: 124.
3. See Bharati:328. Many of the Nepalese manuscripts of Chinnamastā in the Nepalese Archives seem to be copied from the *Śākta Pramoda*.
4. There is some discussion about Kṛṣṇānanda Āgamavāgīśa's dates. See Sircar, *Śākta Pīṭhas*, 1973:74-80; Banerji, S.C., *Tantra in Bengal*, 1978:78-79; and Pal, P., *Hindu Religion and Iconology*, 1981:3. The *Tantrasāra* is not dated; Pal states that it was written between 1585-1600 C.E. and N.N. Bhattacharyya in his *History of Śākta Religion*: 145 states that it was written in the beginning of the seventeenth century.
5. It is of recent origin (2035 Vikram Era, 1979 C.E.).
6. Usually there are ten sections; the eighth section is known as *upaniṣṭa* (mystical knowledge imparted at the feet of the guru), then followed by the hundred and eight names and one thousand names. In the *Śākta Pramoda* the first three and the last Mahāvidyās—Kālī, Tārā, Ṣoḍasī, Tripurasundarī, and Kamalā—have this eighth section but the other six Mahāvidyās do not.
7. For excellent overviews about *mantras* and rituals, see Alper, H., ed., *Mantra*, Albany, SUNY, 1989; Bharati:101 ff.; Chakravarti, P., *Linguistic Speculations of the Hindus*, Calcutta 1933; Gonda, "The Indian Mantra", *Oriens*,vol. 16, 1963: 244-97; Padoux, A., *Recherches sur la symbolique et l'energie de la parole dans certains texts tantriques*, Paris 1964; and Wayman, A., "The Significance of

Mantras, from the Veda down to Buddhist Tantric Practice", *Buddhist Insight*: 413-30.

8. Gupta:102.
9. The etymology of *pūjā* is considered to be from the Dravidian verbal root which occurs in Tamil as *pucu.* This root means "to smear, to put on sticky substances, to daub, to paint". (See Charpentier, J., "The Meaning and Etymology of Puja", *The Indian Antiquary,* May and July 1927, Vol. LVI:93-99; 130-36. Also See Diehl, C.G., *Instrument and Purpose: Studies on Rites and Rituals in South India*:66.)
10. Gupta:141.
11. The famous Sanskrit phrase is "to worship a deity, one must become a deity" (*devo bhūtvā devam yajeta*).
12. Vidyarnava, S.C., *The Daily Practice of the Hindus*:14.
13. Gupta:169.
14. Woodroffe, *Principles of Tantra*: 485.
15. *Mātṛkā* has several connotations including : (1) a diminutive mother which can be interpreted as a subtle creator (the Great Goddess, Mahādevī), and (2) means a 'slight' measure which can be interpreted as the subtle letters of the Sanskrit alphabet. The latter is frequently discussed as the unfolding of the cosmic process proceeding from its matrix.
16. Woodroffe, *Principles of Tantra*:484. Also Gupta:143 states that "The *mātṛkā* is seen as the essential, mystic form of the Goddess who is the source of all names and forms in the universe".
17. Vidyarnava: 62 and 85.
18. *Nityārcana*:37-38.
19. In Hindu ritual the practitioner must become pure and 'divine' to invite a deity, one must be a deity.
20. See Khanna, M., *Yantra: The Tantric Symbol of Cosmic Unity*:11.
21. Woodroffe, *Introduction to Tantra Śāstra*: 95.
22. The Sanskrit word for triangle is *trikoṇa* which can be understood as three-dimensional triangle though depicted as two-dimensional on a *yantra* drawn on the ground, cloth, or paper.
23. When I visited the Cintapūrṇī Temple, Himachal Pradesh, dedicated to Chinnamastā, the *pujāris* told me that householder worshippers visualize Chinnamastā as Mātā Durgā when they are at home. All the curio shops sold only prints of Goddess Durgā; no prints of Chinnamastā were sold. Only yogis or *sādhus* could meditate on Chinnamastā with form.
24. For a fantastic description of the milk ocean and the jewelled island, see *Śrīmad Devī Bhāgavatam*: 1174ff. Also at the National Museum in New Delhi there is a beautiful Chamba mural illustrating this jewelled island.
25. Kalpavṛkṣa is a tree which grants all desires. It is one of the trees in Indra's heaven (*Raghuvaṃśa* 14.48 and 1.75).
26. According to Abhinavagupta the thirty-six *tattvas* are Śiva, Śakti, Sadāśiva, Īśvara, Śuddhavidyā, Māyā, Kalā, Vidyā, Rāga, Kāla, Niyati, and the twenty-five Sāṅkhya categories: Puruṣa, Prakṛti, Buddhi, Ahaṅkāra, Manas, the ten senses, the ten subtle and gross elements.
27. Gupta: 144 mentions that the four *ātmans* are various states of self. *Ātman* is Brahman, *antarātman* is enjoying self, *paramātman* is self in essence, and *jñānātman* is Brahman as undifferentiated from self.
28. Gupta:150.
29. *Nityārcana*: 52-58.
30. In most Indian houses one takes off one's shoes before entering.

31. *Nityārcana* includes parched barley grain (*akṣata*) after flowers but this is unusual.
32. See Gupta:145 and Woodroffe, *Great Liberation*:118.
33. Gupta:152.
34. *Nārada Purāṇa* III. 87. 21ff.
35. *Nārada Purāṇa*:1250; also see *Mantramahodadhi*:30a-30b.
36. Bose and Haldar:113ff.
37. This is the translation of the *Śākta Pramoda* from page 221 to 246.
37a. The description and symbolism of the iconography is discussed in chapter 5.
38. The first part of the sentence can be translated as "having bound snakes as her head ornaments". These *nāgas* are not considered ordinary snakes, *nāgas* have jewels inside their heads and are akin to powerful underworld spirits.
39. During the winter of 1986-87 in Sarnath, India Pandit Vraj Vallabha Dwivedi of Varanasi and I read through this text and he made numerous comments on it. (I shall note his comments with "VVD" throughout this translation of the "Chinnamastātantra".) He explained *bhūpūra* as a technical name for the section in the *yantra* which is an unbroken square enclosure with four 'doors'.
40. This means that one writes "*Hūṃ Phaṭ*" at each corner.
41. See Rai, R.K., *Dictionaries of Tantra Śāstra*: 158.
42. (VVD) The Goddess prevents one from committing the five great sins (killing a Brahmin, drinking, theft, adultery, and associating with anyone who committed such a sin) or if a person commits any of these actions, she counteracts their effects.
43. In the *Tantrasāra*:294-95 the *mantra* is presented in numerous ways, the first one being "*Śrīṃ Klīṃ Hrīṃ Aim Vajravairocanīye Hrīṃ Hrīṃ Phaṭ Svāhā*". The meaning is given as *Śrīṃ* (Lakṣmī), *Klīṃ* (Kāmadeva), *Hrīṃ* (Mahāpātakanāśinī), *Aim* (Vāgdevī who is beyond the three *guṇas* and bestows enjoyment and liberation).
44. Ibid.'Ja' (Surendra).
45. Ibid. Pṛthivīpati (king of the earth) is in '*V*'.
46. Ibid. '*C*' is (Candramā) and '*N*' is (Gaṇeśa).
47. Ibid. '*Hrīṃ Hrīṃ*' is (the goddess always with Prakṛti).
48. For a further variation of the *mantra*, see *Mantramahodadhi*:29b (*Om Śrīṃ Hrīṃ Hrīṃ Aim Vajravairocanīye Hrīṃ Phaṭ Svāhā*).
49. The *Tantrasāra*:295 explicitly explains the correspondences as follows: *Śrīṃ*/face, *Hrīṃ*/right nostril, *Hūṃ*/left nostril, *Aim*/ right eye, *Klīṃ*/left eye, *Śrīṃ*, *Hrīṃ*, *Klīṃ*/right ear, *Aim*/left ear, *Om*/navel, *Klīṃ*/heart, *Im*/touch top of the head, and *Krīṃ*/ touch both shoulders.
50. *Nyāsa* is a ritual of touching different parts of the body while reciting various *mantras*. There is no explanation of the six-part *nyāsa*. (Gupta: 144 fn. 35 lists them as the main domain of the goddess: Gaṇeśa, the planets, stars, yoginī, constellations and holy places). See Rai:103-05. Furthermore, the *Tantrasāra* refers to sixteen *nyāsa*.
51. *Śākta Pramoda* does not elaborate but the *Tantrasāra* does present the beginning. "Touch the forehead with '*Śrīṃ Āṃ Śrīṃ Namaḥ*', touch the mouth with '*Śrīṃ, Aṃ, Śrīṃ, Namaḥ*', again touch the forehead with '*Aim, Āṃ, Aim, Namaḥ*', and the mouth with '*Aim, Aṃ, Aim, Namaḥ*', etc. (This contiues until one has completed the entire alphàbet.)
52. The translation is "Homage to Seer Bhairava, homage to the Samrāṭ meter,

homage to Goddess Chinnamastā, homage to '*Hūṃ*', and homage to the *Svāhā* Power."

53. *Tantrasāra*: 296 has the *mantra* as "*Om Aum Krīṃ Netra Trayāya Svāhā*".
54. *Tantrasāra*: 296 states that the *mantra* is "*Om Aḥ Surakṣasurākṣāyāstraya Phaṭ*". In this text the *karāṅga nyāsa* usually begins with the thumbs and ends with the small fingers.
55. *Tantrasāra*: 296 has "bind the ten directions (*digbandha*)".
56. *Tantrasāra*:301 states that the order is *sattva*, *rajas*, and *tamas* with the colours of white, red and black respectively.
57. Hindu Śaivite and Śākta Tantras are classified into *āgama* and *nigama*, respectively. In an *āgama* Śiva reveals the *tantra* to the goddess and in an *nigama* the goddess reveals the *tantra* to Śiva. The texts that follow are *āgamas*.
58. According to the *Mudrānighaṇṭu*, *yoni mudrā* is a hand gesture used in the worship of the goddesses, such as Tārā, Tripurā, etc. (from *Dictionaries of Tantraśāstra* by Ram Kumar Rai:101).
59. The *Chinnamastātantra* does not describe the conch ritual but the *Nityārcana*:45ff. does. This description is a translation from the *Nityārcana*.
60. This *dhenu mudrā* transforms ordinary liquid into nectar (*amṛta*).
61. Gupta: 146-47 states that the diagram symbolizes the source of power of the universe, the tripod as the orb of fire.
62. See Woodroffe, *Great Liberation*:143. The ten parts are *Dhūmurā* (smoky red), *Arciḥ* (flame), *Jvalinī* (flaming), *Sūkṣmā* (subtle), *Jvālinī* (burning), *Viṣphuliṅginī* (shining with sparks), *Suśrī* (very auspicious), *Surūpā* (well-formed), *Kapilā* (tawny), and *Havya-kavya-vahā* (the carrier of oblations to the poets).
63. Once the deity is invoked and received, one sprinkles the deity three times with consecrated water from the conch shell and perform the six-limbed *nyāsa* on her body. 'Vauṣaṭ' is an exclamation spoken when making an oblation to a deity.
64. Gupta:146-47.
65 See translation in the introduction 11) *pīṭhapūjā* section (p.29).
66. The Nityārcana: 51 states "*Āṃ Hrīṃ Kroṃ Yaṃ Raṃ Laṃ Vaṃ Shaṃ Saṃ Haṃ Hauṃ Haṃsaḥ Chinnamastāya Prāṇa Iha Prāṇaḥ/ Āṃ Hrīṃ Kroṃ . . . Hamsaḥ Chinnamastāya Jīva Iha Sthitaḥ/ Āṃ Hrīṃ Kroṃ . . . Hamsaḥ Chinnamastāya Sarvendriyāni/ Āṃ Hrīṃ Kroṃ . . . Hamsaḥ Chinnamastāya Van Manas Cakṣuḥ Śrotra Ghrāna Prāna Padāni Ihāgatya Sukhaṃ Ciraṃ Tiṣṭhantu Svāhā*".
67. *Śākta Pramoda* does not elaborate; this is from the *Nityārcana*:51.
68. The conch and the lotus are two of the eight treasures of the god of wealth, Kubera. Also Jagadisa Ayyar, P.V. in *South Indian Festivities*, Madras, 1921:79-80 states, based on the *Mārkaṇḍeya Purāṇa*, that *padma* is that which gives prowess in warfare and wealth . . . Śaṅkha is that which brings self-realization and eternal bliss.
69. Usually Nirṛti is in the northwest.
70. Usually the lineage of the Gurus follows this step but curiously it is omitted here.
71. *Tantrasāra*: 303 says only one '*Hūṃ*'
72. Kumārī is missing in both the *Śākta Pramoda* and *Tantrasāra* but she appears in the *Nityārcana*. The most common seven mothers include Kumārī but omit Mahālakṣmī. If there are eight mothers, the latter is included.
73. The regular *saṃhāra mudrā* is with the left hand facing downwards placed on an upward facing right hand, the fingers of both hands clasping each other, and the entire gesture is turned upside down.
74. *Śākta Pramoda* only says this much but *Tantrasāra*: 304 gives the entire phrase
75. When performing the *puraścaraṇa* fire offering, the number of oblations to the

deity is one-tenth of the times that the main *mantra* is repeated. For one hundred thousand *mantras*, one offers ten thousand oblations.

76. This is another name for Śiva. He is speaking to his wife who has asked him to reveal this Tantra.
77. All the numbers in parentheses in the following sections refer to the numbered verses in the text.
78. In the *Śākta Pramoda* and *Nityārcana* the word *gāyantī* (singing) occurs in place of *pivanti* (drinking); I am assuming that this is incorrect and have changed it.
79. *Yoganidrām* has numerous connotations including a state of meditation or a goddess personifying sleep.
80. This paragraph refers to the Vīra ritual which consists of sexual-yogic practice with a suitable consort. This is done to harness and sublimate sexual power into awakening the *kuṇḍalinī*. The male partner views himself as Bhairava (a fierce form of Śiva) and female partner views herself as Bhairavī (a fierce form of Śakti). See Bharati:257 ff.
81. This is an epithet of Śiva's wife.
82. These last three goddesses are three forms of Tārā.
83. These are various female spirits.
84. Pārvatī is one of the most common names for Śiva's wife.
85. *Kīla* means an instrument which nails something down, usually referring to a ritual dagger but in this case to the seed syllable '*Hrīṃ*'

Chapter 3

The Divine Play of Chinnamastā

NĀMASTOTRA

The *nāmastotra*, the praise of names of a deity is well known in many religious traditions; such as the Sufi practice of *dhikr* (remembrance of the names of Allah) and the Buddhist Pure Land practice of reciting Buddha Amitābha's name.[1] Though not unique to Hinduism, the praise of names is a special and widespread feature of liturgical literature in the main devotional sects of Śaktī, Śiva, and Viṣṇu. In the *Bhakti Cult in Ancient India* B. K. Goswami states, "The worship, the concentration on and recitation of the *mantra*, and the repetition of the holy names, constitute the main part of the religious life of a *Satwata* worshipper."[2] Most praises with the recitation of names consist of one hundred and eight, three hundred, a thousand, or a thousand and eight names. These names may be recited aloud, repeated inaudibly, mentally repeated, or sung in groups (*nāmakīrtana*). The recitation of the praise of names became popular because it was deemed a facile yet efficacious way of propitiating a deity who will help or protect a devotee especially in these troubled times. In the *Viṣṇupurāṇa* (6.2.27) it says: "That which one obtains in the Kṛtyayuga by meditation, by performing sacrifice in the Tretā, by worship in the Dvāpara, one receives in the Kaliyuga, by reciting (the names) of Keśava."[3]

According to Indian cosmology we are in the age of decline, the Kaliyuga, wherein a person's life-span is limited to a hundred years or so. Therefore many spiritual practices which require a long-term commitment and perhaps costly rituals are no longer suited to this age of decline. The recitation of the *nāmastotra* is a simple ritual which can be performed by anyone who wants to be closer to the deity. Ideally, as one chants the names of the deity, one contemplates the deity and identifies with all the aspects of the deity. This is a personal and intimate ritual which requires no ritual person, costly rituals, or time commitment. In our 'time-conscious' society, it is an excellent and expedient ritual. This type of reasoning was also propounded by the various Buddhist Pure Land sects in East Asia. Since one needed an expedient yet effective method in order to achieve happiness, spiritual attainments, and eventually liberation from cyclic existence, one method offered in Hinduism was the recitation of *nāmastotra*. In the *Chinnamastāsahasranāma* a practitioner is assured happiness, knowledge, and the attainment of great *siddhis* through reciting Chinnamastā's names.

The efficacy of the recitation of a deity's name in a ritual context has its historical antecedent in the Vedas. Renou in his "Etudes sur le Vocabulaire du Ṛgveda" states that "the name above all is that one of a deity" and that the beginning of language occurred when the ancient seers *(ṛṣis)* gave names to all objects (X.71.1).[4] The first chapter in the *Ṛgveda* (1.1.1-ff) mentions Agni's name eight times in the first nine stanzas. In the *Śatapatha Brāhmaṇa* 6.1.3.9, receiving a name frees one from evil, and in 11.2.3.4-6, ". . . he who knows these two great forces (name and form) of the Brahman becomes himself a great force . . .". Furthermore, the *Bhagavadgītā*, instead of repeating Kṛṣṇa's or Arjuna's name, is replete with epithets for them, thereby emphasizing their diverse and accomplished abilities. In the ninth chapter stressing devotion, Kṛṣṇa is described as many things, including the father of this world, the mother, the establisher (9.17), and one must worship Kṛṣṇa as encompassing all these variegated forms. The power of evoking a deity's name and his/her various epithets is emphasized in India's early sacred texts: one of the first specific one thousand names is that of Viṣṇu in dialogue between Bhīṣma and Yudhiṣṭhira in the *Mahābhārata*, chapter 149 of the 'Anuśāsanika Parvan'. From this prototype, the popularity of praising the names grew, as it is evident from the numerous praises found in the *Purāṇas* and Tantras. Some of the more famous ones are the *Lalitāsahasranāma* in the *Brahmāṇḍa Purāṇa*,[5] the *Śrī Gāyatrī Sahasranāma* in the *Śrīmad Devī Bhāgavatam*,[6] the 'Kadistotra' in the *Mahānirvāṇatantra*,[7] the *Śivasahasranāmastotra* in the *Vāyupurāṇa* 1.30.79ff and in the *Brahmapurāṇa* 38, 40ff.

The evocation of a name is efficacious only because the name itself is powerful. Well-attested in archaic societies, it was believed that a name of the person or an object was directly related to the essence of the person or object. Renou states that in many respects the name is considered the essential property of a person.[8] This is one of the reasons why the Vedas are highly revered and consequently the power of words has always played an important role in Indian thought. The power of words is certainly evident in Tantric practice by the frequent use of *mantras* as a potent protection or gaining access to a deity. In the praise of names (*nāmastotra*), the names are either in the nominative or the dative. Frequently they are considered as *mantras* when they are in the dative because the name is preceded by *Aum* and followed by *Namaḥ*.

In Gonda's monograph, *Notes on Names and the Name of God in Ancient India*, he enumerates several ways that knowledge of a name makes one powerful. The name helps one understand facts and events. He cites the *Atharvaveda* (11,8,7): "As long as the former earth remains nameless it cannot be identified so as to become an object of knowledge."[9] All empirical knowledge is based on knowing words and their meaning because without this, one could never relate to what was learned nor could one ever convey this knowledge to another person. In regard to soteriological knowledge according to the Tantric method, when the guru initiates a disciple by conferring a *mantra* (*mantradīkṣā*)[10] and imparting its meaning to the disciple, it is emphasized that this method is only possible because of the long tradition of transmitted knowledge from guru to disciple. For example, a major Śakti seed syllable *mantra* is *Klīṃ*. The *Mantrārthābhidhānam* of the *Varadātantra* explicates *klīṃ* as follows: *ka* stands for Kāmadeva or Kṛṣṇa, *la* for Indra, *ī* for Tuṣṭi and *ṃ* for *sukha*.[11] Thus, one seed syllable symbolizes four important deities with whom one may mentally associate with oneself. Another explanation presented in the *Śivasūtra* divides the syllable into five parts which are related to the creation of the world since the *klīṃ* syllable is the seed syllable of the god of desire, Kāmadeva. The *Śivasūtra* states: "from the letter *ka* water arises, from the letter *la* the world is born, from *ī* fire comes, from the *nāda* the wind and from the *bindu* comes the sky."[12] By knowing the various meanings of a *mantra*, one begins to acquire power because of mental identification with the referents.

If we consider the recitation of praise of names as *mantras*, by performing the repetition of a *mantra*, one strengthens one's association with a deity or deities and gradually becomes more intimate with them.[13] These deities are believed to aid a practitioner; by reciting their name or names, they become a source of help, strength, and encouragement. Already in the *Atharvaveda* we find the belief that uttering a deity's name will bring the deity's protection. *Atharvaveda* (6,76,4) states, "They who are aiming at him, do not kill the *kṣatriya* who, knowing, pronounces the name of Agni in order to (secure) length of life." Moreover the recitation of the name has a consecratory power and imparts a blessing conferred by the deity. In later devotional literature Dimock, describing the Sahajiyās' relationship with Kṛṣṇa, quotes from the *Ānandabhairava* "having said and understood Hari . . . the uttering of the name in the mouth brings the experience of him within."[14] Tulasīdāsa, the great *bhakti* poet, states that ". . . the name acts as an interpreter between the material and the immaterial forces of the deity, and is a guide and interpreter to both."[15] In other words, the name is a linking reference point between the deity in her/his *saguṇa* (form aspect) and *nirguṇa* (formless aspect). But note that the one thousand names of a deity are not all common names nor are they an exhaustive listing. S.K. De states:

> The deity is often called Nameless or Anāman in the scriptures, but this usage is on par with the employment of terms such as 'birthless' (*ajanman*), 'formless' (*arūpa*) or 'actionless' (*akartṛ*). It does not mean that he has no name but that his name . . . is not like the common names we have in the phenomenal world; it possesses a spiritual significance and efficacy.[16]

The names given in the praises are the important ones but a deity cannot be fully described by any number of names, for a deity is nameless and limitless. Thus, by reciting the names of a deity one can: (1) become more familiar with the deity; (2) be protected by the deity, (3) receive blessings and experience the deity in her/his *saguṇa* form; and (4) be directed to the transcendent deity without form. Ramprasad Sen, a Bengali devotional poet, has a poem which exemplifies many of the reasons to recite the names of deities.

> Kālī's name is the wishing-giving tree.
> My heart is seeded with it.
> I've peddled my bones in the marketplace
> Of this world and brought up Durgā's name . . .
> Tārā's name is the best remedy.
> I've tied it to my topknot.
>
> Ramprasad says:
>
> I have begun my journey
> calling on the name of Durgā.[17]

In the *Bhakti Cult of Ancient India*, B. K. Goswami states, "To chant therefore the holy names with the help of the sacred rosary of beads is better in one sense than every other formal act of religious life. It may be then viewed as the essence of worship and the culmination of worship."[18] In many of the praises of names, such as the *Lalitāsahasranāma* and the *Viṣṇusahasranāma*, it is said in the *phalaśruti* (results) section that a reciter of the thousand names will be free from evil, all accumulated sins will be destroyed, one will achieve prosperity, eloquence, and whatever one desires.[19] Furthermore, the *Lalitāsahasranāma* states that if one 'mesmerizes' ashes with the thousand names and applies these ashes over a sick person, the person will be healed. Or if water 'mesmerized' with the thousand names is poured over a possessed person, the *graha* (the possessor) will flee at once.[20] Most importantly, in both the *Lalitāsahasranāma* and *Viṣṇusahasranāma*, the reciter of the praises will be free of all suffering and achieve liberation.[21] In the 'Chinnamastātantra' of the *Śākta Pramoda*, in the introduction of the thousand names, Mahādeva (Śiva) tells Devī (his wife), "even without worship (*pūjā*), without meditation, without repetition, . . . only by reciting (the thousand names), one will obtain *siddhis*." In the *phalaśruti* (results) section, it stresses the attainment of *siddhis*, as well as the elimination of all sins, control over others, strength, beauty, wealth, respect from others, etc.

The attainment of *mokṣa*, however, is only indirectly mentioned in connection with the attainment of knowledge. In the *Viṣṇusahasranāma*, it comments that "one should not think that by merely reciting (this hymn) salvation is insured; because it is by knowledge alone that one attains *mokṣa*."[22] Consistent with the Tantric viewpoint that the individual's power and understanding are needed to attain liberation, one cannot rely solely on the grace of the deity. Therefore the recitation of the praise of names is an expedient and efficacious means in reaching the threshold of liberation, i.e., having the knowledge of Brahman (*Brahmajñāna*).

Classification of the Thousand Names

Indians are fond of the practice of systematization and classification of names, terms, concepts, etc., and the *nāmastotra* genre was not exempt from classification. In the aforementioned *Kadistotra*, the hundred names all begin with *ka*, the first consonant in Sanskrit. In the *Chinnamastāsahasranāma* a loose alphabetical order, occasionally interspersed with names beginning with other letters, begins with name #95 *Karālī* and continues to the name #807 *Huṅkārabījarūpam*.[23] The *Lalitāsahasranāma* does not have names in alphabetical order but according to Bhāskararāya's commentary, an order according to subject-matter does prevail. The first hundred and twelve names comprise an exemplary group. The first five names reveal her real (*prakāśa*) form;[24] names 6 to 52 enumerate her manifested (*vimarśa*) form from her head to feet;[25] names 53 to 63 describe the seat of the Devī;[26] names 64-85 exalt her actions which have both an explicit meaning and implicit meaning;[27] and names 86-112 describe her subtle forms.[28] Thus in the *Lalitāsahasranāma* the classification is primarily according to subject-matter. In the article "Śrīrādhikānāmasahasram" Chemburkar classifies Rādhā's names also according to subjects, namely, the twofold main classification of Rādhā as Gopī and of Rādhā as a female deity worshipped by the Vaiṣṇavas.[29] This is subdivided into different classifications, e.g., Rādhā as a Gopī who is beloved of Kṛṣṇa, or Rādhā as a Gopī associated with the Rāsa-dance;

and the deity Rādhā as Śaktī or the deity Rādhā identical with the deity of the Śāktas.[30] Hence there are numerous ways to classify the praise of a thousand names.[31]

Another approach in systematizing the thousand names of a goddess is to view these epithets which are descriptions of her form according to iconography, mythological allusions, exaltation of her prowess, talents, extraordinary protection, etc., as a great *līlā* (divine play) of the goddess, i.e., the Goddess' manifesting herself in a myriad forms in order to instruct, help or protect her devotees. As Ramprasad says:

> O Mother, who really knows Your magic? You're a crazy girl driving us all crazy with these tricks. No one knows anyone else in a world of your illusions. . . . If she decides to be kind, this misery will pass.[32]

Chinnamastā is a wonderful example of a goddess who understands the illusions (*māyā*) of the phenomenal world and can assume various forms, such as a warrior, magician, beauty, protectoress, etc. Chinnamastā is limitless as are the manifestations of the phenomenal world; this is simply a marvellous performance—*līlā*. By thinking of the thousand names of Chinnamastā as divine play, one can classify her thousand names according to the nine *rasa* (sentiments) of the Indian aesthetical theory.[33] The nine *rasas* are the: (1) erotic, (2) comic, (3) pathetic, (4) furious, (5) heroic, (6) terrible, (7) odious, (8) marvellous, and (9) peaceful.

In the preface to the *Theory of Rasa in Sanskrit Drama*, Gopinath Kaviraj states:

> The Śiva Sūtras appear to suggest that the ancient Indian conception of Drama consists in the realization that Ātmā (self) endowed with its inherent Power and playing all possible parts is the Naṭa (actor), the senses are the spectators (Prekṣakāni) and the Anatarātmā (innermost self) is the Prekṣāgṛha or stage. The object of Abhinaya (dramatic representation) is evidently taken to be the manifestation of Rasa.[34]

Gopinath Kavirāj is referring to the aesthetical theory propounded in Kashmir Śaivism, initially presented by Abhinavagupta. Abhinavagupta was a major proponent of a profound philosophical way of linking religion and drama. Influenced by the Tantric ritual of Kashmir Śaivism, he developed an aesthetic theory which incorporated the spiritual aspects of drama, and all later aesthetic theorists followed his lead.[35] Abhinavagupta was interested in how the actor, the spectator and the sentiment evoked in the play interacted. If one applies this theory to the thousand names, the goddess depicts the actress, the practitioner is the spectator, and the feeling of transcendence or holiness is the sentiment evoked. Abhinavagupta considered the actor to represent the *paramātman* who is never affected by the *rasa* portrayed, but evokes the *rasa* in the spectator, who represents the senses according to Kaviraj's interpretation.[36] *Ātman* always remains unaffected but the senses do react to emotion. The Goddess represents the *ātman* who can assume a myriad of forms and evoke emotions in her practitioners while she essentially remains unaffected. In contrast, her practitioners become very involved in her various forms and do react to them. However, Abhinavagupta states that a spectator becomes mentally attuned to the drama and the actor's depiction of a particular *rasa*, and by contemplating it, becomes absorbed by it and identifies with the actor. Furthermore, in the *Dhvanyālokalocana* he comments that some people are capable of identifying with the subject-matter because the mirror of their heart has been polished through *constant recitation*. If one applies this to the recitation of the thousand names of Chinnamastā, a sensitive reader can be affected by the repetitions of the names by sympathetically responding to her myriad manifestations, her paradoxes, her exploits, her limitless energy to protect, to help, to be kind, etc. One can become overwhelmed, forget oneself and experience the bliss of Chinnamastā. By reciting Chinnamastā's names one can experience the bliss of Chinnamastā and unconsciously identifies with Chinnamastā or experiences her essence. To the reciter of her names Chinnamastā is the sacrificer and the sacrifice which feeds her essence, reminiscent of feeding her two attendants.[37] Though this poem is not addressed to Chinnamastā, it evokes the same sentiment:

> She's playing in my heart.
> Whatever I think, I think Her name.
> I close my eyes and She's in there
> Garlanded with human heads.[38]

For anyone who recites the 108 or 1000 names, certain emotions will be evoked. Though the nine *rasas* might all be present in the 108 or 1000 names, certainly some *rasas* will be dominant. Since Chinnamastā is such a paradoxical deity, I assume that her 108 or 1000 names will also entail an inherent paradox. Though classifying the deity's names according to *rasas* is not an Indian tradition, it is a provocative means to assess whether one *rasa* does dominate in the 108 or 1000 names of Chinnamastā.[39]

These nine *rasas*, (1) the erotic (*śṛṅgāra*), (2) comic (*hāsya*), (3) pathetic (*karuṇa*), (4) furious (*raudra*), (5) heroic (*vīra*), (6) terrible (*bhayānaka*), (7) odious (*bībhatsa*), (8) marvellous (*adbhuta*), and (9) peaceful (*śānta*), are the basis of classifying the 108 and 1000 names of Chinnamastā from the *Śākta Pramoda*.[40]

One Hundred and Eight Names

The following is a translation of Chinnamastā's one hundred and eight names.

Śrī Pārvatī spoke:[41]

"The one who is named 'overcoming the enemies', please now tell me the best hundred and eight names which are dear to Chinnamastā. (1)[42] For those who cannot recite the thousand names, O Lord that I honour, O giver of mercy , I ask you again. (2) O merciful one, tell me, O esteemed one, who should recite these names."

Śrī Sadāśiva spoke:

"One should always recite the hundred and eight names. (3) Without doubt one will attain the same results by reciting the hundred and eight names as by reciting the thousand names. *Aum* to the praises of the hundred and eight names of Chinnamastā, the *ṛṣi* is Sadāśiva, the metre is Anuṣṭubh, the goddess is Chinnamastā, and the results obtained by this recitation will be all accomplishments.

"*Aum* 1. Chinnamastā 2. Mahāvidyā (great knowledge goddess), 3. Mahābhīmā (great fierce one), 4. Mahodarī (great bellied one)[43] / 5. Caṇḍeśvarī (fierce goddess), 6. Caṇḍamātā (mother of fierce beings or the fierce mother), 7. Caṇḍamuṇḍaprabhañjinī (killer of demons Caṇḍa and Muṇḍa) // (4)

"8. Mahācaṇḍā (great fierce one), 9. Caṇḍarūpā (fierce form), 10. Caṇḍikā (fierce one), 11. Caṇḍakhaṇḍinī (destroyer of Caṇḍa)/ 12. Krodhinī (wrathful one), 13. Krodhajanani (creator of wrathful beings), 14. Krodharūpā (wrathful form), 15. Kuhūḥ (new moon day i.e., darkness), 16. Kalā (skillful one) // (5)

"17. Kopāturā (afflicted with rage), 18. Kopayutā (filled with rage), 19. Kopasaṃhārakāriṇī (destroyer of rage) / 20. Vajravairocanī, 21. Vajrā (adamantine one), 22. Vajrakalpā (competent with a *vajra*), and 23. Ḍākinī // (6)

"24. Ḍākinīkarmaniratā (involved with the work of *dākinīs*), 25. Ḍākinīkarmapūjitā (worshipped as the work of *ḍākinīs*, / 26. Ḍākinīsaṅganiratā (delighted in the company of *ḍākinīs*), 27. Ḍākinīpremapūritā (filled with love of *ḍākinīs*)// (7)

"28. Khaṭavāṅgadhāriṇī (holder of a *khaṭvāṅga*), 29. Kharvā (mutilated one),[44] 30. Khaḍgakharparadhāriṇī (holder of a scimitar and a skullcup) / 31. Pretāśanā (feeder of *pretas* [hungry ghosts]), 32. Pretayutā (united with *pretas*), 33. Pretasaṅgavihāriṇī (plays or dwells in the company of *pretas*) // (8)

"34. Chinnamuṇḍadharā (holds a severed head), 35. Chinnacaṇḍavidyā (fierce *mantra* [holder]) of the one with the severed body), and 36. Citriṇī ī(having variegated forms) / 37. Ghorarūpā (terrific form), 38. Ghoradṛṣṭā (terrific to behold), 39. Ghorarāvā (having a terrific roar), 40. Ghanodarī (firm abdomen, i.e., beautiful) // (9)

"41. Yoginī, 42. Yoganiratā (practitioner of yoga), 43. Japayajñaparāyaṇā (absorbed in sacrifice and recitation) / 44. Yonicakramayī (possessing *yonicakra*), 45. Yoniḥ (embodying the *yoni*), 46. Yonicakrapravarttinī (arising from the *yonicakra*) // (10)

"47. Yonimudrā (has the *yonimudrā*), 48. Yonigamyā (accessible to the *yoni*, [knowing the *yoni*]), 49. Yoniyantranivāsinī (abides in the *yoniyantra*)/ 50. Yantrarūpā (has the *yantra* form), 51. Yantramayī (possesses the *yantra*), 52. Yantreśī (goddess of the *yantra*), 53. Yantrapūjitā (worshipped with a *yantra*) // (11)

"54. Kīrtyā (renowned one), 55. Kapardinī (has matted hair, [i.e., Śiva's wife in yogi form]), 56. Kālī, 57. Kaṅkālī (emaciated, [i.e., one who practises austerities]), 58. Kalavikāriṇī (constantly transforming)/ 59. Āraktā (being slightly red), 60. Raktanayanā (having red eyes), 61. Raktapānaparāyaṇā (quaffing blood continuously) // (12)

"62. Bhavānī (Pārvatī), 63. Bhūtidā (gives prosperity), 64. Bhūtiḥ (prosperity), 65. Bhutidātrī (bestows prosperity), and 66. Bhairavī (formidable one) / 67. Bhairavācāranirată (engaged in the practice of *bhairavas*, [i.e., practices in cemeteries]), 68. Bhūtabhairavasevitā (served by fierce beings) // (13)

"69. Bhīmā (formidable one), 70. Bhimeśvarīdevī (goddess who is lord of the formidable ones), 71. Bhimanādaparāyaṇā (having continuous formidable sounds) / 72. Bhavārādhyā (praised by Śaṅkara, [i.e., Śiva]), 73. Bhavanūtā (worshipped by all), 74. Bhavasāgaratāriṇī (crosses over the ocean of existence, [i.e. liberation]) // (14)

"75. Bhadrakālī (a form of Kālī), 76. Bhadratanuḥ (having a beautiful body), 77. Bhadrarūpā (beautiful form), and 78. Bhadrikā (goodness) / 79. Bhadrarūpā (embodies goodness), 80. Mahābhadrā (magnanimous), 81. Subhadrā (wonderful goodness), 82. Bhadrapālinī (protectoress of goodness) // (15)

"83. Subhavyā (exceedingly beautiful [a name of Pārvatī]), 84. Bhavyavadanā (having a beautiful face), 85. Sumukhī (good face or mouth), 86. Siddhasevitā (served by *siddhas*) / 87. Siddhidā (gives *siddhis*), 88. Siddhanivahā (has the collection of *siddhis*), 89. Siddhā (accomplished one), 90. Siddhaniṣevitā (honoured by *siddhas*) // (16)

"91. Śubhadā (gives auspiciousness), 92. Śubhagā (elegant), 93. Śuddhā (pure), 94. Śuddhasattvā (has pure *sattva*), 95. Śubhāvahā (bearer of auspiciousness), 96. Śreṣṭhā (excellent), 97. Dṛṣṭamayī (embodies [the right] view), 98. Devī, 99. Dṛṣṭisaṃhārakāriṇī (capable of destroying by [her] gaze) // (17)

"100. Śarvāṇī (Śiva's wife), 101. Sarvagā (omnipresent), 102. Sarvā (complete), 103. Sarvamaṅgalakāriṇī (creator of all auspiciousness, [a name of Pārvatī]) / 104. Śivā (pacifier), 105. Śāntā (peaceful), 106. Śāntirūpā (embodiment of peacefulness), 107. Mṛḍānī (gladdened, [a name of Pārvatī]), 108. Madanāturā (indomitable by Kāmadeva) // (18)

"These are rare praises which I have told you, O Devi. With great effort you must not reveal this secret section. (19) It is necessary to have said so much to you, O Beloved. You will obtain the ability to kill, delude, eradicate others, (20) perturb, along with the *ṛddhis* and *siddhis*. Recite these names three times a day and undoubtedly you will obtain all the *siddhis*. (21) This is the highest praise, O beautiful one; recite it with faith. Being the most supreme person, you are invincible to enemies. (22) This completes the praises of the hundred and eight names of Chinnamastā."

The following is my classification according to the nine *rasas*.

(1) Erotic: 16, 40, 62, 76, 77, 83, 84, 85, and 92;
(2) Comic: none;
(3) Pathetic: none;
(4) Furious: 3, 5, 8-12, 14, 17, 18, 23, 37, 39, 56, 60, 61, 66, 71, 75, and 99;
(5) Heroic: 7, 19, 22, 28, and 69;
(6) Terrible: none;
(7) Odious: 21, 41, 42, 55, 57, 67, and 88[45];
(8) Marvellous: 1-3, 6, 13, 15, 20, 24-27, 29-36, 44-53, 58-59, 63-65, 70, 72-74, 78-82, 86-87, 89-91, 95, 97-98, 100-104, 107, and 108; and
(9) Peaceful: 43, 54, 79-81, 93, 94, 96, 105 and 106.

In the one hundred and eight names there are nine in the erotic *rasa*, twenty-one in the furious *rasa*, five in the heroic *rasa*, seven in the odious *rasa*, fifty-six in the marvellous *rasa*, and ten in the peaceful *rasa*.

Thus in this classification of names according to the nine *rasas*, more than half are subsumed under the eighth *rasa*, the marvellous. For a deity, the dominant *rasa* must be the marvellous one because a deity can perform extraordinary acts, has amazing abilities, and is superior to other beings, especially humans. Certainly many goddesses would also have names included in the erotic *rasa* but one would not expect this from Chinnamastā. Indeed, the erotic *rasa* is less prominent than the furious and peaceful *rasas*. There are no names of Chinnamastā in the categories of comic, pathetic, and terrible.[46] Rather there is a predominance of the awesome, combining of the marvellous and furious.

REFERENCES

1. See Wilson, Martin, *In Praise of Tārā*: 94-104 for one hundred and eight names of Tārā. Wayman, Alex, translated and annotated; *Chanting the Names of Mañjuśri*, Boston, Shambala, 1985.
2. Goswami, B. K., *The Bhakti Cult in Ancient India*: 302.
3. Sastry, R.A. trans., *Viṣṇusahasranāma*, Adyar, Adyar Library, 1980:14.
4. Renou, L., *Etudes sur le Vocabulaire du Ṛgveda*:10.
5. Sastry, R.A., trans., *Lalitāsahasranāma*, Madras, Adyar, 1976.
6. Swami Vijñānānanda, trans., *Śrīmad Devī Bhāgavatam*,: 1146-54.
7. Woodroofe, J., trans., *Great Liberation*: 185ff.
8. Renou: 10. Dimock, in his *The Place of the Hidden Moon*, has a subsection entitled "The Power of the Name" wherein he discusses the concept that the relationship between the word and its meaning is not arbitrary, but natural: 226-27.
9. Gonda (1970): 61.
10. There are many kinds of Tantric Hindu initiations, See 'Initation', *Studies in the History of Religions*, vol.10, 1965: 71-80.
11. Rai, *Dictionary of Tantraśastra*: 96.
12. Dimock: 233.
13. Basu, A., 'Dikṣā', Initiations:85. He quotes Śrī Aurobindo as describing *mantra* as "a supreme rhythmic language which seizes hold upon all that is finite and brings into each the light and voice of its own infinite."
14. Dimock: 228.
15. Gonda: 99.
16. Gonda: 94.
17. Ramprasad; Nathan L. and Seely, C. trans., *Grace and Mercy in Her Wild Hair*, Boulder, Great Eastern, 1982: 55.
18. Goswami: 302.
19. Ramprasad; Nathan and Seely, trans.: 59. In poem 51 of Ramprasad, he says, "He mows the grass of sin with the honed blade of Kālī's name."
20. Sastry, R. A., trans., *Lalitāsahasranāma*: 24-25.
21. The *Lalitāsahasranāma* states that one will have *brahmajñāna* (pp.396-97) and the *Viṣṇusahasranāma* states one will attain the ultimate (*prāpnotyanuttamam*) (p.423).
22. *Viṣṇusahasranāma*: 419.
23. There are a thousand names but the first 94 names and the names after #807 have no alphabetical order.
24. *Lalitāsahasranāma*: 46.
25. Ibid: 56.
26. Ibid: 56.
27. Ibid: 64-65. For example, name 65 is Bhaṇḍāsuravadhodyataśaktisenāsamavṛtā which is translated as "she is endowed with an army of *śaktīs* for the sake of slaying Bhaṇḍāsura" The first part of the compound, *bhaṇḍāsura*, is a fierce

demon who fights with the goddess. This is the exoteric meaning. However the esoteric meaning is that *bandha* (lit., shameless) means the embodied soul (*bhaṇḍiman*) with life and *asura* means life (*asu*) and to take away (*ra*)—he who takes away life, i.e., one who imprisons the real nature of life.

28. Ibid: 85.
29. Chemburkar, J., "Śrīarādhikānāmasahasram", *Annals of the Bhandarkar Oriental Research Institute*, Vol. LVII, 1976: 107.
30. Ibid: 108-9.
31. Also see Lalye, P.G., *Studies in Devī Bhāgavata*, Bombay, Popular Prakashan, 1973: 207ff.
32. Nathan and Seely: 30.
33. I thank Alex Wayman for this ingenious suggestion of classification.
34. Misra, H.R., *Theory of Rasa in Sanskrit Drama*, Chatarpur, Vindhyachal Prakashan, 1964.
35. See Masson, J.L. and Patawardhan, M.V., *Śāntarasa and Abhinavagupta's Philosophy of Aesthetics*, Bhandarkar Oriental Series, no.9, Poona: Bhandarkar Oriental Research Institute, 1969: 38-43.
36. In the *Bhagavad Gītā* 4:13 Kṛṣṇa states:"I am . . . the actor who never acts".
37. One definition of *rasa* is taste, the names of the deity let the reciter 'taste' Chinnamastā.
38. Ramprasad, trans. by Nathan and Seely: 63.
39. There are endless discussions about how a *rasa* is protrayed. I am certain that many will disagree with my classification of a particular name but few will disagree that the marvellous *rasa* is the predominant one. To complicate matters, many of the names are compounds. I have only presented one translation and did not indicate how I interpreted the compound. A book devoted to the topic of Chinnamastā's names would have included more meticulous detail.
40. The 1000 names will be given in Appendix 1.
41. This is an *āgama* since Śiva's wife is asking Śiva for instruction.
42. The numbers in parentheses are the verse numbers from *Śakta Pramoda*.
43. This name has various connotations, such as one who can contain all beings, a sign of yogic ability, or a possible connection with *yakṣas*.
44. This name also means that she has the *siddhi* to make herself small.
45. The odious category includes all yogic abilities.
46. One can argue for including some of the names under the furious in the terrible category but I opted for the furious. Chinnamastā is not terrifying to her devotees; however, she may display fury in order to make a devotee aware of his/her wrong actions.

Chapter 4

The Question is Not—To be or not to be

TANTRIC BUDDHIST PRACTICE

Mahāyāna Buddhism is comprised of two divisions entailing different methods: the Perfection Vehicle or Pāramitāyāna; and the Tantric Vehicle or Vajrayāna, also frequently called Mantrayāna. The ultimate goal of Buddhahood is the same for all Mahāyāna practitioners. According to Pāramitāyāna one accomplishes the goal of Buddhahood by perfecting the six perfections—generosity, ethical conduct, patience, effort, meditation, and transcendental insight with the realization of voidness as the necessary underlying basis. This process takes at least three incalculable aeons. In sharp contrast, in Vajrayāna which utilizes the realization of voidness and deity yoga (Skt. Deva Yoga; Tib. lha'i rnal 'byor), one can achieve the final goal of Buddhahood in seven lifetimes or even within one lifetime. In accordance with the Mahāyāna ideal, one seeks Buddhahood to benefit all sentient beings. The Vajrayānists believe that the quickest way to Buddhahood is the best because one can help more beings. The ultimate or supramundane goal of Tantric practitioners is Buddhahood but this is facilitated by the acquisition of mundane goals, such as the eight great *siddhis*, the six supranormal powers, and the four means of action. In consequent to the Mahāyāna vows to help all sentient beings in achieving Buddhahood, these mundane goals should not be ends in themselves but expedient means of overcoming obstacles to the ultimate goal such as poor health, ignorance, or other worldly hindrances.

The eight great *siddhis* are as follows:

(1) *Khaḍga* is the power to be invincible with a sword empowered with specific *mantras*;
(2) *Añjana* is an eye salve which removes ignorance;[1]
(3) *Pādalepa* is to be 'swift-footed' or an ointment applied to make one a 'speed-walker';[2]
(4) *Antardhāna* is the ability to become invisible;
(5) *Rasa-Rasāyana* is the alchemical ability to transform base metals into gold or having the elixir of immortality;

(6) *Khecara* is the ability to fly through the air;
(7) *Bhūcara* is the power to go anywhere in an instant;
(8) *Pātāla* is the power to go to the nether worlds.[3]

One may also acquire the six suprasensory perceptions (*ṣaḍābhijñāna*) which are clairvoyance (*divyacakṣurvijñāna*), clairaudience (*divyaśrotram*), knowing other's thoughts (*cetaḥparyyāya*), understanding of illusions and miracles (*ṛddhividdhi*), remembering one's previous lives (*pūrvanivāsānusmṛti*), and knowledge of how to eradicate the 'fluxes' (*āsravakṣaya*). Another attainment is the four means of actions (*catuḥkarma*) which are pacifying (*śānti*), increasing (*pauṣṭika*), dominating (*vaśīkaraṇa*), and destroying (*māraṇa*).[4] All these extraordinary abilities should be applied to achieve Buddhahood and to help others achieve Buddhahood; these abilities should not be used for self-glorification. This is one of the reasons why Tantra is known as the quickest but most dangerous path. The temptation to use these abilities for fame, domination, and so forth, can be overwhelming and eventually destructive to the practitioner.

Buddhist Tantra Classification[5]

In Tantric Buddhism the four principal kinds of Tantra are *kriyā* (action), *caryā* (performance), *yoga* (union), and *anuttarayoga* (supreme union).[6] Tsong kha pa states, "because the main trainees in the Vajra Vehicle are of four very different types, four doors of entry are poisted."[7] Each of these four kinds of Tantra uses desire, the chief emotion in the realm of desire.[8]

> Practitioners of the four Tantras have the same intention in that they all are seeking others' welfare .... All four have deity yoga .... All use desire for the attributes of the desire realm on the path.[9]

These four Tantras are explained sometimes as four aspects of a relationship between a woman and a man: exchange of looks (*kriyā*), exchange of smiles and laughs (*caryā*), holding hands or embracing (*yoga*) and sexual union (*anuttarayoga*).[10] Also they are explained as reflecting the different mental capacities and religious propensities of practitioners. All four classes of Tantra emphasize deity yoga but they vary in their method. *Kriyā* or action *tantra* stresses external purification and ritual action. The majority of *kriyā* practitioners imagine the deity in front of themselves and makes offerings, recites prayers, and *mantras* to the deity. In action *tantra* one thinks of oneself as the servant of the deity. *Caryā* or performance Tantra stresses the need for a balance between external performance (as in Kriyā Tantra) and internal yoga. A practitioner visualizes the deity in front of oneself or imagines oneself as the deity. There is a more equal relationship between the deity and practitioner; the practitioner considers the deity as a friend or a close relative. Yoga or union Tantra emphasizes the practice of internal yoga by transforming one's ordinary body, speech, mind, and actions into extraordinary or divine body, speech, mind, and actions. The procedure involves the generation of oneself as the deity in the form of the pledge being (*samayasattva*) and then invokes the wisdom being (*jñānasattva*) to merge with the pledge being. Then one applies the four seals: the pledge seal (*samayamudrā*), *dharmamudrā*, action seal (*karmamudrā*), and great seal (*mahāmudrā*). The application of these seals transforms one's ordinary mind, speech, body, and actions into divine ones. In Yoga Tantra one visualizes oneself as a deity during meditation sessions but not on a continual basis as in Anuttarayoga Tantra. Anuttarayoga Tantra, which is only for the most intelligent and dedicated practitioners, emphasizes a complex internal yogic practice. One visualizes oneself as a deity and employs internal yogic practice which culminates in sexual union with either a visualized or actual *vidyā* (a knowledge consort). The practitioner visualizes him/herself as a deity at all times and places. This is the supreme path, unequalled by any other.[11]

Anuttarayoga Tantra is subdivided in various ways; one of the most common is into Father, Mother, and Non-Dual Tantras[12] which emphasize method (*upāya*), insight (*prajñā*) or equal balance, respectively. All Anuttarayoga Tantras teach about the inseparability of method (*upāya*) and insight (*prajñā*). The Father Tantras, which include, *Guhyasamājatantra* and *Yamāntaka*, teach the non-duality of bliss and void but emphasizes the method; the Mother Tantras, which include, *Cakrasaṃvaratantra* (or *Saṃvaratantra*) and *Vajrayoginī*, stress the transcendental insight (*prajñā*) brought about by the experience of non-duality of bliss and void, rather than the method. A Non-Dual Tantra combines insight and method equally. The Chinnamuṇḍā *sādhanas* are classified as Anuttarayoga Mother Tantra since their root is in the *Cakrasaṃvaratantra* and they emphasize *prajñā*, rather than *upāya*.[13]

Notes on Sādhana Translation

Numerous *sādhanas* of Chinnamuṇḍā are extant in Tibetan, Newari, and Sanskrit. No one *sādhana* seems to be more famous or popular than another, but three *sādhanas* are remarkably similar. These three are (1) *Chinnamuṇḍā Vajravārāhī* by Śrīmatidevī in the Tibetan Tangyur,[14] 2) *Lakṣmīsādhana* from a collection of Nepalese Buddhist *sādhanas*, and (3) *Vajrayoginī Sādhana* in the *Sādhanamālā*.[15]

The introduction and translation here is based on the *Chinnamuṇḍā Vajravārāhī Sādhana*, the most elaborate of the three. This *sādhana*, as with most Buddhist practice of Chinnamuṇḍā, consists primarily of the ritual worship section (*pūjā*). A second *sādhana* is a praise (*stuti*) to Trikāyavajrayoginī (i.e., Chinnamuṇḍā and her attendants) written by a disciple of Lakṣmīṅkarā, the Siddhācārya Śrī Virūpa (not the Mahāsiddha Virūpa of the eighth century) from the Nepalese Buddhist collection. Unlike the Hindu *sādhanas* of Chinnamastā, I have not found any *kavacas* ('armour' section). The essence of the practice section (*hṛdaya*) is contained in abbreviated *sādhanas* which are available. Though there are hundred and eight names, or thousand names of deities in Buddhism, none have been found for Chinnamuṇḍā.[16]

CHINNAMUṆḌĀ VAJRAVĀRĀHI SĀDHANA BY ŚRĪMATIDEVĪ

The colophon of the *Chinnamuṇḍāvajravārāhī sādhana* states that this *sādhana* is by Śrīmatidevī, translated by the Newari Paṇḍitācārya Bharendraruce and the (Tibetan) Blo-ldan Shes-rab (1059-1109). It does not elaborate who Śrīmatidevī is. In the Nepalese manuscript entitled *Lakṣmīsādhana*, which is almost identical with the *Chinnamuṇḍāvajravārāhī sādhana*, there is no colophon. Usually, however, a *sādhana*'s name indicates the deity or the author of the *sādhana*. Lakṣmī is a well known deity who is also known as Śrī.[17] Since this *sādhana* is not about the deity Lakṣmī, one deduces that Lakṣmī must be the author. Furthermore, Lakṣmīṅkarā is known as Bhagavatī Lakṣmī. Śrīmatidevī must be an epithet for Lakṣmī or Lakṣmīṅkarā. There are several well known Lakṣmīṅkarās, including the sister of King Indrabhūti and the eleventh-century Kashmiri nun. The lineages of the *sādhanas* of Chinnamuṇḍā indicate that they must have been practised in the ninth century; therefore indicating Lakṣmīṅkarā of the ninth century as the author. Evidence is that, according to one lineage of a Chinnamuṇḍā *sādhana*, one of Lakṣmīṅkarā's disciple was Virūpa. There is a very famous Virūpa who is the patriarch of the Tibetan Buddhist Śākya lineage but he lived during the eighth century. This Virūpa lived in the ninth century.[18] Thus Śrīmatidevī and the ninth-century Lakṣmīṅkarā are shown to be the same woman—one of the eighty-four Mahāsiddhas.[19]

The following is the mode of practice according to this *sādhana*:

The preliminaries

(1) Homage to the deity,
(steps 2 to 5 are not explicit in the text)

(2) Homage to one's guru;
(3) Refuge in the Three Jewels;
(4) Generation of *bodhicitta*;
(5) Four immeasurables;
(6) Vajrasattva meditation;
(7) Consecration of one's body;
(8) Visualized meditation on the deity;
(9) Drawing of the *maṇḍala*.

The actual meditation on the deity

(1) Visualization of the deity;
(2) Offerings to the deity and her attendants;
(3) Praises to the *pīṭhas* and *kāyas*;
(4) Repetition of the root *mantra*;
(5) *gTor ma* offering;
(6) Dedication of one's merit.

Preliminaries

As in the Hindu Tantras, the preliminaries are not elaborated since it is assumed that a Tantric practitioner is well acquainted with them.[20]

(1) Homage to the deity begins all Tantric Buddhist *sādhanas*. One prostrates oneself, usually three times, as one offers homage to Chinnamuṇḍā.

(2) Homage to the guru or one's spiritual teacher is of tantamount importance in Vajrayāna Buddhism because one's guru is indispensable in guiding one on the path to enlightenment. A Tantric disciple is trying to overcome mental obscurations and gain insight. Only an experienced teacher will know which kind of teaching or method is necessary to eradicate these mental defilements and accomplish these realizations.[21] Secondly, in Vajrayāna a disciple needs to receive initiations from a qualified teacher and blessing from the teacher in order that the practice be successful.[22]

(3) Refuge in the Three Jewels is obligatory for all Buddhists; in fact, the definition of a Buddhist is one who has taken refuge in the Three Jewels. The Three Jewels are the Buddha, the Dharma (his teachings), and the Saṅgha, the noble community. The teacher comprises all Three Jewels since she/he is the living embodiment of all three, through whose efforts the disciple receives the Buddhist teachings.[23] *The Beautiful Ornament of the Three Visions* describes the Three Jewels in this way:

> The place of refuge is the Master and his lineage of Preceptors who have revealed to one the transcendentally exalted path . . . . The Buddha is one

> who has accomplished the Body of Reality (Dharmakāya) . . . . which is endowed with every kind of virtue and free from every kind of imperfection . . . . attained the Form Body (*Rūpakāya*) . . . which acts solely for the welfare of beings . . . . The Dharma is the precepts . . . . The Saṅgha comprises the noble ones who dwell on the stages of irreversibility and those ordinary beings who have entered the doctrine prior to oneself.[24]

(4) Generation of the Bodhicitta is the practice at the heart of Mahāyāna Buddhism. Mahāyāna Buddhism developed the *bodhicitta* practice which in turn created the ideal of the Bodhisattva—beings who help all sentient beings to become liberated from cyclic existence and eventually to attain Buddhahood. Based on loving kindness and compassion the *bodhicitta* attitude is the wish to attain enlightenment in order to help all beings become free from suffering. After one has nurtured this wish, one is ready to enter and train on the path of developing this enlightenment thought. As it is stated in the *Bodhicaryāvatāra*:

> Just as a distinction is perceived between one who wishes to travel and one who actually travels, so the wise should recognize a graded distinction between these two (the wishing and entering enlightenment thoughts).[25]

The path consists of (1) meditating on the equality between self and others, (2) meditating on exchanging self for others, and (3) training in the conduct of these two.[26] Successfully completing the path, one concentrates on the actual *bodhicitta* with the understanding of the lack of any intrinsic nature. Without understanding this voidness of intrinsic nature, a being could never become a Bodhisattva who works selflessly for all beings. Thus the actualization of *bodhicitta* is a prerequisite in attaining Buddhahood for the sake of helping all sentient beings.

(5) The Four Immeasurables are compassion, love, joy, and equanimity. The cultivation of the four immeasurables aids one in developing *bodhicitta*. They are considered 'immeasurables' because "The field with respect to which one is meditating is the infinite field of all sentient beings throughout all space."[27] With refuge one cultivates virtue in relation to a 'pure field' of beings; with the four immeasurables one does so in relation to the 'field' of ordinary beings.

(6) Vajrasattva meditation is a practice of purification of one's body, speech, and mind. The practice consists of cleansing one's sins, obscurations, faults, failings, and impurities through regret for wrong doings and a pledge not to repeat these aided by the power of the pure being, Vajrasattva, and the meditation ritual. The Vajrasattva meditation is an essential

foundation practice in Tantric Buddhism. *The Opening of the Lotus* states that: "If you desire a good crop, you must first sow the seeds properly. Likewise, without the seed of proper purification, the crop of enlightenment will not grow."[28]

(7) Consecration of one's body is performed by reciting *om* as one touches the top of the head or forehead, *āḥ* as one touches the throat, and *hūṃ* as one touches the heart. By the recitation of 'oṃ *āḥ*, *hūṃ*' and touching the appropriate place, one purifies one's body, speech, and mind, transforming them into adamantine body, speech, and mind, respectively.

(8) Meditation on the deity will be discussed fully in the section of the actual meditation.

(9) Drawing the *maṇḍala* is equivalent to the Hindu drawing of the *yantra*. The Buddhists refer to a deity's abode as a *maṇḍala*, rather than a *yantra*.[29] Though *maṇḍala* has many meanings in this practice here, it is referring to the residence of Chinnamuṇḍā. Padmavajra in his *Tantrārthāvatāravyākhyāna* (96b-3ff) states that *Maṇḍala* means an enclosing of essence because of having the 'essence' (*maṇḍa*) in the sense of 'enclosing' (*-la*) it."[30] Thus Chinnamuṇḍā's *maṇḍala* is enclosing the 'essence' of Chinnamuṇḍā within a particular confine in order to perform the ritual.

Actual Meditation of the Deity

(1) Visualization of the deity is discussed in chapter 5.

(2) Offerings to the deity and attendants: In Buddhist Tantra the basic number of offerings is seven—the offering of saffron water, flowers, incense, lamps, scent, food, and music.[31] These can be actual liquid, flowers, etc. or they can be imagined. Furthermore, these offerings are explained differently by various Tibetan scholars, such as Sakya Chogyal Phagpa, Buddhaguhya, and the third Karmapa, Rangjung Dorje.[32]

Offering	*Phagpa*	*Buddhaguhya*	*Karmapa*
water	ocean of hearing		defilement cleansing
flowers	good qualities	*samādhi*	pleasing senses
incense	moral conduct	morality	morality
lamp	insight	insight	insight
scent	faith	*bodhicitta*	*bodhicitta*
food	contemplative trance		nectar (*amṛta*)
music	songs of praise		liberation melody

Phagpa does not explain his associations but the third Karmapa, Rangjung Dorje does. From the three lists, only certain items are explained by the three *blamas* in the same terms. All agree that incense refers to morality because in Tibetan Buddhism, as well as other religions, a sign of a moral person is that she/he exudes a wonderful fragrance.[33] The lamp is associated with insight (*prajñā*) because wisdom is the light which dispels the darkness of ignorance. This scent can be interpreted as incense which seems to be Phagpa's interpretation, but it can also be understood as kindness or *bodhicitta*. Karmapa stated, "Pure water with perfume and herbal ingredients is the bathing water of the victorious ones . . . May kindness, raining continually from the cloudbanks of wisdom, purify the multitude of foul odours."[34]

Water is usually understood as purification and Karmapa elaborates that it represents purification of the defilements (*kleśas*) of body, speech, and mind.[35] Wayman interprets Buddhaguhya's association of flowers with *samādhi* as referring to the incident where the Buddha teaches by holding a flower and is only understood by Mahākaśypa.[36] Phagpa explains food as contemplative trance (*samādhi*); a great yogi needs *samādhi*, not ordinary food.[37] Also food keeps the body healthy and in Tantra one needs a healthy body to achieve liberation.[38] By using the Tantric method, one experiences bliss or nectar of deathlessness (*amṛta*). Finally, music includes songs of praise to Bodhisattvas and Buddhas as well as songs of insight, such as the Tibetan yogi Milarepa's songs or the Mahāsiddhas.[39]

(3) Praises to the *pīṭhas* and the *kāyas* of the Buddha: In Buddhism, as in Hinduism, the goddess has special seats which are both external, geographically located in Asia and internal, located within each person's body. One of the earliest mentions of these *pīṭhas* is in the Hevajra Tantra which enumerates Oḍḍiyāna, Pūrṇagiri, Kāmarūpa, and Jālandhara.[40] The probable geographical locations for these are Oḍḍiyāna in Swat Valley in present North Pakistan, Pūrṇagiri in the Bījāpur region in Karnataka in south India,[41] Jālandhara in the Kangra Valley in Himachal Pradesh in north India, and Kāmarūpa in Assam, India. In the *Chinnamuṇḍā sādhana* the four *pīṭhas* mentioned are Oḍḍiyāna, Pullirāmalagiri (or Pūrṇagiri), Kāmāla (or Kāmarūpa) and Śrīhaṭṭa. Śrīhaṭṭa replaces Jālandhara. These latter four *pīṭhas* are consistent in many of Chinnamuṇḍā *sādhanas*.[42] According to Sircar Śrīhaṭṭa is modern Sylhet in Assam.

In Tantric Buddhism a Buddha manifests in four types of bodies—the Emanation Body (*nirmāṇakāya*) which associated with the navel, the Complete Enjoyment Body (*sambhogakāya*) associated with the throat, the Truth Body (*dharmakāya*) associated with the heart, and the Great Happiness Body (*mahāsukhakāya*) associated with the forehead, i.e., the place of the third eye. The most commonly known body is the Emanation Body, such as that of Śākyamuni Buddha who appeared in the human world, though it also includes manifold other Emanation Bodies which help beings in ways appropriate their circumstances. The Complete Enjoyment Body is only perceptible by high-level Bodhisattvas, and the other two bodies can be experienced only by other Buddhas. This ability of manifesting different bodies is one of the talents of a Buddha. Furthermore, each of the manifestations is connected with a *cakra* in one's body, whereby each person has the potential to become a Buddha and to manifest these bodies. These are the praises to the *pīṭhas* and the *kāyas*.

(4) Repetition of *mantras* is a common practice in the both Hindu and Buddhist Tantric traditions. In Buddhism usually a practitioner undergoes a retreat and makes a determination to recite 100,000 times, or a multiple of 100,000 times, the syllables in the root *mantra* of the deity accompanied by ritual worship including the visualization meditation. Sometimes the practitioner does this retreat in order to establish a stronger spiritual bond with the chosen deity, or a practitioner may have more mundane intentions, e.g., acquisition of power and boons. Upon successful completion of a retreat, a fire ceremony is performed as a thanksgiving to the deity, and "to pacify excess and omission that may have occurred during the retreat and for the welfare of sentient beings".[43]

(5) *gTor ma* offerings (*bali*) are equivalent to the sacrificial offerings in the Hindu practice. These *gtor ma* are ritual cakes which in Tibet are made of barley flour, butter, and frequently brown sugar. As one offers the *gtor ma*, one must imagine that one is a deity. Then offerings emanate from space and are transformed into nectar (*amṛta*). One offers these to many different deities and protectors, both benign and malevolent—gods, *nāgas, bhūtas, pretas, piśācas*, etc.[44] These offerings are made to appease the deities and to propitiate their aid. Tucci states:

> An imaginary plane is reached, on which the sacrificer and the whole feast (*mgron*) to which the imagined divine guests are invited to come together in an apotheosis transcending space and time This series of innerconnected visions however always remain within the structure of the ritual architecture of a supranormal world which opens before the participants in these meditations.[45]

A practitioner, if desired and time permits, can present these 'ritual cakes' daily but usually they are offered only on certain days and for particular reasons.

(6) Rejoicing and the dedication of merit is the conclusion of any Buddhist Tantric practice. One rejoices in the accumulation of virtues in oneself and in all other sentient beings. The Dalai Lama states:

> Although all phenomena lack any states apart from nominal existence on the conventional level, yet since positive fruits are produced from positive cause, I shall rejoice in the deeds of others.[46]

Moreover, the merit one has gained by this practice should be shared with all sentient beings.[47] In the *Innermost Essence Preliminary Practice* 'Jigs med gLing pa states:

> If one dedicates merit for the ultimate benefit of others the virtues will never decrease, they will only increase . . . The exceptional means of dedicating merit is to do so in conjunction with the realization of their non-reality—without the practice being defiled by attachment to any reality in the merit to be dedicated, in the objects to whom it is being dedicated, and in the purpose for which it is dedicated.[48]

Introduction to the Praises to Trikāyavajrayoginī by Siddhācārya Virūpa

These praises to Trikāyavajrayoginī were written by Siddhācārya Virūpa, a disciple of Mahāsiddhā Lakṣmīṅkarā.[49] They consist of an invocation, visualizations, praises, and supplications. As with Hindu praises, most Buddhist practitioners have not pledged to perform these praises daily; however, they are encouraged to do so. The praises contain a description of Trikāyavajrayoginī (lit., three-bodies of Vajrayoginī, i.e., Chinnamuṇḍā, Vajravairocanī, and Vajravarṃinī) which state that blood is issuing from the three subtle channels (*nāḍīs*). This demonstrates that Chinnamuṇḍā's iconography is a visual depiction of the yogic practice of controlling the subtle winds within the main subtle channel and its two ancillaries. The praises are self-explanatory and the objects of supplication include the attainment of the *siddhis*, becoming Vajrasattva,[50] and the attainment of Buddhahood for all sentient beings.

Chinnamuṇḍā Vajravārāhī Sādhana[51]

Here is the meditation on Chinnamuṇḍā Vajravārāhī. I pay homage to Vajravārāhī, the chief of the *maṇḍala* of the yoginīs, who adorns the three worlds and is the source of benefit for all sentient beings. O Vajrayoginī, to you I pay homage.

The Tantric adept rises at dawn and sits on a comfortable seat conducive to (meditating upon) Vajrayoginī. One faces in the direction previously explained.[52]

Firstly, the Tantric adept should recite, *Oṁ, Āḥ, Hūṃ* in order to protect the dwelling, oneself, and one's practice. Then in the centre of one's navel meditate on the one who is pledge-bound (*samayasattva*) who is on a fully blossomed white lotus. Seated on top of this (lotus) one visualizes a sun disc whose rays are radiantly glowing. Upon this sun disc is the syllable *Hrīḥ* which looks like an *argha* flower. From this syllable *Hrīḥ* there emanates a multi-coloured lotus upon which is a sun disc.

Upon this (sun disc) meditate on the *dharmodaya* (a three-dimensional triangle, lit., the source of *dharmas*). Then in this triangle is a syllable *Hrīḥ* which transforms into Bhagavatī Vajravārāhī who is yellow with a reddish lustre. She has severed her own head with a scimitar (*kartṛ*) that she holds in her hand. She holds her head in her left hand and the scimitar (in her right hand) which is pointing downward. Her right leg is extended, her head is adorned with skulls, she has her hair loose, and her nude body is adorned with the five *mudrās*. Meditate on this Buddhaḍākinī in the centre.

Then a stream of blood flows upward from the neck of her severed head and enters her mouth. Similarly streams of blood enter the mouths of the two yoginīs (who stand beside her on each side). To the left (of Bhagavatī Vajrayoginī) stands the green Goddess Vajravarṇinī and to the right is the yellow Goddess Vajravairocanī.

The left one (Vajravarṇinī) holds a scimitar and skull in her left and right hands respectively. The right one (Vajravairocanī) holds a scimitar and skull in her right and left respectively. The right one's (Vajravairocanī's) right leg is extended and the left one's (Vajravarṇinī's) left leg is extended. Their hair is loose and they are nude. Meditate on the formidable Vajrayoginī in the centre who is flanked by these two terrifying and charming yoginīs. This is the focus of the meditation.

Then make offerings. Having created a *maṇḍala* in front with red sandalwood water, draw a triangle which rests on a sun disc. Then from the syllable *Hrīḥ* on that (triangle) arises the adamantine and venerable Goddess with all the attributes previously explained. Make offerings in accordance with the ritual in proper sequence. Offer flowers in the centre of the triangle with the *mantra--Oṁ Sarvabuddhaḍākinyai Svāhā.* Then offer libation, flowers, incense, perfume, light, and other items of good quality. Likewise on Bhagavatī Vajrayoginī's left recite, *Oṁ Vajravarṇinyai Hūṃ Svāhā* and on her right, *Oṁ Vajravairocanyai Hūṃ Svāhā.*

Then make praises with offerings to the four holy places as one recites, *Udhila* (*Oḍḍiyāna*), *Phullirāmalagiri, Kāmalakhyā,* and *Śrīhaṭa.* Then recite this *mantra* while offering praises to *Dharma, Saṁbhoga, Nirmāṇa, and Mahāsukhakāyas.* Then recite this *mantra,* (*Oṁ*) *Sarva-buddhaḍākinyai, Oṁ Vajravarṇinyai, Oṁ Vajravairocanyai Hūṃ Hūṃ Hūṃ Phaṭ Phaṭ Phaṭ Svāhā.* If one recites it 100,000 times while in retreat, it will pacify all obstacles. If one recites it 200,000 times, one will be able to captivate all women. If one recites it 300,000 times, one will be able to conquer cities. If one recites it 400,000 times, one will be able to captivate kings. And if one recites it 500,000 times, all one's wishes will be fulfilled. Practise this by a river, at a charnel ground, by a solitary tree, at a sanctified place, in the house of a *caṇḍikā*, or in the outskirts of a city.

Resolve, 'Until I have abandoned all thought constructions, I will remain as a fortunate, naked yogin practising austerities.' Then offer the ritual cakes (*gtor ma*) saying (in Sanskrit), *Oṁ Sarvabuddhaḍākinyai, Oṁ Vajravarṇinyai, Oṁ Vajravairocanyai, take* the flowers, incense, light, perfume, and sacrificial offerings. *Protect* me, *Hūṃ Hūṃ Hūṃ Phaṭ Phaṭ Phaṭ Svāhā*. This completes the *sādhana* by Śrīmatidevī, translated by Nepalese Paṇḍitācārya Bharendraruce and the (Tibetan) translator Blo-ldan-Shes-rab (1059-1109).

TRIKĀYAVAJRAYOGINĪ STUTI[53]

Homage to Śrī Vajrayoginī. Homage to the Buddha, Dharma, and Saṅgha. Homage to the Guru, Buddhas, and Bodhisattvas. Homage to Locanī, etc., the ten adamantine women. Homage to Yamāntaka, etc., the ten fierce heroes and their consorts (*prajñā*). *Oṁ, Āḥ, Hūṃ*. (Homage) to the body, speech, mind, five sense perceptions, speech, and thoughts, mind consciousness, supranormal faculty of knowing the minds of others, and supranormal faculty of entering others' bodies.

Visualize at the navel a lotus surmounted by a red solar disc upon which is a *dharmodaya* upon which is a lotus with a tawny red triangle connected with the four *pīṭhas* (i.e., *cakras*) in its centre. In the middle portion (of this triangle) is a yellow *Hrīṃ* where that yellow being (Vajrayoginī) stands alone in the *avadhūtī* channel. In the *lalanā* channel stands the dark one and in the *rasanā* channel stands the white (*gaurikā*) one. In the middle of the pleasing seat (*pīṭha*) standing in the three paths is the Goddess Trikāyavajrayoginī in a *pratyālīḍha* stance. The main figure is Sarvabuddhaḍākinī who has a divine form in the three worlds and who fulfils all hopes. In her right hand is a scimitar (*kartṛ*) with which she has severed her head which is held in her left hand. She removes the sorrow of the world. The figure on her left is dark green Vajravarṇinī who holds a skull in her right hand and a scimitar in her left. The figure on her right is yellow Vajravairocanī who holds a scimitar in her right hand and a skull in her left. The two are in the *pratyālīḍha* stance and are nude. As the hands are reversed so are the feet of the two[54] who stand on each side of the Mother of the Buddhas (Sarvabuddhaḍākinī) who is conjoined with the form of enlightenment. Eternally auspicious, she destroys birth and death.

and has the form of the Dharma, Saṁbhoga, Nirmāṇa, and Mahāsukha Bodies of a Buddha. In the three worlds, the Goddess presides always like the moon.

From the headless body out of the *avadhūtī* channel comes blood which enters her own mouth and also gushes from the *lalanā* and *rasanā* channels. The red blood symbolizes compassion and she drinks for peace. She extinguishes the sufferings of the worlds, destroys the four Māras, and severs with her scimitar the mental afflictions, etc.

"Praises to you, O Mother of the Victorious Ones, you are so pleasing. I will do my best for myself and others who are in the ocean of cyclic existence. Please, O Goddess, be kind to me; I am foolish, ignorant, and commit faults with my body, speech, mind. I do not know how to be devoted to my teacher or to you. So in this world, please be kind to me. Please purify my body, speech, and mind and make them tranquil. By this I shall be released from *saṃsāra* and no longer dwell in the six realms. I shall be free and my body will be like a *vajra* (adamantine). When my body is abandoned by all Māras, then my body will be illusory and have all *siddhis* without obstacles. All *siddhis* will be accomplished and my body will not be subjected to old age and death. By frightening all Maras and fulfilling all hopes, give me the excellent *siddhi*." The Goddess dissolves into the mind with the five senses. "May I become Vajrasattva, have a youthful life without disease and with happiness. By your grace, may all achieve Mahāmudrā and wherever the gods, *asuras*, and humans dwell, may they be happy. May all obtain the result of brilliant Buddhahood." This concludes the praises of Trikāyavajrayogini in the *Śrī Guhyasamaya Tantra* written by Siddhācārya Virūpa.

Comparison of Buddhist and Hindu Tantra

The goal of Buddhism and Hinduism reflect the understanding and experience of the unconditioned or ultimate reality of each tradition. For the Hindus, generally speaking, the goal is for one's *Ātman* to become liberated from cyclic existence and to merge with the impersonal Brahman or to be eternally with one's chosen deity.[55] Each individual will eventually achieve this permanent state and does not return to cyclic existence. The main exceptions are the avatars who continually "descend" to earth when chaos and evil prevail. Tantric Buddhists desire to achieve Buddhahood in the shortest time possible, not to escape cyclic existence, but in order to help other beings in achieving Buddhahood as quickly as possible. In Vajrayāna *sādhanas*, including the *Chinnamuṇḍā Vajravārāhī Sādhana*, explicitly or implicitly the generation of the *bodhicitta*, the four immeasurables, and the dedication of merit are the sections of a *sādhana* which stress this altruistic intention of achieving Buddhahood for the sake of all sentient beings. The concept of *bodhicitta* and the Bodhisattva ideal are some of the most distinctive features of Mahāyāna Buddhism.[56] Another important difference between Hinduism and Mahāyāna is that all Mahāyāna methods operate with the underlying premise of the understanding of voidness of intrinsic existence.

To achieve these goals there are many methods and some of these methods can lead a practitioner astray. Many Hindu and Buddhist Tantric *sādhanas* warn the practitioner not to become enamoured by the acquisition of *siddhis* and other supranormal powers. These powers are so attractive that some practitioners seek to acquire these worldly aims and are not interested in liberation for themselves or others. A true and pure practitioner would consider them only as means to the goal but not the goal itself.[57] The Hindus have eight *siddhis*, but these are not identical to the Buddhist ones. (See the beginning of the chapter for the Buddhist *siddhis*.) The Hindu *siddhis* are:

(1) *Aṇiman*—the ability to become very small to the size of an atom;
(2) *Mahiman*—the ability to become very big;
(3) *Laghiman*—the ability to become very light;
(4) *Gariman*—the ability to become very heavy;
(5) *Prāpti*—the power to obtain everything;
(6) *Prākāmya*—the power of irresistible will,
(7) *Īśitva*—the power of supremacy; and
(8) *Vaśitva*—the power to subdue anything.[58]

Comparing these mundane accomplishments with the eight *siddhis* and the six supranormal powers of the Buddhists, similarities are evident. These include the basic interest in dominating or subduing, in changing one's form, in controlling elements or at least, not being subject to their influence, and generally in controlling of animate and inanimate things. Although these *siddhis* and supranormal powers should not be sought for the motive of acquiring power, they may be utilized to attract a person to the Hindu or Buddhist path.[59]

Let us look at specific methods described in two *sādhanas* of the Hindu Chinnamastā and the Buddhist Chinnamuṇḍā Vajravārāhi. The "Chinnamastātantra" of the *Śākta Pramoda* is divided into nine sections from the visualization of the deity to the repetition of thousand names. Among all the Buddhist *sādhanas* of Chinnamuṇḍā, none is as complete as the Hindu one and some sections such as the *kavaca* and thousand names sections are rarely found in the Buddhist *sādhanas*. If one contrasts the ritual worship section (*pūjā*) which is the heart of all daily Tantric practice in both traditions, one can formulate both basic patterns which are common to all Tantric practices and distinct differences between Buddhism and Hinduism.

The Hindu *pūjā* section begins with the regular preliminaries which include homage to one's guru and one's chosen deity (*iṣṭadevatā*) and then proceeds to the Tantric preliminaries. The Buddhist *pūjā* section of regular preliminaries also begins with homage to one's deity and to one's guru but it adds in the specifically Buddhist practice of taking refuge in the Three Jewels, generating *bodhicitta*, and cultivating the four immeasurables all with the underlying premise of the voidness of inherent existence. The Hindu *pūjā* continues with the cleansing of oneself through ablution which in Buddhism is represented by the purification of oneself by reciting the hundred-syllable *mantra* of Vajrasattva. The next Hindu section consists of various *nyāsa* which empower oneself and transform one's body into a divine body.[60] This is a very elaborate section compared to the Buddhist consecration of one's body;[61] however, both traditions of Chinnamastā insist that one's ordinary self must be transformed into an extraordinary self in order to worship. In the Hindu rite of *bhūtaśuddhi*, the practitioner imagines that his/her body composed of the five elements are being reabsorbed gradually into Brahman, then progressively in reverse order, the body becomes manifest again indicating that she/he is cosubstantial with Brahman. In the Buddhist rite of purification, a practitioner visualizes that his/her body is completely cleansed of impurities and after purification, his/her body is blessed gradually by Vajrasattva and consort. The blessing begins with the head, then throat, heart, and the entire body. Upon completion of the purification and consecration, one can meditate on Chinnamastā/Chinnamuṇḍā and draw or visualize her 'residence' which in Hinduism is known as a *yantra* and in Buddhism as a *maṇḍala*. The Hindu *sādhana* elaborates on Chinnamastā's residence with the special conch ritual which is very important in Hindu Tantric worship. This special couch is frequently filled with wine indicating the blissful nature of the Goddess. This is followed by the *pīṭha pūjā*. Although the *maṇḍala yantra*, special conch, and *pīṭha* (the goddess' throne) are known as her residence, she is everything in the ceremony. The practitioner should identify everything with Chinnamastā. Thus both Hinduism and Buddhism have three main preliminaries: (1) purification of oneself, (2) consecration of oneself, and(3) visualizing Chinnamastā/Chinnamuṇḍā and the creation of her residence.

Proceeding to the actual meditation session of the deity, one begins in both traditions with an invitation to the deity. Here we encounter two major differences between the Hindu and Buddhist *sādhanas*. In the Buddhist *sādhana*, the practitioner imagines or experiences (depending on ability) the voidness of inherent existence prior to the actual visualization. Then one visualizes oneself as Chinnamuṇḍā. By contrast, in the Hindu practice, there is no mention of voidness of inherent existence and Chinnamastā remains in front of the practitioner. Since in Hindu Tantra Chinnamastā is in front, the practitioner who has already been transformed into a deity can instill the vital breath (*prāṇapratiṣṭhā*), and consecrate her six limbs, whereas in the Buddhist *sādhana*, the practitioner has already undergone this consecration, so does not need to perform this ritual while she/he is visualizing her/himself as Chinnamuṇḍā.

In the conclusion section both *sādhanas* have some similarities. An important difference is that in the Buddhist *sādhana* which upholds the Mahāyānist ideal of altruism, a practitioner concludes with the dedication of merit. Although many sections of the actual meditation on the deity are similar in both traditions, differences are apparent. The two main differences are the method generating the deity and the dedication of merit; the latter is a fundamental Buddhist component not found in the Hindu *sādhana*.

In regard to the fire ceremony in both traditions the practitioner offers certain items in the fire, repeats certain *mantras*, and performs the ceremony for specific reasons. The concept of performing a fire sacrifice (*yajña*) originated in the Vedic times and eventually was incorporated in both the Tantric traditions. According to the Hindus there are six types of accomplishments as a result of performing specific versions of the fire ceremony. These six are: (1) appeasing (*śānti*), (2) influencing (*vaśyam*), (3) 'stunning' (*stambhanam*), (4) causing division or hating (*dveṣam*), (5) causing to flee (*uccāṭana*), and (6) killing (*māraṇa*). The Buddhists have four divisions of accomplishments, which are: (1) appeasing (*śānti*), (2) increasing or prospering (*pauṣṭika*), (3) dominating (*vaśīkaraṇa*), and (4) destroying (*māraṇa*). The first (appeasing) and last (destroying) of each tradition are the same and all the other Hindu ones can be classified under the 'dominating' category in Buddhism. Furthermore, the dominating and killing categories are under the rubric of the 'dreadful rites' (*abhicāra*).[62] The *sādhanas* do not have specific fire ceremonies for each type of accomplishment specifically tailored to Chinnamastā/ Chinnamuṇḍā.[63] Although many of the basic components of the practice to Chinnamastā/Chinnamuṇḍā are similar in the two traditions, there are some fundamental differences.

REFERENCES

1. The *Sādhanamālā* (vol.II, p.lxxxv) states that this "evidently means the magic unguent which enables the wearer to perceive the treasures buried under the earth or otherwise hidden from the eyes." Lessing and Wayman (p. 220) state that this 'enables one to see all the *devas* and *nāgas*.'
2. Ibid.
3. *Sādhanamālā* Vol.II: 350 (no. 172).
4. Lessing and Wayman:136.
5. This is based on the Tibetan Tantric tradition, not the East Asian Tantric traditions.
6. Tibetan Buddhism is divided into four major schools—Nyingma, Kargyu, Sakya, and Gelug. The Nyingma differ in their classification from the other three; they classify the Tantras as outer and inner. The outer ones are *kriyā, caryā*, and *yoga*; the inner ones are *mahāyoga*, *anuyoga*, and *atiyoga*.
7. Gyatso, *Tantra in Tibet*:156.
8. In Buddhist cosmology the worlds are divided into the desire, form, and formless realms. Since human beings dwell in the desire realm; Tantra harnesses and maximizes the force of desire as a means to liberation.
9. Gyatso, *Tantra in Tibet*:74.
10. Ibid.:156ff.
11. There are many discussions about these four classifications and the reasons why they are classified as such. See Lessing, F. and Wayman, A.: 165-69; Gyatso, *Tantra in Tibet*:151-64, and Tulku Thondup, *Buddhist Civilization in Tibet*:20.
12. Lessing and Wayman:253ff.
13. The *rGyud sde kun btus*:410 states that Vajravārāhī Tantra is from the Cakrasaṃvara root Tantra and is the summary Tantra. However, in the Nepalese Buddhist manuscripts, the Chinnamuṇḍā *sādhanas* are from the *Guhyasamayādhāna-saṃgraha* which I find suspect.
14. *Tangyur*, Vol.23:409-11.
15. The Nepalese Buddhist *sādhana* is from the late Jagannath Upadhyaya's collection in Varanasi. This collection was acquired in Nepal for the Dhīḥ project based at the Institute of Tibetan Studies in Sarnath, U.P. It is listed under *Guhyasamayādhānasaṃgraha* #22:66a-67a. I thank the Dhīḥ project for allowing me to copy all their manuscripts of Chinnamuṇḍā. The *Vajrayoginī sādhana* is from *Sādhanamālā* : 453 (#232).
16. *Kavacas* do not seem very popular in Buddhist Tantras; recitation of hundred and eight names do exist but are certainly not as ubiquitous as in the Hindu Tantra; recitations of the thousand names are rare. (See Lessing and Wayman:121-23 for hundred and eight names of the eight main Bodhisattvas, Mañjuśrī, and Amitāyus.)
17. See Kingsley:19-34.
18. Also in a personal communication with Sakya Trizin, he stated that he was certain that there are no lineages of Chinnamuṇḍā which include Virūpa, the Sakya patriarch.
19. See chapter 1 and also see Dowman:375 and Wayman, *The Yoga of the Guhyasamāja*:96.
20. For the prelīminaries preceding refuge, see H.H.Dalai Lama Tenzin Gyatso, *The Union of Bliss and Emptiness*:32-42.
21. See Snellgrove:176-80.

22. In Tibetan Buddhism the exemplary teacher/disciple relationship is Marpa Milarepa. Milarepa tries to practise under one of Marpa's disciples, Lama Ngokpa who initiates him and explains the practice. When Milarepa has no result, Lama Ngokpa realizes that he does not have Marpa's blessing. He exclaims, "Without the *lama*'s permission you will not achieve results. There is nothing to be done." Lhalungpa:65 and see xiiiff.
23. For excellent descriptions of the Three Jewels and why one should seek refuge in them, see Lhundrub, N.K.: 9-17; Amipa:91-100; Gyatso, *The Union of Bliss and Emptiness*:42-50.
24. Lhundrub, N.K.:10-11.
25. Ibid.:138.
26. Ibid.:140ff.
27. Sopa and Hopkins, *The Practice and Theory of Tibetan Buddhism*: xviii.
28. Amipa:129.
29. See Tucci, G., *The Theory and Practice of the Mandala* : 45-46.
30. Lessing and Wayman: 270.
31. See Gyatso, *Union of Bliss and Emptiness*:100-102.
32. Phagpa's explanation is from a Hevajra *sādhana* published in Rajpur, India, 1985; the third Karmapa's is from a Vajrayoginī *sādhana* (see Klimburg-Salter:236 & 241); and the Buddhaguhya's is from the *Artha-vyañjana vṛtti* (PTT. Vol.76, pp.35-42) cited in Wayman, *Buddhist Tantras* : 74.
33. Benard, 1988:41.
34. Klimburg-Stalter:236.
35. Ibid.
36. This incident is frequently considered as the origin of Ch'an or Zen.
37. Benard, 1990:49. In Ma gCig Lab sGron's biography, her son was asked by a yogi whether he was hungry or cold. Her son replied, "I am eating meditational food (*samādhi*) . . . and I am wearing *tum-mo* (internal heat yoga) clothes."
38. In the Japanese Tendai tradition, the six offerings excluding music are connected with the six perfections—giving and water, morality and scent, patience and flowers, effort and incense, meditation and rice (food), insight and light. I thank Professor M. Ichishima of Taisho University for this information.
39. See Kvaerne and Dowman.
40. Snellgrove, *Hevajra Tantra*, I:14ff.
41. See Sircar:94.
42. See the *Sādhanamālā*: 453 and 455. Note that Śrīrhaṭṭa is not mentioned in many of the *Tantras*. (See 'Dhīḥ', vol.1: 140-41.)
43. Sharpa Tulku and Perrott: xi. The fire ceremony (*homa*) can be performed also for any of the four actions—pacifying, enriching, dominating, and eliminating.
44. *Sādhanamālā*:458 (no.238).
45. Tucci, *The Religions of Tibet*:115ff.
46. From *A Method of Offering to the Guru, The Profound Path Entitled the Indivisibility of Bliss and Emptiness* (cited from Gyatso, *Union of Bliss*:114).
47. Ibid:176.
48. 'Jigs med gLing pa, *The Dzogchen: the Innermost Essence Preliminary Practice*, Dharamsala, Library of Tibetan Works and Archives, 1982:78-79.
49. Roerich, *Blue Annals*:390.
50. See Wayman, *Buddhist Tantras*: 83, "Vajrasattva is the synthetic paragon of all Buddhist accomplishments."
51. *Tangyur*, Vol.23:409-11 (#2262). See plate 3 for an illustration of Chinnamuṇḍā and her two attendants.

52. The direction is not mentioned in the text because the adept knows this.
53. This is from the 'Dhīḥ' collection, vol.1 #25 (68b-69b).
54. Vajravaraṇinī's right leg is extended and Vajravairocanī's left leg is extended.
55. An explanation of the goal of each of the six *darśanas* is beyond the scope of this work.
56. In Vajrayāna Buddhism the method is different from that of the Perfection Vehicle though the goal is the same.
57. In modern India a popular connotation of a Hindu Tantric practitioner is one who practices 'black magic'.
58. Bose:173-74.
59. One well known Buddhist example is Sakya Phagpa performing miracles for the Mongolian Emperor Kublai Khan to demonstrate the supremacy of Buddhism.
60. Gupta: 136 states the cleansing of the self (*ātmaśuddhi*) consists of several parts and only a minor part is the physical acts. The major part is *bhūtaśuddhi* (consecrating one's physical body) and *nyāsa* (transmutation and accommodation).
61. Deshung Rimpoche stated that Buddhists emphasize the purification of the mind rather than external purification because everything ultimately depends on the mind.
62. See Lessing, F.D., *Yung-Ho-Kung*:139-61.
63. For the general rite, see the twenty-fifth chapter of the Hindu *Mantramahodadhi* which presents explicit details of nineteen items connected with each specific accomplishment rite. These include the deity and its colour, season, directions, day, seat, posture, etc.

Chapter 5

Visualization of Chinnamastā/ Chinnamuṇḍā

Tantric practice includes an important aspect of spiritual practice (*sādhana*)—the visualization of the deity. In a Tantric *sādhana*, worship of a deity involves either imagining oneself as the deity or visualizing the deity in front of oneself. An oft-quoted verse in the Hindu tradition is "In order to worship a deity, one must become a deity."[1] In Buddhist Tantra, one must visualize oneself as a specific deity in order to acheive Buddhahood. In *Tantra in Tibet*, the 14th Dalai Lama, Tenzin Gyatso states:

> In order to attain the definite goodness of the highest achievement, Buddhahood, deity yoga is needed. Also, in order to attain the common achievements, the eight feats and so forth, one must view one's body clearly as a divine body and train in the pride of being a deity. Without deity yoga the Mantra path is impossible; deity yoga is the essence of Mantra.[2]

Imagining oneself as a deity is not unique to the Tantric method, but it is a major component. Why must one visualize oneself as a deity? According to the Tantric method a practitioner, whose motives are pure, seeks the most expedient means to liberation or Buddhahood.[3] These means consist in visualization of the deity. The deity represents the ideal, the refined form, which has no defilements or obscurations preventing liberation from cyclic existence. How does one become like the deity? In order to understand this Tantric method, one must remember that the Tantras inherited much from Upaniṣadic thought. One central concept is the Upaniṣadic hypostasy of macrocosmic equivalents in the human body; each part of the body is a homology of a place or thing in the universe.[4]

By accepting this macrocosm/microcosm homology, a Tantric practitioner mentally merges the self and a deity because the deity's body is an undefiled microcosm of the universe. One's ordinary body is considered defiled and these defilements must be transformed in order to have a pure homology. One's body becomes the principal instrument in this transformation in order to achieve the ultimate goal of the *sādhana*, liberation or Buddhahood. A. Bharati states:

> What distinguishes tantric form from other Hindu and Buddhist teaching is its systematic emphasis on the identity of the absolute (*paramārtha*) and the phenomenal (*vyavahāra*) when filtered through the experience of the *sādhana*.[5]

Both Tantric traditions do agree that the *sādhana* is of central importance and that the imagining of oneself as the deity is the essential part of the *sādhana*. Furthermore, in Hinduism and Buddhism, someone or something becomes distinct by name and form (*nāmarūpa*). In chapter 3 the name and its significance was discussed and in this chapter the aspect of form will be explored. In this study of Hindu Chinnamastā and Buddhist Chinnamuṇḍā, the particular visualization and its interpretations of form are dependent on the particular Tantric tradition. This chapter will compare and contrast various hermeneutics which reflect the particular religious tenets of Hinduism or Buddhism; also herein will be demonstrated the commonality of the two Tantric traditions.

Though there are many *sādhanas* of Chinnamastā/Chinnamuṇḍā, commentaries are rare. The earliest commentary is from one of the older Hindu texts, *Mantramahodadhi*, by Mahīdhara in 1589 C.E. Chronologically, the next one is the Buddhist one by 'Jam dbyangs mkhyen brtse'i dbang po (1820-1892) in the *rGyud sde kun btus* (Vol.23). The other three are recent Hindu commentaries—"Daśa Mahāvidyā" by S. G. Śrīmotilal in the *Śākti Aṅka* (1934), the Kashmir Śaivite commentary of 'Chinnamastā' by J. Misra in *Bhāratīya Pratīkavidyā* (Patna, 1959), and the aforementioned "Śrī Chinnamastā Nityārcana" commentary by Śrī Swamiji Mahārāja. Of these five only Misra gives a word for word or line for line commentary; the rest only emphasize a few salient points. Commentaries on Chinnamastā are difficult to find because she is an uncommon Tantric deity. Frequently Tantric *sādhanas* were kept secretly and were only revealed to initiates who took the vow (*samaya*) to practise the *sādhana*. Some of the *sādhanas* state that this *sādhana* should not be revealed to anyone who does not cherish it more than one's own life. With this injunction, public accessibility to this material was limited until this century when scholars began to compile and translate these texts. In recent decades some of the Hindu gurus and Buddhist *blamas* have been more willing to bestow initiations and impart commentary on many Tantric *sādhanas*. Thus as the *sādhanas* are revealed, perhaps oral commentary and eventually written commentary will become more readily available for lesser known deities, such as Chinnamastā. The hermeneutics will depend on written commentaries, oral commentary, and general Tantric scholarship to interpret the *sādhanas*, as well as the Upaniṣadic "inheritance".

THE SĀDHANAS

The first *sādhana* is from the Buddhist *Sādhanamālā* which contains 312 *sādhanas* of various Buddhist deities.[6] The *sādhana* of the headless Vajrayoginī is as follows:[7]

> The practitioner should visualize (lit., meditate) at one's navel an opened white lotus surmounted by a very red solar disc. On top of that is a *sindūra* (red) colored *Hrīṃ*. This *Hrīṃ* transforms into Bhaṭṭārikā Vajrayoginī (the practitioner imagining him/herself as Goddess) who is of yellow color, who holds in her left hand her own self-severed head with the scimitar (*kartṛ*) held in her right hand. Her left hand is raised upwards while the right is extended below. She is nude (*vasana śūnyā*), and her right leg is outstretched while the left is bent. The practitioner meditates on the streams of blood issuing from the severed body as falling into the mouth of her severed head and into the mouths of the two Yoginīs on either side of her.
>
> The practitioner should also visualize the two Yoginīs to the left and right (of the principal goddess), the green (*śyāmā*) Vajravarṇinī and the yellow Vajravairocanī, both of whom hold the scimitar (*kartṛ*) in their left and right hands respectively, and the skullcup (*karapa*) in the right and left hands respectively. Their left and right legs respectively are outstretched, while the other legs are bent, and their hair is dishevelled. On all sides, between the two Yoginīs and in the intermediate space (*antarikṣa*) is the very frightening cremation ground.

The second *sādhana* is a Buddhist meditation which is a combination of two earlier meditations. It is from the *Yidam rgya mtsho'i sgrub thabs rin chen 'byung gnas* by Tāranātha and reads as follows:

> From space, light rays emanate from the letter 'Ram' in your navel. Your body has become a red triangle *maṇḍala*; in the center is a four petalled white lotus, in its centre is your mind of enlightenment (*bodhicitta*) as a moon and on the moon is the sun. The sun and moon combine, from the middle of this combination emanate three 'Hrīḥ' which transform into three scimitars (*kartṛ*) inscribed with a 'Hrīḥ'. All merge into one. In the midst of this merging emanates a reddish yellow Buddhaḍākinī whose right leg is extended and left leg is bent as she stands on Kālī (T. *dus mtshan ma*). In her right hand she brandishes a scimitar which hangs downwards and in her left hand she holds a skullcup of blood; under her left arm is a white

> *khaṭvāṅga* which symbolizes method (including *bodhicitta*). On her left side stands Vajravarṇinī (*rDo rje rab bsngags ma*) who is green and has her left leg extended; she brandishes a scimitar in her right hand and a skullcup in her left. To the right of the main deity stands Vajravairocanī who is yellow, has her right foot extended, holds a knife in her right hand and a skullcup in her left one. All (three deities) are wearing an ornament of five dried skulls (as a tiara) on their heads and fifty freshly severed heads as a garland. Each has the five ornaments (*mudrās*). All are nude, inexhaustible, have three eyes, dishevelled hair, and faces which are both angry and smiling; they are frightening to those who are terrifying to others. They are sitting in the middle of the great burning grounds.
>
> The main *ḍākinī*'s right hand brandishes a scimitar with which she has severed her own head which she holds by the hair strands in her left hand. Her three eyes look downwards. At the place where the head has been severed, three subtle channels have been cut. From the central channel red and white drops are mixed and blood spurts into her mouth. From the left channel blood mixed with Akṣobhaya falls into the left *ḍākinī*'s mouth and from the right channel blood mixed with ordinary blood falls into the right *ḍākinī*'s mouth. You should meditate with clarity and strong effort in this manner as long as you can.

The third *sādhana* is from one of the older Hindu texts, the *Mantramahodadhi*, by Mahīdhara.[8] In addition he wrote a commentary named *Naukā* (lit., boat).[9] In chapter 6 one finds the meditation of Chinnamastā as follows:

> I pay homage to goddess Chinnamastā who shines in the middle of the solar disc, who holds in her left hand her own severed head with dishevelled hair, whose mouth is open wide and who drinks her own blood dripping down from her neck, who is stationed above Rati and Smara who are engaged in sexual intercourse, and who is extremely pleased in seeing her attendants, Ḍākinī and Varṇinī.

Mahīdhara's only comment on this meditation is that *yabha* means sexual intercourse and that Chinnamastā is standing on Rati and Kāma who are indulging in sexual intercourse.[10]

The second Hindu *sādhana* is from another Hindu Tantric compendium, the *Tantrasāra*, written by Kṛṣṇānanda Āgamavāgīśa at the end of the sixteenth century.[11] This *Tantrasāra* is a digest for serious Hindu Śākta Tantric practitioners. N. N. Bhattacharyya states that the *Tantrasāra* is the "most comprehensive and popular of the numerous digests that are in Bengal. A few manuscripts of this work are found in non-Bengali scripts, and outside of Bengal, indicating thereby the extent of its popularity."[12] In the *Tantrasāra*, Chinnamastā is not listed as a deity; however, Pracaṇḍa-caṇḍikā is.[13] Pracaṇḍa-caṇḍikā is another name for Chinnamastā because from the first verse, the deity is referred to as Chinnamastā. In this Pracaṇḍa-caṇḍikā section there are four visualizations of the deity. The most elaborate is the first one which is as follows:[14]

> Visualize in your navel, a half-opened white lotus and in its centre is a solar disc red as a hibiscus flower and resembling a red *bandhūka* flower. This disc is decorated with an equilateral triangle pointing downward which is formed by three lines, each representing a *guṇa* (beginning in the left in an counter-clockwise direction) *rajas, sattva*, and *tamas*. Standing in the middle is the Great Goddess (Mahādevī, i.e. Chinnamastā) who is as effulgent as ten million suns. In her left hand she holds her own head; her mouth is wide open, and the tip of her tongue is lolling. She drinks the sanguine stream issuing from her recently-severed throat. Her hair is loose, dishevelled and decorated with various flowers. In her right hand she brandishes a scimitar (*kartṛ*); she is nude, extremely fierce to behold, decorated with a skull rosary, and stands in the *pratyālīḍha* stance. She wears a bone necklace and has a snake as her sacred cord. She is a perpetual sixteen-year-old with full firm breasts. She stands on Rati and Kāma who are in reverse sexual embrace (i.e. Rati is above Kāma). One visualizes in this manner saying the *mantra*.
>
> She is flanked by Ḍākinī and Varṇinī to her left and right respectively. Varṇinī is drinking from the nectar-like sanguine stream which is shooting up from the Goddess' neck. She is red with a smiling face, has loose hair and is nude. She holds a skull and a scimitar in her left hand and right hands respectively. She wears a snake as her sacred cord and has a fiery splendour. Decorated with various ornaments and a bone rosary, she stands in the *pratyālīḍha* stance and is a perpetual twelve year old.
>
> On the goddess' left side is Ḍākinī whose brilliance equals the fire at the end of an aeon. Her matted hair glistens like lightning, her teeth with protruding canines are as white as cranes and she has swelling breasts. This great goddess is terrible to behold—nude with loose hair, has a great flickering tongue and is ornamented with a skull rosary. Her left and right hands hold a skull and a scimitar respectively. She drinks the ambrosial sanguine stream issuing from Chinnamastā's neck. She is extremely terrifying and holds a terrible skull. A wise devotee should meditate upon this Goddess attended by these two, Varṇinī and Ḍākinī. The *Bhairava Tantra* states: She holds in her left hand her own head with a skull and drinks her blood with her mouth. The Tantra states that whoever performs this worship without meditating on Chinnamastā, the Goddess will sever his (or her) head and drink his (or her) blood.

These four *sādhanas* are the basis of interpreting how Chinnamastā is depicted and the significance of the various items depicted. The interpretation is divided into three categories: (1) the deity's location, (2) the deity and her implements, and (3) the deity's attendants.

THE DEITY'S LOCATION

Although no location is given in Mahīdhara's *sādhana*, he does imply a location by referring to the solar disc. In the other three *sādhanas*, the practitioner must visualize the deity at the navel. Tāranātha's meditation begins with the visualization emanating from space. In accordance with Buddhist belief in the lack of an inherent self, in most Buddhist Tantric *sādhanas*, the visualization of the deity is preceded by the words 'from space' or a mantra, such as, *Oṁ Svabhāvaśuddhāḥ Sarvadharmāḥ Svabhāvaśuddho 'Ham.*[15] These words remind the practitioner that neither the deity nor the meditator have a permanent, eternal nature. The Hindu meditations do not begin like this because they do believe in an unchanging eternal self, the *ātman*. This is a major philosophical difference between the two traditions.

The Navel

In J. Misra's commentary, he states that the navel is the centre of consciousness (*nābhi* [*cetanā ke vistāra ke bindusthāna*] *meṃ*). In the beginning of creation is consciousness; as the first vibration expands itself (Skt. *spanda*), it becomes equated with the *bindu* in the navel.[16] Since the navel is equated with creation, this implies that Chinnamastā's location is in the source of creation.

A Tantric explanation of the navel, specifically the *maṇipūra cakra* located at the navel, is that the *maṇipūra cakra* is the locus of creation and also dissolution, its necessary complement.[17] The navel is not ordinarily associated with dissolution; but for a Tantric practitioner, it is. According to both Hindu and Buddhist Tantra, a practitioner must eliminate the concept of duality in order to be liberated. Both Tantric traditions accept that duality is caused by the subtle winds which are located in the two subtle channels. At the *maṇipūra cakra* the right subtle channel, *piṅgalā nāḍī* (in Hinduism) or *rasanā nāḍī* (in Buddhism), and the left subtle channel, *iḍā nāḍī* (in Hinduism) or *lalanā nāḍī* (in Buddhism), converge with the central subtle channel, *suṣumṇā nāḍī* (in Hinduism) or *avadhūti nāḍī* (in Buddhism). The subtle winds traverse the side channels but these winds are impeded in entering the central channel because the opening at the *maṇipūra cakra* is closed. As long as the entrance is closed, a person experiences duality. This duality can be understood in many ways but at the *maṇipūra cakra*, duality indicates the duality of creation and dissolution. People who do not know how to manipulate the opening of the central channel will not experience the dissolution aspect until the time of death. At the time of death the winds enter naturally and effortlessly into the central channel, but a person usually does not remember this because she/he dies. Conversely, a Tantric practitioner practises bringing the subtle winds into the central channel in order to gain mastery of this process. Why? By mastering this manipulation, one can transcend the entrapment of duality—birth and death—thereby rendering the potent bonds of cyclic existence ineffective. Eventually by this practice, a Tantric practitioner becomes liberated from Saṃsāra, cyclic existence. This does not indicate that one need die to experience this unity or non-duality. By becoming familiar with the death process, one can control it when one dies, thereby becoming able to consciously choose rebirth or not.

First, the navel is the centre of consciousness—the consciousness which is the pivotal point between the collapsing of consciousness thereby destroying duality as well as the reaffirmation of consciousness creating duality. Second, the *maṇipūra cakra* is also a pivotal point between liberation or enslavement to cyclic existence. If one knows how to open the central channel at the *maṇipūra cakra*, one can achieve salvation; conversely, if one does not, one remains in the continual cycle of births and deaths. Thus Chinnamastā is placed at this pivotal point; indicating that she is connected with the power to either enslave or liberate the practitioner.

The Lotus

According to the *Tantrasāra* meditation, the correct order of visualization is a white lotus which in its centre has a red solar disc which is decorated with a downward-pointing equilateral triangle. In Tāranātha's meditation the visualization begins with Raṃ, whence the practitioner's body is transformed into a red triangular *maṇḍala* which at its centre is a four-petalled white lotus topped by a moon and a sun.[18] In Hinduism and Buddhism, the lotus as a symbol or implement is ubiquitous. Both the religions associate the lotus with purity and beauty. Frequently a deity is said to have lotus-eyes (*padmākṣī*), lotus-thighs (*padma-ūru*); moreover they hold lotuses and have a lotus as a seat cushion. In Buddhism the lotus is a powerful symbol because it represents the mind of enlightenment, *bodhicitta*. This symbolism developed because a lotus grows from the mud but remains untainted by it. Similarly, the lotus of the mind is originally pristine, yet it becomes adventitiously defiled. A Buddhist practitioner is encouraged to realize this mind of purity for the sake of all sentient beings. In Hinduism this concept of *bodhicitta* is not important, but in Mahāyāna Buddhism (including Tantra) it is a major concept. All beings must cultivate *bodhicitta* in order to become enlightened for the sake of all sentient beings. Thus in the two traditions the lotus symbolizes purity but in Tantric Buddhism it is also associated with *bodhicitta*.

Fire Element

In the Hindu Tantric text, *Ṣaṭ Cakra Nirupaṇa* enjoins "Meditate there on the region of fire, triangular in form and shining like the rising sun . . . ."[19] The navel area, specifically the *maṇipūra cakra*, is associated with the *tejas tattva* which is characterized by expansion, the production of heat and stimulation of the visual sense of colour and form.[20] In this text on the six *cakras*, the *maṇipūra cakra* is the region of fire and heat. Furthermore the *cakra*'s seed syllable is *Raṃ* known as the Agni *bīja*, the fire god's seed syllable.[21] The Buddhists also state that *Raṃ* is the seed syallable of the *maṇipūra cakra* and that this *cakra* is associated with the goddess Caṇḍālī, the fire goddess who is propitiated for the attainment of mystical or yogic heat (Tib. *gtum mo*).[22] This fire located in the *maṇipura cakra* region is not gross fire which is familiar to us but a pure form of the fire element. As Wayman cites in the *Buddhist Tantras*, E.H. Johnston shows that these elements (wind, fire, water and earth) are already regarded as divine forces in Upaniṣadic literature.[23] Fire is very important because when the central channel is opened this fire eventually reaches the top of the head where according to the Tantric traditions nectar (*amṛta*) is located. When this nectar is heated, it descends the channel and the practitioner experiences bliss in various degrees. Thus one can see that the *maṇipūra cakra* is a major pivotal point in regard to bliss and liberation.

The Inverted Triangle

The three-dimensional inverted triangle (i.e., downward pointing) is frequently a symbol of a womb (*bhaga*) and the feminine.[24] The inverted triangle can be found in many *yantras* of goddesses, such as the Daśa Mahāvidyās.[25] In the meditations on these goddesses the triangle symbolizes a more abstract concept. The *Tantrasāra* meditation states that the triangle is composed of three lines representing *rajas*, *sattva* and *tamas guṇas*. These three 'distinct powers' are found in various proportions in every composed entity. The beings dominated by *rajas guṇa* exhibit turbulence, instability, volatile actions and pain; those dominated by the *sattva guṇa* are calm, pleasing and usually illuminating; those dominated by the *tamas guṇa* display delusion, confusion and inertia. Since the triangle consists of the three *guṇas* which are in every composed entity, this indicates that the triangle symbolizes the source of creation. In the centre of the triangle is the *bindu*, the place of the Goddess.[26] This *bindu* is known as the *mahāśakti pīṭha*, the principal abode of the great feminine power.[27] In *Yantra*, Khanna states that the *bindu* is a 'Whole', or 'Full' (*pūrṇa*), the undifferentiated, all-embracing reservoir of the infinite.[28]

In the Buddhist meditations the three-dimensional triangle is called *dharmodaya*, a specific type of triangle which symbolizes the source of all phenomena (*dharmas*).[29] Furthermore, there are two types of triangles associated with Vajrayoginī—the single or the double. Tucci states in *The Theory and Practice of the Maṇḍala* that the *dharmodaya* signifies a double intersecting triangle, sometimes referred to by others as a tetrahedron since it is three dimensional. The *dharmodaya* is not always a double intersecting triangle but the double version is definitely more prevalent.[30] On the other hand, Mallmann states in the *Niṣpannayogāvalī* (1:141-142 n.6.) that the *dharmodaya* signifies one triangle.[31] In a Tibetan Buddhist meditation on Vajrayoginī, it states:

> All the *dharmas* comprising grasping and fixation become empty. From within emptiness . . . arises the source of *dharmas*, a triangle . . . . On that is the nature of my consciousness . . . like a fish leaping from water, I arise in the body of Jetsun Vajrayoginī.[32]

This quote, states that one's visualization, begins with the visualization of Voidness, that all *dharmas* are void (of intrinsic nature), and that from the Voidness the triangle appears which represents the source of *dharmas*. On this triangular source of *dharmas*, the nature of one's consciousness appears in the body of Vajrayoginī. In both the Hindu and Buddhist meditations there is a progression or evolution from the source to individual differentiation.

According to Misra, who also has written about the progression in Kashmir Śaivitic terms, the white lotus symbolizes creation: as the initial vibration expands, creation occurs. The next step is visualization of the solar disc which represents the universe with form as a reflection (of consciousness) (*vimarśa*). This is followed by the triangle which represents the three *śaktis* (powers) known as *icchāśakti* (will power), *jñānaśakti* (knowledge), and *kriyāśakti* (action).[33] These three are the sources of impulses which begin the process of differentiation.[34] Hence in Misra's commentary, one sees again this process of differentiation from one source; the initial vibration (*spanda*) inducing creation, followed by specific forms with specific impulses or powers.

In sum, as to the location of Chinnamastā, both the Tantric traditions agree that the Chinnamastā's abode is at the navel in the *maṇipūra cakra,* specifically in the centre of the triangle. Both agree that this *maṇipūra cakra* is the locus for yogic heat symbolized by the seed syllable *Raṃ*. However the two traditions vary in their interpretations of what the triangle represents. The Hindu texts state the triangle is composed of the three *guṇas*. The *guṇas*, an ancient concept in Indian thought, remains important to the present time. In several Indian philosophical schools the *guṇas* are the basic components of animated beings; these *guṇas* are the first evolutes of differentiation.[35] Though this is an ancient Indian concept found in the Upaniṣads, the Tantric Buddhists never accepted or adapted this theory. The theory of *guṇas* play a minor role in Buddhism compared to its major influence in Hinduism. What becomes important in Buddhist philosophy is the concept of *dharma* (phenomena).[36] This concept is incorporated in Tantric Buddhism as seen in the Chinnamuṇḍā Vajrayoginī meditation. For the Tantric Buddhists the inverted triangle does not represent the three *guṇas* or *śaktis* which are the Hindu concepts but symbolizes the source of *dharmas* (*dharmodaya*), a Buddhist concept. Thus both the Tantric traditions agree that Chinnamastā stands in the centre of the triangle and that the triangle is the source where differentiation begins; however, both traditions interpret this source according to their own philosophical tenets.

THE DEITY AND HER IMPLEMENTS

In all four meditations treated herein the description of Chinnamastā follows the description of her abode in the navel of the body. All these meditations describe Chinnamastā as effulgent and shining like the sun (in *Tantrasāra* as 10 million suns); sometimes she is described as yellow in colour (*Sādhanamālā*) or as reddish yellow (Tāranātha), indicating the colour of the setting or rising sun. In Tantric Buddhism the sun is associated with insight (*prajñā*)—the insight needed for liberation, the red element, and the female gender.[37] This reddish yellow colour is also associated with passion. Trungpa states in his Vajrayoginī commentary: "Such passion is immensely powerful; it radiates its warmth in all directions. It simultaneously nurtures the welfare of beings and blazes to destroy the neurotic tendencies of ego."[38] In Hindu Tantra the sun is interpreted in various Tantras, such as in *Prapañcasāratantra*, which explains the Gāyatrī mantra, *tat savitur vareṇyaṃ bhargo devasya dhīmahi dhiyo yo naḥ pracodayāt* as follows:

> *Tat* refers to the first cause of all substance in the form of the fiery energy in the disc of the sun, that is *sadānandaṃ paraṃ brahma*: the true bliss, the highest Brahman. *Savitur* ('of the sun') refers to: Always the producer of all animate beings.[39]

Another interpretation is found in the *Śāradātilaka* (1,40) which associates the right side in general with the sun and with Agni; in the

Rudrayāmalatantra (17, 97f.) Agni is associated with the *kuṇḍalinī.*[40] The *sādhanas* explicitly state how luminous she is and want to emphasize her effulgence. As the sun is the major source of illumination and growth in its positive value, the practitioner is reminded to regard Chinnamastā this way. After describing Chinnamastā's effulgence and colour, three meditations continue with "holding her own head in her left hand". This is significant in two respects: (1) most meditations of Tantric goddesses stress the left, the left being associated with the female.[41] (2) By beginning with Chinnamastā's severed head, the authors of the *sādhanas* are stressing the importance of this act; Chinnamastā is one of the few goddesses in Tantric Hinduism and Buddhism who is depicted as holding her own severed head. The symbolism of one's own severed head is complex in Tantra and should be preceded by an overview of head symbolism in Hinduism and Buddhism.

The Importance of the Head

Throughout Indian thought and literature the importance of the head is indisputable. In the famed Puruṣa Sūkta of the *Ṛgveda* (10.90) where Puruṣa creates the universe by his own dismemberment, many major creations originated from his head. His mouth became the Brahmin, Indra and Agni emerged from his mouth, from his eye the sun was born, from his mind the moon, and from his head the sky evolved (10.90.12-14). Also in the *Śatapatha Brāhmaṇa* (6.1.1.4) seven persons were needed to form the head "Because (in it) they concentrated the excellence (*śrī*)". The *Bṛhadāraṇyaka Upaniṣad* begins with the chapter, "The world as a sacrificial horse" wherein "*Auṁ*, the dawn, verily is the head of the sacrificial horse (1.1.1)". In all these quotes the head symbolizes supremacy, the ruler or leader. It is associated with *Auṁ*, the most important Indian mystical syllable which symbolizes totality.[42] As in Hinduism, the importance of the head is indisputable in Buddhism. The head is considered the best part of the body. Wayman states in his *The Buddhist Tantras*, ". . . because the Tantras inherited the viewpoint that a man is a microcosm corresponding to the macrocosm. . . . The head is the highest and best member. . .".[43]

The Head as an External Identifying Factor

In Indian mythology some stories illustrate how the head is the decisive factor for identifying a person. The two stories which I shall cite are about transposed heads. The first is from the popular *Vetālavikrama* series known as the 'Transposed Heads'.[44] A brief synopsis of the story is that since washerman Dhaval wanted to marry washerwoman Madanasundarī, he went to propitiate the great goddess, Gaurī, and made an oath that he would offer his head if his wish was granted. Indeed his wish was granted and the two wed. Later when his wife, her brother and he went to visit his father-in-law, they passed by the Gaurī Temple. When he entered the temple, he remembered his oath and severed his head.[45] A while later, his brother-in-law entered the temple and seeing what happened to Dhavala, he also severed his head. Madanasundarī was waiting outside and wondering what happened to her husband and brother. When she entered the temple and saw what had occurred, she decided to sever her head. However, Goddess Gaurī intervened and commanded her to join the heads with their respective bodies. In her haste, she inadvertently misplaced the heads. The *vetāla*, who is narrating the story to King Vikramasena, asked him, "Who is to perform the service of Madanasundarī's husband?" The King replied, "O Vetāla, the head is the seat of the five senses, the five motions, the hands and feet and so on. The head is the basis for the parts. Therefore the woman belongs to the head."[46]

Another story is a version of Reṇukā's beheading.[47] In this version two women are beheaded; one is the high caste Reṇukā and the other is a low caste woman. Paraśurāma pleaded with his father to revive his mother, Reṇukā. When his father did give permission, it was very dark and Paraśurāma accidentally transposed the heads. As in the *Vetālavikrama's* 'The Transposed Heads', the head determined who was whom. Reṇukā was determined to be the one with Reṇukā's head and the low caste woman's body. Both stories emphasize that the head and its external characteristics are crucial in identifying the person.[48]

The Head as an Internal Identifying Factor

In Buddhism external characteristics of persons or objects are caused by *karma* but manifest in form. Form is one of the five aggregates (*skandhas*) which as a whole creates a semblance of an eternal self (*ātman*). Each aggregate is assigned a particular place in the body; the form aggregate is placed in the head. Wayman in his "Five-fold Ritual Symbolism of Passion" quotes Tsong-kha-pa's commentary, '*Dod 'jo*, on the *Śrīcakrasaṃvaratantra* as follows:

> The Viśeṣadyota (Toh.1510) explains that since the aggregate of form (*rūpa skandha*) is the basis of seeds, the chief place of the *rūpa skandha* is the middle of the head; and explains that the forehead is the place of the *bindu*: hence one contemplates it (i.e., the *skandha* of form) there. . .[49]

Furthermore, in Hindu and Buddhist philosophies the concept of form coupled with the concept of name (*nāmarūpa*) are major components in establishing individuality or differentiation. This concept is well-developed in the early Upaniṣads, such as in *Bṛhadāraṇyaka Upaniṣad* (1.4.7.): "At that time this (universe) was undifferentiated. It became differentiated by name and form . . ." Thus these statements show that the form aggregate is located in the head and that the coupling of form and name create differentiation.

Furthermore, in Tantric Hinduism, as in Tantric Buddhism, the head is the source of seed.[50] This creates differentiation by invoking the illusion of a separate individual; by having such an illusion, an individual does not feel connected with the great soul (*parātman*) which pervades everything. The *Kauṣītaki Brāhmaṇa Upaniṣad* (1.6) states : "All this, whatever there is. All this you are." Unlike Hindus, Buddhists do not accept any eternal self (*parātman*) yet the grasping at the concept of an individual inherent self (*ātmagraha*) is a major impediment to liberation. A Tantric Buddhist must realize that there is no individual inherent self (*ātman*) nor any great self (*parātman*) by experiencing the voidness of intrinsic nature in all persons (*pudgala nairātmya*) and phenomena (*dharma nairātmya*). In summation both the religious traditions do accept that the concept of an individual self is an impediment to liberation. However the Hindus believe that the individual self and the great self do exist eternally and one only has to realize that the individual self is part of the great self.[51] In contradistinction the Buddhists do not accept the belief in a permanent inherent self (*ātman*) and instead stress the realization of voidness of an inherent self.

The Symbolic Significance of Severing the Head

The Buddhist and Hindu religious traditions want to sever the concept of the individual self, but for different reasons. The following stories illustrate the realization of voidness of intrinsic reality of persons (*pudgala nairātmya*) by Buddhist practitioners who severed their grasping at the concept of an individual self (*ātmagraha*). In the following story Gam-po-pa, a main disciple of the Tibetan yogin, Milarepa, is meditating and attempting to gain some sort of realization.[52] The story is as follows:

> Thereupon Gam-po-pa set up hermitage three miles removed from Milarepa's cave and began meditating. After six weeks, he had visions; the first day the Buddha appeared, the second day a *maṇḍala*, and so on. Each time, he reported his visions to Milarepa, who kept on saying, "It is nothing! Go back to your practice." After a few more weeks, Gam-po-pa had a vivid vision of all six worlds, and naturally he thought that he hit the mark. He ran to Milarepa to report, but Milarepa was sleeping. The

> Milarepa merely said, "Let me sleep! I am not a scholar like you. But I know that the Prajñāpāramitā says all this is mere illusion. I suggest that you go back and practise!" Gam-po-pa, crestfallen and frustrated, returned to his meditation. At length, he dreamt one day that he had cut off his own head and that he saw it rolling down the hill. Thereafter there were no more visions, for the root of '*ātmagraha*' was cut off.[53]

In this episode one learns that the severing of the head symbolizes the destruction of the erroneous belief in a permanent self. Gam-po-pa no longer has visions because he transcended the duality of subject and object. This understanding can be found also in the Tibetan Buddhist Tantric collection, *rGyud sde kun btus* (vol. 23: 412), wherein 'Jam dbyang mkhyen brtse'i dbang po states, "The understanding of the non-existence of apprehended and apprehender is symbolized by her (Chinnamuṇḍā's) form".[54] This explanation is the *raison d'etre* to practise the *sādhana* of Chinnamuṇḍā, i.e., a practitioner's goal is to understand the illusory nature of the dichotomy of subject and object.

The ultimate reality is the non-duality of form and voidness as illustrated in another story. This story describes the realizations of the two Mahāsiddha yoginīs, Mekhalā and Khanakalā (see chapter 1). In this story they sang this song of realization as they severed their heads and offered them to their teacher, Mahāsiddha Kanhapā. They sang:

> Through the grace of the Guru's instruction, uniting creative and fulfilment meditation, we destroy the distinction between *saṃsāra* and *nirvāṇa*; vision and action united in co-incident harmony we destroy the distinction between acceptance and rejection;
> In the union of vast space and pure awareness we destroy the distinction between self and others.
> As tokens of the indeterminate, we offer these gifts.

The guru exclaimed:

> Behold these two great Yoginīs!
> They have reached their goal in joy!
> Now forgetting your own peace and happiness, live for
> the sake of others![55]

These two yoginī's were able to sever their heads when asked by their teacher. This act of severing their heads, as in Gam-po-pa's meditation, revealed their understanding of voidness of intrinsic reality of persons. The two yoginī sisters realized the non-duality of opposites: *saṃsāra* and nirvāṇa, self and others, etc. They had transcended this illusory dichotomy and were equipped with the proper insight and means to help others in achieving enlightenment.

In Hinduism, one finds many statements in the Upaniṣads of severing one's concept of an individual self (*ātman*) because this individual self is, in reality, part of the great self (*paramātman*). Though this great self is pervasive, it is extremely subtle and cannot be easily perceived. In the *Chāṇḍogya Upaniṣad* (6.13.1) Śvetaketu is instructed by his father about the great self. This is a description of the essence illustrated by nyagrodha tree.

> 1. "Bring here a fruit of that nyagrodha tree. . . Break it . . . What do you see there?" "These very small seeds, Venerable Sir." "Of these, please break one. . . . What do you see?" "Nothing at all, Venerable Sir."
> 2. Then he said, "My dear, that subtle essence which you do not perceive, verily, my dear, from that very essence this great nyagrodha tree exists. Believe me, my dear.
> 3. That which is the subtle essence, this whole world has for its self. That is true. That is the self. That is you Śvetaketu.

This example illustrates that the self is pervasive such that even if it is broken into the smallest parts and becomes imperceptible to the senses, it does exist. Also the *Kaṭha Upaniṣad* 1.2.18 says:

> The knowing self is never born; nor does it die at any time. It sprang from nothing and nothing sprang from it. It is unborn, eternal, abiding and primeval. It is not slain when the body is slain.

In both these quotes, the annihilation of the seed or the body does not destroy the essence—the unborn, eternal, abiding, primeval self. Moreover, it stresses that what a person believes to be the self—the individual unit, the seed, or the body—is part of a greater whole. Yet one must ask if Chinnamastā with her decapitated head is dead or alive? Everyone would agree that without one's head, one could not exist. This is the paradox of Chinnamastā. Ernest Payne in his *The Śāktas* quotes Ronaldshay as stating that Chinnamastā "symbolized the Motherland (India) 'decapitated by the English, but nevertheless preserving her vitality unimpaired by drinking her own blood'." Kinsley also feels that she is alive and thriving but not by her own means. Kinsley states, "She is shown being nourished or sustained not by death (or sacrifice) but by the copulating couple beneath her."[56] This frozen moment of temporarily decapitating her head indicates her ability to transcend the relative dichotomy of life and death.

Before discussing the severing of the head in sacrificial terms, I shall mention a popular psychoanalytical interpretation initially propounded by Freud.[57] This interpretation of the severing of the head as a castration symbol is applied by prominent authors, such as Wendy Doniger and Gananath Obeyesekere.[58] Obeyesekere states that a castration symbol for a woman is to sever her breasts which can be identified with the penis.[59] The Buddhist Goddess Pattini does sever her breasts but Chinnamastā does not. Though there is no 'displaced' castration in Chinnamastā's iconography or myths, O'Flaherty does discuss the head held by Chinnamastā under the heading of 'Beheading and Castration'. She states in *Women, Androgynes and Other Mythical Beasts* that though Chinnamastā appears to be holding her own head, it could be Śiva's.[60] "The question remains ambiguous, perhaps purposely ambiguous . . . but it is possible that some Tantric texts may identify the head as Śiva's." I agree with O'Flaherty that Chinnamastā's decapitation is ambiguous and, indeed, purposely ambiguous. Chinnamastā's temporary decapitation is a *koan*. However all *sādhanas* explicitly state that she holds her own head which she has severed with her own knife. Moreover according to the *sādhanas* Chinnamastā has only temporarily severed her head. Near the end of the *sādhana*, a practitioner must visualize the severed head being put back on the body. If this act of Chinnamastā's decapitation symbolizes castration, then why would the head be replaced at the end of *sādhana*?[61]

Courtright in his *Gaṇeśa* also discusses the severing of the head in terms of castration symbolism but he is not satisfied with this explanation alone. He presents some very insightful discussions about the symbolism of a severed head and his concluding words from the section on the severed head are especially pertinent to interpreting Chinnamastā's self decapitation.

> Personal fulfilment comes when personal idiosyncratic attachments give way to acceptance of the transpersonal divine order, an order made apparent only at the moment in which the particular self surrenders itself. The Maharashtrian poet-saint Tukārāma expressed this theological vision succinctly (*Tukārāma Gāthā* no. 3414, 3171)
>
> If we want to enjoy God, we should lop off our head from our body and hold it in our hands.
> When the body has been sacrificed to god, says Tuka, all worship has been accomplished.[62]

Another modern commentator, S.G. Motilal, discusses the severing of Chinnamastā's head as significant of the head offering sacrifice.[63] Motilal enumerates five methods of sacrifice (*yajña*) of which the fifth is the splitting of the head sacrifice. He emphasizes that according to *śruti* the sacrifice of the severed head is the essence of sacrifice because in every sacrifice there is a head ritual. A story connected with the head ritual is in the *Śatapatha Brāhmaṇa* (14.1.1.ff) which recounts the legend when Viṣṇu gained glory (*śrī*) but was unable to contain it, thereby losing his head by his own bow. His head became the sun. When he lost his head, vital sap emerged which was wiped up by the gods, especially Indra who arrived first. Indra wanted all the glory for himself; however Dadhyañc Athārvana knew the sweet essence of the 'pravargya sacrifice' which is how to restore the head and how the sacrifice becomes complete (*Śatapatha Bārhmaṇa* 14.1.1.19). Indra threatened to sever Dadhyañc's head if he divulged this secret to anyone. The Aśvins heard of Dadhyañc's knowledge and offered themselves as his disciples. He refused until the Aśvins promised to protect him with a ruse of putting a horse's head on him when he revealed the secret. Then when Indra severed Dadhyañc's head (the horse's head), the Aśvins replaced Dadhyañc's own head (14.1.2.9). This 'pravargya sacrifice' is involved with the severed head and how to join it sacrificially again to the body.[64] In this ritual the severed head represents the sun, the illumination of the universe. In Tantric thought this sun could be understood as the eradicator of the ignorance which prevents release from cyclical existence. The symbolic act of severing one's head signifies the realization that one is not separate from others but part of the great self. However the severing of the head is not the final step, since one must be able to restore one's head to complete the 'sacrifice' which brings immortality.

Restoration of the Head

Indian mythology has many stories of decapitation and of transposed heads, but few exist of self-decapitation and restoration of the same head.[65] The legends of Chinnamastā and the Mahāsiddhā sisters are important examples of this unique motif.[66] In an article by J.C. Heesterman, "The Case of the Severed Head", he discusses the Vedic sacrifice—the dismemberment and restoration of a sacrificial victim. His insights can be applied in understanding Chinnamastā's self decapitation and subsequent restoration. He states:

> The sacrifice is a cosmos which is violently broken up to be put together again . . . the constantly alternating movement between the two poles of disintegration and reintegration, death and birth. . . . The pivotal point, however, is that actual death and disintegration have been eliminated.[67]

In Vedic sacrifices the restoration of the head is merely symbolic because the victim is indeed sacrificed; therefore, one wonders why the restoration of the head is included. *Śatapatha Brāhmaṇa*, a sacrificial text, terminates with the 'pravargya sacrifice', is this statement:

> And, verily, whosoever either teaches, or partakes of this (Pravargya) enters that life, and that light: the observance of the rule thereof is the same as at the creation.[68]

This indicates when one receives a new head, a transformation occurs which is usually interpreted as receiving a better head. Courtright states that when Gaṇeśa received his elephant head, he received his 'real' one which 'expresses his true nature'.[69] One can apply this to Chinnamastā. She illustrates that having the ability to sever one's head and to restore it leads not to death but to immortality. Chinnamastā displays the ultimate; though it appears as a disunity, it is a unity. The *Kaṭha Upaniṣad* (2.1.14-15) states:

> As water rained upon a height flows down in various ways among the hills; so he who views things as varied runs after them.
> As pure water poured forth into pure becomes the very same, so the self, O Gautama, of the seer who has understanding becomes (one with the Supreme).

Three Eyes

In the *sādhanas* quoted, only Tāranātha's states that Chinnamuṇḍā has three eyes—right, left, and a centre vertical one frequently referred to as the third eye, the eye of transcendent knowledge. Misra's commentary, however, does discuss Chinnamastā's three eyes and all pictorial illustrations depict Chinnamastā/Chinnamuṇḍā as triocular. Misra comments that these three eyes represent the sun, moon, and fire.[70] In the *Doctrine of Vibration*, Dyczkowski quotes from Abhinavagupta's *Tantrāloka* as follows:

> This Wheel of the Absolute (*anuttaracakra*) flows out from the Heart through the void of the eyes, etc. onto each sense object. The rays of this Wheel progressively engender the Fire (of the subject), Moon (of the object), and the Sun (of the means of knowledge), in each phrase of destruction, creation, and persistence of the external world.[71]

In this quote Abhinavagupta speaks of the flowing out of the Absolute through the orifices. In stating this, he indicates that the Absolute can be found in the heart, within an individual, thereby implying that introspection is needed to discover the Absolute. One should not direct the senses to externals, which create the illusion of duality and multiplicity, but withdraw the senses into oneself. This is a continuation of the yogic method propounded in the Upaniṣads. The *Kaṭha Upaniṣad* (2.1.1) states:

> The self is not sought through the senses. The Self-caused pierced the openings (of the senses) outward; therefore one looks outward and not within oneself. Some wise person, however, seeking eternal life with his eyes inward, saw the self.[72]

The direction of a deity's eyes are important in Hinduism. Diana Eck in *Darsan* states:

> The prominence of the eyes of Hindu divine images also reminds us that it is not only the worshipper who sees the deity, but the deity sees the worshipper as well. The contact between devotee and deity is exchanged through the eyes.[73]

In pictorial representations, Chinnamastā does not look directly at her devotees. By looking at herself, she directs her devotees to look within themselves. This is a brilliant and profound aspect of Chinnamastā's iconography.

Likewise in Buddhism, the downward-cast eyes can indicate an emphasis on introspection. Buddhism does not accept that an *ātman* (a permanent self) can be found within the body but by accepting the Upaniṣadic yogic method, it does advocate that the yogic process is beneficial in achieving liberation. The third Karmapa, Rangjung Dorje (1284-1339), comments about the three eyes, "Because she is the knower of past, present, and future, she rolls her three furious bloodshot eyes".[74] Trungpa elaborates that having "three eyes means that nothing escapes the vision of Vajrayoginī"; furthermore, one can say that she looks down with compassion on all sentient beings.[75] As in Hinduism the third eye located in the centre of the forehead indicates the realization of transcendent knowledge which is necessary in order to help beings effectively.[76] In summation both the religious traditions stress that having three eyes as does Chinnamastā, indicates a transcendent knowledge which aids one to liberation.

Blood as a Destructive Vital Fluid

All four meditations state that Chinnamastā is drinking the blood which is spurting from her severed throat. The Buddhist meditations do not mention the widening of the mouth or the lolling tongue as the Hindu ones do. The extended mouth and darting tongue are common characteristics among several of the Daśa Mahāvidyās, such as Kālī and Tārā. In the *Devī Māhātmya* episode of Durgā's battle with the Asura Raktabīja (lit., blood seed), whenever Durgā pierced Asura Raktabīja's body and a drop of his blood fell on the ground, immediately another Raktabīja appeared *ad infinitum.* Since any attempt to kill Raktabīja had the reverse effect, only generating more Raktabījas, Durgā asked Kālī and other wrathful manifestations (*mātṛkās,* etc.) to open their mouths very wide and to drink the blood of Raktabīja before it touched the ground. When the goddesses defeated Raktabīja through this technique and eventually were triumphant over all the *asuras* (rivals to the gods), the *devas* (gods) reigned again.[77] V. S. Agrawala glosses Raktabīja's name:

> The name is significant, viz. the Asura who is born from the seed as churned out of the blood. . . . Raktabīja is the symbol of the physical man. The cosmic blood reservoir of the life principle has the potency of creating a Raktabīja from each single drop of blood in its body. If the same is soiled by matter it becomes an Asuric force (8.51) but the Goddess Cāmuṇḍā who had made short the work of Caṇḍa and Muṇḍa sublimates the blood of Raktabīja by drinking it herself, that is, making an offering of it to the sacrificial process symbolized in the body of Kālī-Cāmuṇḍā. Thus the possibility for evil engrained in the animal blood is exhausted.[78]

Thus by opening her mouth wide and drinking the blood, the goddess indicates her ability to transmute a potentially negatively charged force into a positively-charged force. Agrawala's thesis of sublimation is not supported explicitly by the Hindu meditations of Chinnamastā. No Hindu *sādhana* states that the blood is *amṛta* (nectar); however, one Buddhist *sādhana* describes the bloodstream as nectar (*niḥsṛtāmṛtadhārā*).[79] Thus this blood, a vital essence of being, has the potential to be destructive if embodied by *asuras* but conversely can be transformed into a positive power by the Goddess. As Chinnamastā drinks her own blood, it indicates a self-transformation of potential negativity and by internal transmutation, external negativities are also transformed.

Blood as a Beneficial Vital Fluid

The *Brāhmaṇas* discuss the vital fluid; however, it is not always stated that blood is this essence. Since the *Brāhmaṇas* are sacrificial ritual texts, however, we may assume that this vital fluid is blood. As in aforementioned 'pravargya sacrifice' when Viṣṇu was beheaded, the vital sap emerging from his head was wiped up by the gods. Furthermore, in the construction of the Mahāvīra's pot which symbolizes Viṣṇu's severed head, in the *Śatapatha Brāhmaṇa* (14.1.2.9), it states:

> O divine Heaven and Earth, when the sacrifice had its head cut off, its sap flowed away, and entered the sky and the earth . . . (14.1.2.19) when the sacrifice had its head cut off, its vital sap flowed away, and therefrom those plants grew up: that vital sap thus supplies and completes it.

This vital sap is desired by the gods; it is a part of the sky and the earth; it is a necessary component in a sacrifice and also completes it.[80] Noting these different aspects of the vital sap or essential fluid, we understand that transmutation of this vital sap is possible. For the Tantrics, the ultimate transformation is the formation of *amṛta*, the nectar of immortality for the Hindus and the nectar of bliss for the Buddhists.

In order to create this transformation, a Tantric practitioner must master *prāṇāyāma*, the manipulations of the subtle winds in the body.[81] *Prāṇāyāma* is a similar process in both the Tantric traditions; however, the results are interpreted differently. In Hinduism, there are five major subtle winds known collectively as *prāṇa* and of the five, two of the most important are the *prāṇa* and *apāna*.[82] As long as the subtle winds circulate in the subtle veins (*nāḍīs*), the consciousness is preoccupied with the external world because then it 'rides' on the winds. When the consciousness travels through the *iḍā nāḍī*, the consciousness is introverted and when it flows through the *piṅgalā nāḍī* the opposite occurs. These two *nāḍīs*, the *iḍā* and the *piṅgalā*, which are located on the left and right side respectively of the main subtle channel, the *suṣumṇā*, create a sense of polarity or duality when *prāṇa* and *apāna* traverse them. The practitioner must excercise retaining her/his breath (*kumbhaka*) in order to prevent the winds from traversing the two side channels. By retaining the breath, the practitioner forces the subtle winds to enter the *suṣumṇā* at the base of the spine where the *kuṇḍalinī*, hypostatized as a female serpent, 'sleeps'. This *kuṇḍalinī*, "symbolizes cosmic energy; due to the individual's ignorance the cosmic energy remains powerless and limited, as the individual energy (*jīvaśakti*)".[83] By ejecting the subtle winds into the base of the *suṣumṇā*, the *kuṇḍalinī* is aroused and after arduous practice, the *kuṇḍalinī* ascends to the fontanelle, the *sahasārara cakra*, which symbolizes the Supreme Self (*parātman*). When the practitioner accomplishes this unification, one is released from fetters of cyclic existence and attains immortality by uniting with the *Parātman*. As Gupta states, "We can see in the process that symbolically (the practitioner) has reversed the process of creation and effected the reabsorption of the world (and himself) into an undifferentiated unity".[84] In sum, the blood issuing through the three subtle channels of Chinnamastā can be interpreted as the vital essence in its subtlest form, *prāṇa*. Furthermore, since Chinnamastā drinks the blood from the central channel, the *suṣumṇā*, this can be interpreted as drinking *amṛta* thereby illustrating to her practitioners that she has achieved the goal, salvation or undifferentiation, through the Tantric method of awakening the *kuṇḍalinī* in order to reunite with the *Parātman*.

In Tantric Buddhism, the technique of *prāṇāyāma* is also applied but the interpretation is different. Moreover, the Buddhist *sādhanas* (e.g. Tāranātha) are explicit in stating that these three channels are the *nāḍīs*. The *lalanā* on the left side of the *avadhūtī*, begins at the left nostril and joins the *avadhūtī* below the navel; it is white, represents the absolute aspect, the corporeal aspect, the objective pole and is symbolized as the moon. The *rasanā* on the right side of the *avadhūtī* begins at the right nostril and joins the *avadhūtī* below the navel; it is red in colour, represents the relative aspect, speech aspect, the subjective pole and is symbolized by the sun. The *avadhūtī* is the central channel which runs straight from the perineum up the spine to the fontanelle where it arches and terminates between the two eyebrows. This channel is also known "as the two abandonments because gathering the winds into this channel causes the negative activity associated with the winds of the right and left channels to be abandoned".[85] In the biography of Mahāsiddha Jālandhara, his teacher who was a *ḍākinī* said to him, "Empty the *lalanā* and *rasanā* into the *avadhūtī*, then eject all the constructs of your mind through the 'gate of purity' on the crown of your head. Thereafter meditate upon the indivisibility of appearances and emptiness."[86]

In Chinnamuṇḍavajrayoginī *sādhanas* there is mention of the subtle drops, as well as the subtle winds and channels. Tāranātha states, "After the three channels are severed, the white and red drops are mixed in the central channel. . .".[87] In *The Clear Light of Bliss* a short explanation is given about the white and red drops (Skt. *bindu* and T. *thig-le*). The white drop is the pure essence of the white seminal fluid and its principal seat is the crown of the head; the red drop is the pure essence of blood and its principal seat is the navel. There are both gross and subtle forms of these drops. The ones in the vacuole of the central channel found in the heart are the subtle ones while the gross ones flow through other channels. When these drops melt and flow through the channels, they give rise to the experience of bliss.[88]

The severing of the three channels and the mixing of the white and red drops are very important in eliminating the notion of duality which creates the erroneous belief of a permanent and unique self. The Tantric Buddhists state that while the winds remain in the two channels flanking the central one, one has the sense of duality—subject and object, female and male, etc. This sense of duality creates a polarized tension or a struggle for dominance. In the *Caryagīti*, a collection of realization songs by the great Mahāsiddhas, there is a song rich with imagery about duality.[89]

1. The river of existence (M: the three *nāḍīs*), fathomless (or frightening) and deep (M: due to the evil of opacity), flows (M: carries urine, excrement, etc.) swiftly; on the banks (*lalanā* and *rasanā*) there is mud (M: the evil of opacity), in the middle (*avadhūtī*), no support (M: it cannot be grasped by inexperienced yogins).
2. For the sake of Dharma/dharma Cāṭila builds a bridge (M: oneness of relative and absolute truth); people (M: yogins desiring release), going to the other shore, safely cross over (M: the ocean of Saṃsāra).
3. Splitting (M: destroying the grasping at sense-objects of) the tree of delusion (M: *bodhicitta*), the planks are joined (M: the *bodhicitta* is united with Perpetual Light); with the strong axe of non-duality (*yugānaddha*), Nirvāṇa is spilt (?).
4. When going on the bridge (M: oneness of the *svādhiṣṭhāna* and Clear Light), be not on the right or on the left (M: sun or moon); Enlightenment (M: the perfection the Great Seal) is near, do not go far!
5. If you, O people (M: yogins) are to cross over to the other shore (M: cross the river of the triple false appearance), ask Cāṭila the incomparable lord.

Though a commentary on this profound song of realization cannot be presented here; a few salient points will be discussed. The song emphasizes that the concept of duality sunders reality and prevents recognition of this delusion. Most people, except for experienced yogins, stay on the two mud banks symbolizing this duality. Only the experienced yogin can make the bridge, i.e., manipulate the winds to enter into the *avadhūtī*, and experience the Great Seal (Mahāmudrā), or enlightenment.

Her Stance

In most *sādhanas*, Chinnamastā stands in either the *ālīḍhapada* or the *pratyālīḍhapada* stance.[90] The former is the bowman's stance of the right leg lunging forward and slightly bending of the left leg and the latter is the same stance with the reversal of the legs. This bowman's stance indicates that she is prepared to defend her devotees, ready to strike their enemies and be ever vigilant in protecting them. A more esoteric Hindu explanation is that Chinnamastā is ever alert in destroying the internal enemy—ignorance which creates the illusion of separateness between a being and Brahman. Likewise a practitioner must be constantly aware and prepared to strike whenever ignorance dominates and deludes.[91] The *Muṇḍaka Upaniṣad* states:

> Taking as the bow the great weapon of the Upaniṣads, one should place in it the arrow sharpened by meditation. Drawing it with a mind engaged

> in the contemplation of that (Brahman), O beloved, know that Imperishable Brahman as the target.[92]

In both traditions Chinnamastā is standing on a deity; in Buddhist *sādhanas* she stands on (Kālī) and in Hindu *sādhanas* she stands above Rati, goddess of desire, and Kāma, god of desire, who are in sexual union with the woman on top of the man (*viparīta*).[93] Standing defiantly on these deities indicates that not only does she triumph over them but she has overcome or conquered what they symbolize. Standing on a prostrate Kālī, Chinnamuṇḍā has transcended time and is beyond the dualities of birth and death. Also this symbolizes that a Buddhist deity has supremacy over a Hindu deity and Hinduism. Moreover, a Hindu deity symbolizes the concept of *ātman*, a major tenet refuted by Buddhists. Thus Chinnamuṇḍā is victorious over one of the most deeply-rooted impediments to liberation—*ātmagraha*. In contrast Rati and Kāma in the Hindu depiction represent the main impetus for creation and the perpetuation of cyclical existence, *Saṃsāra*. Hence by standing on them, Chinnamastā triumphs over the craving for cyclical existence and indicates to her devotees that they, too, must be unaffected by worldly desire in order to attain liberation. D. Kinsley presents another view:

> Chinnamastā takes life and vigour from the copulating couple, then gives it away lavishly by cutting off her own head to feed her devotees.[94]

This is a plausible interpretation in Hinduism because the woman on top in a sexual embrace represents *śakti*, the power to create.[95] This is not applicable in Buddhism because there is no copulating couple under Chinnamuṇḍā and because woman in Mahāyāna symbolizes, *prajñā*, transcendent wisdom. Thus the deities under Chinnamastā's feet symbolize different concepts in the two religions. In Hinduism these concepts are both positive and negative and in Buddhism they are impediments.

Dishevelled Hair and Nudity

These two characteristics of Chinnamastā are best described as a pair because in this context they represent an abandoning of societal values. Chinnamastā as a yogin knows the relativity of societal values of respectability and non-respectability. Poems by the great devotee of Mother Kālī, Ramaprasad, poignantly express the rejection of societal values by Kālī.

> Mother, incomparably arrayed
> Hair flying, stripped down.[96]

Kālī, why are you naked again?
Good grief, haven't you any shame?[97]

Also it is not a coincidence that in the *Mahābhārata* Draupadī's garments and hair were pulled (*keśāmbarakarṣaṇam*); these two aspects indicate a loss of public respectability.[98] In Draupadī's case, the pulling of her garments and hair were forced upon her, but in Chinnamastā's (or Kālī's) her nudity and dishevelled hair represent freedom. Hiltebeitel discusses Draupadī's dishevelled hair as symbolizing dissolution: "itself (dishevelled hair) (is) an image of Kālarātri, the Night of Time, the night of dissolution (*pralaya*) of the universe".[99] Such dissolution also indicates an aspect of pervasiveness. One of the Sanskrit words for nudity is *digambara* (lit., clad with the quarters of the sky) symbolizing that Chinnamastā is so pervasive that it is as impossible to cover her as it is to cover the sun. Vast space alone is her vesture.[100]

In Buddhism, Chinnamuṇḍā is also a yogin who rejects societal values with her nudity and dishevelled hair. However in Buddhism, where compassion is stressed, her nudity indicates that she is unencumbered by defilements; "she has no armour of ego to clothe her".[101] By having this realization she can benefit sentient beings and extend absolute compassion, indicating that their welfare precedes her own.[102] In summation, both the traditions represent Chinnamastā as a yogin and the Buddhist tradition emphasizes the yogin's power to help beings through compassionate means.

DEITY'S IMPLEMENTS

The Kartṛ

In both the religions the knife is seen as cutting through major obstacles to liberation. With the *kartṛ* (sacrificial knife) held in her right hand, Chinnamastā severs her own head thereby committing a 'self-sacrifice'.[103] By this severance she sacrifices the illusory, yet firmly established concept of the individual 'I'. The concept of individual self (*ātman*) must be severed in order for one to merge with Brahman, becoming liberated. In contradistinction a Buddhist explanation is that this *kartṛ* is not a sacrificial knife but a hook of mercy which protects one from falling into either the extreme of cyclic existence (*saṃsāra*) or the quiescient state of Nirvāṇa. Other interpretations are severing the concept of *ātmagraha*, grasping to a notion of the self or, as Mañjuśri's sword destroys ignorance, Chinnamuṇḍā's *kartṛ* severs the concept of discursive thought, another major impediment to enlightenment. According to Kazi Dawa Samdup (p.20), the *kartṛ* indicates that her wisdom cuts all reasoning, destroys all fiends (*māras*) and defilements. This ability indicates that Chinnamastā is connected with wisdom (*jñāna*) In Buddhism Chinnamuṇḍā is the *jñāna ḍākinī* (wisdom 'sky-goer') or *sarvabuddha ḍākinī* (all-enlightened 'sky-goer') and in Hinduism Chinnamastā is a *mahāvidyā*.

Skull Rosary, Bone Necklace, Serpent as Sacred Cord

In Hinduism the skull rosary, bone necklace and serpent sacred cord are symbols of transcending the concept of time, i.e., the fear of death. Life and death are human constructions which bind beings to cyclical existence. Chinnamastā is able to fuse these concepts by wearing the symbols of death on an animated body. By this fusion she illustrates that these categories are not absolute and neutralizes their effects, thereby indicating a way to salvation. The serpent as her sacred cord is significant because it is associated with temporality and immortality. Since a serpent has the ability to slough off an old skin without dying, it is a symbol of immortality. By having a serpent as a sacred cord, Chinnamastā indicates that she is not part of the ordinary Hindu class (*varṇa*) system and its obligatory duties.

Skull, Five Mudras, Khaṭvāṅga

The Buddhist *sādhanas* describe Chinnamuṇḍā as holding a skull, having a five-skull tiara, wearing a fifty-skull garland, and holding a *khaṭvāṅga* (Tantric staff).[104] The tiara of five dried skulls symbolizes the five wisdoms of the Pentad Buddhas (Akṣobhya's mirror-like wisdom, Ratnasambhava's wisdom of equality, Amitābha's discriminative wisdom, Amoghasiddhi's wisdom of all-accomplishing action, and Vairocana's wisdom of the Dharmadhātu.) The fifty-head-garland represents the fifty completely purified *saṃskāras*. The five *mudras* or five ornaments (head ornament, earrings, necklace, bracelet and anklets, and belt) symbolize the five perfections of giving, morality, patience, perseverance, and meditation; the sixth is represented by the female body—insight (*prajñā*).

Under Chinnamuṇḍā's left arm is a white *khaṭvāṅga* which symbolizes method. The holding of the *khaṭvāṅga* represents Chinnamuṇḍā's union of skilful means (*khaṭvāṅga*) and insight (her body); these two are needed to achieve liberation. The *khaṭvāṅga* includes many symbols. The three heads topping the *khaṭvāṅga* are respectively a dried skull representing the Dharmakāya, the decaying one for the Sambhogakāya, and the recently severed one for the Nirmāṇakāya.[105] The eight sides symbolizes the eightfold path propounded by the Buddha.[106]

DEITY'S ATTENDANTS

In both the traditions Chinnamastā is flanked by two goddesses who, in contrast to Chinnamastā's sixteen years, an indication of maturity and completeness, are twelve years old, symbolizing a transitional phase from immaturity to maturity. Their names vary according to the *sādhanas*. In some Buddhist *sādhanas* the goddess flanking Chinnamuṇḍā's left is green Vajravaraṇinī and the one on her right is yellow Vajravairocanī. Mahīdhara does not indicate their colour, age, or position but refers to them as Ḍākinī and Varṇinī; in the *Tantrasāra's sādhana* the one on Chinnamastā's left side is the black Ḍākinī and on the right side the red Varṇinī. Though the two traditions do not agree on the names, both agree there is a triad with the central figure as the main deity flanked by two attendants depicted in different colors.

In the section on blood symbolism, the three channels emiting blood from Chinnamastā symbolize the three subtle channels (*nāḍīs*). This symbolism is reiterated by the hypostatization of the three *nāḍīs* as the three goddesses. In Buddhist terms, the *rasanā* is hypostatized Vajravaraṇinī, the *lalanā* as Vajravairocanī, and the *avadhūtī* as Chinnamuṇḍā; in Hindu terms the *iḍā* is hypostatized as Ḍākinī, the *piṅgalā* as Varṇinī, and the *suṣumnā* as Chinnamastā.[106a] This is further demonstrated by the way the three goddesses stand; they are inter-locked with each other at their feet just as the three subtle channels are connected at the navel *cakra*. Though each one's body is free-standing and not intertwined with the other's, the two attendants drink the blood issuing from Chinnamastā's severed throat thereby indicating their dependence on Chinnamastā. As the two side subtle channels do not become separated from the central subtle channel until the yogin can manipulate the subtle winds in entering and remaining in the central subtle channel, the two attendants cannot become independent until they reach yogic maturity.

A mature or adept yogin knows how to manipulate these subtle winds so they enter the central channel. By accomplishing this, the dichotomy of subject and object is eradicated and the relativity of duality is realized. For instance, if there is a subject, then there must be an object; if there is a night, then there must be a day; if there is a left, then there must be a right. All these divisions are dependent on each other for definition. Chinnamastā's two attendants are described in various terms indicating duality. In the Buddhist *sādhanas* the two attendants have different names, different colors and mirror each other in the way they stand. In the Hindu *sādhanas* the differences are more pronounced. Varṇinī is red, has a smiling face, and a fiery splendour; whereas Ḍākinī is black and exceedingly frightful to behold. Moreover in all the *sādhanas*, the attendants have their heads intact which indicate that they do not have the yogic ability to sever their heads; this represents the clinging to an 'I' concept.[107] The delusion of duality is iterated by their drinking of

Chinnamastā's blood. Hence in both the traditions the two attendants represent an spiritually 'immature' person who is not liberated because she has not realized the relativity of duality.

Another way to interpret Chinnamastā and her two attendants according to the Hindu conception is presented by Misra. He states that Varṇinī or Yoginī represents the *rajas guṇa*, Ḍākinī or Bhoginī represents the *tamas guṇa*, and Chinnamastā represents the *sattva guṇa*.[108] According to *The Doctrine of Vibration*, an excerpt from the *Spanadanirṇaya* by Kṣemarāja: "that liberated soul recognizes that these three (*guṇas*) are natural and uncreated powers of pure consciousness."[109] He continues to elaborate that (1) *sattva* corresponds to Śaṅkara's (Śiva's) power of knowledge (*jñāna*)—the light of consciousness (*prakāśa*); (2) the *rajas* to the power of action (*kriyā*)—the reflective awareness of consciousness (*vimarśa*); (3) the *tamas* to the power of Māyā . . . the initial subtle distinction which appears between subject and object in pure consciousness. This explanation demonstrates a liberated soul's recognition of the interaction of the three *guṇas*. Since Chinnamastā is in the centre, drinking her own blood and feeding her blood to her two attendants, she indicates that she is a liberated soul whereas her two attendants are not liberated because they drink her blood instead of their own. In other words, Chinnamastā has severed the notion of duality while the others have not.

These interpretations of Chinnamastā's location, physical appearance, and attendants are certainly not exhaustive. Though more interpretations could be presented, I highlighted the symbolism of the navel, fire, triangle, head, blood and attendants which demonstrates Chinnamastā's centrality as a Tantric goddess. Furthermore these aspects clearly show that to comprehend her, one needs to incorporate many facets of the Indian tradition which are explicitly esoteric or have been adapted for the esoteric Indian traditions, such as the Upaniṣadic "inheritance". One can see how Hindu or Buddhist tenets are embedded in the hermeneutics of the iconography.

Differences between the two religion's beliefs are apparent: *ātman* as opposed to the lack of an eternal self, the *guṇas* versus *dharmodaya* as source, and self-liberation versus the motivation of *bodhicitta*. However, what is also striking is the commonality of certain techniques in both Hindu and Buddhist Tantric traditions, e.g. the manipulation of the subtle winds in the subtle channels. This knowledge of manipulating the winds is one of the major Tantric methods employed to experience bliss and eventual liberation.

By using the tantric lens, one learns that Chinnamastā and her two attendants not only represent the three subtle channels but reveal a profound tantric teaching of liberation. It is a masterful illustration of the interaction of the three subtle channels and the manipulation of the winds entering the central channel. Tantric adepts frequently used drawings to convey the subtlest teachings. Chinnamastā is certainly one of these *mahāyoginīs.* Thus this great *yoginī,* the texts that discuss her, and her iconography distinctly demonstrate her importance in the Indian and Tibetan esoteric traditions and in understanding the great goddess tradition which has influenced the entire Asian continent as well as more and more Western scholars in this century and certainly in the next century.

REFERENCES

1. *Devo bhūtvā devaṃ yajeta.*
2. Tenzin Gyatso, *Tantra in Tibet*: 68.
3. I use the phrase 'pure motivation' because some Tantric practitioners are interested in acquiring supra-normal powers as ends in themselves which are only ancillary results of the Tantric method. Texts contain constant warnings to practitioners not to be averted from the path by these worldly attainments.
4. See *Bṛhadāraṇyaka Upaniṣad* 1.1.; Bharati: 90ff; Eliade "Cosmical Homology and Yoga", and Wayman, *Buddhist Tantra*:203.
5. Bharati:18.
6. B. Bhattacaryya edited the *Sādhanamālā* and translated many *sādhanas* in *The Indian Buddhist Iconography.* He states that *Sādhanamāla* is very valuable because it is a product of Buddhism just before its destruction in Bengal by the Muslims.
7. This translation of the headless Vajrayoginī is from the *Sādhanamālā*:452-53. Also see Bhattacharyya's translation from *The Indian Buddhist Iconography*:247-48. In this section she is not named Chinnamuṇḍā Vajrayoginī but simply Bharṭṭārikā Vajrayoginī (Noble Goddess Vajrayoginī). However, if one compares this meditation with others of Chinnamuṇḍā, it clearly refers to the same deity.
8. The colophon states that he concluded *Mantramahodadhi* on the eighth lunar day of the Jyeṣṭha month (May-June) in the Vikram Era 1645 (1589 C.E.).
9. *Mantramahodadhi* (lit., Great Ocean of Mantras) is a compendium of twenty-five chapters (Skt. *taraṅgas* [lit., wave]) which describes mantras and meditations of many Hindu deities. The symbolism of an ocean as a vast repository and a wave as an individual manifestation is a common metaphor in Hinduism. By naming his commentary, *Naukā*, Mahīdhara is implying that by practising the meditations and knowing the commentary, one can cross over the vast ocean and achieve salvation (*mokṣa*).
10. This concept of 'reversed' sexual union (*viparīta*) is discussed on p.106.
11. There is some discussion about Kṛṣṇānanda Agamavāgīśa's dates. See Sircar: 74-80; Banerji:78-79; and Pal (1981):3. Moreover the *Tantrasāra* is not dated; Pal states that it was written between 1585-1600 C.E.. and N.N.Bhattacharyya: 145 states that it was in the beginning of the seventeenth century.
12. Bhattacharyya, N.N.:145.
13. This is from Agamavāgīśa, K., Hindi *Tantrasāra*:293-310 (section 63).

14. See Āgamavāgīśa: 296 and Pal (1981):79-83.
15. The translation is "*Oṁ*, the nature of all phenomena is pure; pure, too, is my own nature."
16. Misra, *Bhāratīya Pratīkavidyā*:229.
17. The earlier *cakra* systems such as *Yoga Sūtra*, had 4 *cakras*, namely navel, heart, throat and forehead. Later six cakra systems equated the navel with the *maṇipūra cakra*.
18. In other Buddhist Vajrayoginī *sādhanas* a red or multi-coloured lotus is very frequent.
19. Woodroofe, *Serpent Power*:366 (*Dhāyedvaiśvānarasyāruṇamihirasma maṇḍalam tat trikoṇam*).
20. Ibid:141. Also see *Ṛgveda* 10.5.3. for the homology of "Agni is the navel of all that moves and is firm . . . ".
21. See Bose, D.N., and Haldar, H.:161-62.
22. Wayman, *Buddhist Tantras*:188-89.
23. Johnston, E.H., *Early Sāṃkhya*, London, 1937:20.
24. Khanna :32. He states that the inverted triangle is the "symbol of the creative-genetrix feminine power (*śakti*), whose kinetic dynamism gives impetus to the inert force in existence. It is the female emblem (*yoni maṇḍala*) . . . ."
25. Ibid.: 57-60. Also the famous Śrī Yantra which consists of nine interpenetrating triangles, five pointing downward and four pointing upward a symbol of Śakti and Śiva in the process of continuous creation.
26. The *bindu* also is the central dot found in the Śrī Yantra which symbolizes the source and base of the universe. (See the introduction to *Tantrarājatantra*: 4-8 by A. Avalon and Gupta, *Hindu Tantricism*:114.) It is exactly at the *bindu* which is the source of the universe where the process of differentiation begins. (See *Brahmayāmalatantra* (Gupta:13.) Also names 458-60 establish Chinnamastā in the triangle and name 794, Śaktibindunivāsini (dwells in the point of power), indicates that she is in the centre of the triangle.
27. In many Tantric texts, Śiva is assigned the *bindu* as his domain (See Gupta: 86, 94, 98, and 105). By allocating the *bindu* to the goddess implies that she has the supreme position among the Śāktas.
28. Khanna: 31.
29. Some scholars say that the *dharmodaya* is synonymous with the womb. M.T. Mallmann, states that it is synonymous with the *bhaga* (vulva) or the *yoni* (the womb); see *Etude Iconographique sur Mañjśuri*, Paris, Ecole Francasie D'Extreme Orient, 1964:256. She also cites Snellgrove's translation of *Hevajra Tantra*:58-59 as considering the word as *bhaga*.
30. Tucci:135. When one visits Vajrayoginī shrines in Nepal, frequently on the side wooden window a double triangle is carved; also, if there is a *maṇḍala* in front or above, it is frequently a double one. Moreover this double triangle is an ancient symbol found throughout the Middle East and known as the Seal of Solomon, the king of wisdom. Vajrayoginī is frequently referred to as a *jñānaḍākinī*, a wisdom 'sky-goer'.
31. Mallmann: 71.
32. Trungpa:238.
33. Abhinavagupta, tr. by Singh, J., *A Trident of Wisdom*:123-24. He states that Icchā pertains to *saṃhāra* (dissolution or retraction), *jñāna* to *sthiti* (continuance), and *kriyā* to *sṛṣṭi* (manifestation or expansion).
34. Misra:230 (He also gives other triads.) See Sinha, J., *Śākta Monism*, Calcutta, Sinha Publishing, 1966:7.

35. For instance, in the Sāṃkhya philosophical system, the three *guṇas* are the constituents of Prakṛti and through it of worldly objects. See Sharma, Chandradhar, *A Critical Survey of Indian Philosophy*, Delhi, Motilal Banarsidass:154.
36. *Dharma* has many definitions but here we are concerned with the definition of *dharma* as phenomena. In Buddhism the two major impediments to liberation or Buddhahood are the incorrect view of self and phenomena as inherently existing.
37. According to Tantric Buddhism, at conception, one receives from one's mother a red drop and from one's father a white drop. The red element becomes associated with the female gender and *prajñā* and the white element with the male gender and method (*upāya*).
38. Trungpa: 238.
39. Gupta, *Hindu Tantricism*: 111.
40. Ibid:59.
41. The left subtle channel is associated with the female as the right subtle channel is with the male.
42. See *Māṇḍūkya Upaniṣad* for what *Auṁ* represents.
43. Wayman, *Buddhist Tantras*: 203.
44. This *Vetālavikrama* originally from the *Kathāsaritsāgara* has been translated numerous times in English from many languages—Nepali, Mongolian, etc., as well as from the original Sanskrit. This version is from T. Riccardi, Jr., trans., "A Nepali Version of the *Vetālapañcaviṃsati*", *American Oriental Series*, Vol.54, 1971:142-44.
45. Though this is a legend, there are sculptures which indicate that devotees did offer their heads to the goddess. See Vogel, J. Ph., "The Head-offering to the goddess in a Pallava Sculpture", *Bulletin of the School of Oriental Studies*, London, VI, 2 (1930-32):539-43. Srinivasin, P.R., "Two Noteworthy Sculptures in the Madras Museum", *Journal of Indian Museum*, Vol. XVI-XVII (1958-60).
46. This story inspired a delightful novella by Thomas Mann, *The Transposed Heads: A Legend of India*.
47. See chapter 1 p.6. See O'Flathery, W., *In Origins of Evil in Hindu Mythology*:351 and Courtright, P., *Ganesa*:93.
48. There seem to be exceptions, as when a human receives an animal's head, such as Dakṣa, Gaṇeśa, Hayagrīva, etc. In these cases the selective factor is that of a human body which supersedes the animal head; the transposed animal head did not cause the person to be classified as an animal.
49. Wayman, *Buddhist Tantras*:208; Tsong-kha-pa *Bka'-'bum*, Lhasa ed. Vol TA '*dod 'jo* (27a-b ff). Furthermore, Wayman states that according to Greeks, the life spirit active in procreation was believed to be in the head; the Romans . . . believed that the head was the source of seed and concerned in procreation.
50. O'Flaherty (1980):17-61.
51. Many examples are given to Śvetaketu in the *Chāṇḍogya Upaniṣad*, see VI.9.1.ff
52. Prior to this, Gam-po-pa was meditating for six hours per day and when asked by Milarepa what he had experienced, he replied, 'Nothing at all'. Milarepa laughed and asked, "How were there no signs of progress? You should change meditations." (Rao, S.:87)
53. Ibid. I have changed the word 'ego' to *ātmagraha*.
54. *rGyud sde kun btus*, Vol.23:412 states: "*gzung 'dzin gyi snang wa dbyings/ su thim pa'i brdar dbu bcad ma'i tsul du bsnengs pa ste*".

55. Dowman:318.
56. Kinsley, *Hindu Goddesses*: 175.
57. Freud, S., *Interpretations of Dreams*, 1961: 366-67.
58. O'Flaherty, W. Doniger; *Women, Androgynes and Other Mythical Beasts*: 81ff and Obeyesekere, G., *The Cult of Pattini*, University of Chicago:478.
59. Obeyesekere cites Flugel, J.C., " Polyphallic Symbolism and the Castration Complex", *International Journal of Psychoanalysis* 5 (1924):176. "There is one way in which it is possible to carry out a fairly satisfactory (displaced) castration of the female, . . . by cutting off the breasts. . . ." (Obeyesekere does not discuss Chinnamastā.)
60. O'Flaherty:85.
61. When reading O'Flaherty I wonder also why one needs to be decapitated in order to have sexual intercourse. According to her account, "She (Chinnamastā) decapitates herself in order to copulate with the male figure lying beneath her. Decapitation in this context leads to total freedom and release, for her or for her worshippers."
62. Courtright, *Gaṇeśa*:122.
63. *Kalyāṇa Śakti Aṅka*: 108-9.
64. See an interesting article about the Mahāvīra ritual by Stella Kramrisch entitled "The Mahāvīra Vessel and the Plant Putika" in Wasson R.G., et al., *Persephone's Quest: Entheogens and the Origins of Religion*, New Haven, Yale University Press, 1986:95-116. (Reprinted from the *Journal of the American Oriental Society*, Vol.95 #2 Apr-June 1975.)
65. See Das, Kunjabehari, "The Study of Orissan Folklore", *Visvabharati Studies* 16 (1953):58-59 for a story about a goddess who is worshipped with only a horse's head. A well known Tamil story of devotees offering their heads is the *Silappadikaram*, tr. V.R. Ramachandra Dikshitar, 1939, 'Canto' XII, Vettuvavari 180-89.
66. See the *Prāṇatoṣiṇītantra* and the Mahāsiddhā sisters' legend in chapter 1.
67. Heesterman:24.
68. *Śatapatha Brāhmaṇa* 14.3.2.31. The last part of the phrase refers to the renewal of Prajāpati after his sacrificial dismemberment.
69. Courtright:70.
70. Misra: 230.
71. Dyczkowski:125.
72. Duessen:77.
73. Eck, D., *Darsan: Seeing the Divine Image in India*, Chambersburg, Penna., Anima Press, 1985.
74. Cited from Trungpa: 241. (Tib. *dus gsum mkhyen phyir rab tu gtum pa'i spyan gsum khrag ltar dmar zin zlum la gyo ba*.)
75. Ibid: 239. The Buddhist deity who epitomizes this quality is Avalokiteśvara, especially in his thousand-eyed form. Also see Kazi Dawa-Samdup:19. He comments that three eyes symbolize that all three worlds (desire, form, formless) are under Vajravārāhī's vision.
76. In Tibetan Buddhism there is an initiation known as the mirror initiation which 'opens up the third eye', i.e., the eye of wisdom. See Wayman, *Buddhist Tantras*: 69. Furthermore, in the Bodhisattva path, the third of the five paths is known as the Path of Insight (which implies one has developed the third eye) wherein one has direct vision of no-self (*anātman*) in the four Noble Truths. (See 14th Dalai Lama, Tenzin Gyatso, *The Opening of the Wisdom Eye*:108.)

77. See *Devī Mahātmya* 88.39-62. "From the stream of blood which fell on the earth from his body . . . hundreds of Asuras were born. And . . . filled the world.// Seeing the gods dejected, Caṇḍikā exclaimed . . to Kālī, O Cāmuṇḍā, open thy mouth." (8.50-52.)
78. Agrawala, V.S., *Devī Mahātmya: The Glorification of the Great Goddess*, Ramnagar Varanasi, All-India Kashiraj Trust, 1963:211. Also see Ibid:19-20.
79. See the *sādhana* entitled the *Chinnamastāsādhana*, listed in *Dhīḥ* (no.23, 67a-68) has the complete title in the colophon is *Trīkāyavajrayogīncitta Chinnamastā Sādhana* by Siddhācārya Virūpa.
80. See O'Flaherty:17-62 for mutiple interpretations of vital fluids. She also cites *Chāndogya Upaniṣad* 6.5.2 which states that the water which is drunk becomes divided into three parts: urine, blood, and breath (*prāṇa*).
81. There are many books on yoga, *prāṇāyāma*, etc. One on which I have based my information is Gupta: 162-85.
82. *Prāṇa* is both an individual wind and the collective name for the five winds. *Prāṇa* wind ascends and *apāna* descends; the combination is respiration.
83. Gupta:164.
84. *Ibid.* 171.
85. See Gyatso, Kelsang; *The Clear Light of Bliss: Mahāmudrā in Vajrayāna Buddhism*, London, Wisdom Publications, 1982:20ff.
86. Dowman:245.
87. Tāranātha: 216. (*dbus nas byang sems dkar dmar dras pa'i . . .*)
88. Gyatso, K.: 28.
89. *Kvaerne, P., An Anthology of Buddhist Tantric Songs: A Study of the Caryagīti*:91. This is Kvaerne's translation and arrangement of song five and whatever is in parentheses is from a commentary by Munidatta.
90. One notable exception is Mitrayogi's *sādhana* where she is in the dancing form of a slightly bent right leg and a completely bent upward left leg.
91. See Sinha, J., *Śākta Monism: The Cult of Sakti*:9-10.
92. Radhakrisna:683.
93. See B. Miller's "Divine Duality" in the *Divine Consorts*, ed. by J.S. Hawley and D.M. Wulff, Boston, Beacon Press, 1982:24 and D.H.H. Ingalls, trans., *An Anthology of Sanskrit Court Poetry*, Harvard Oriental Series 44, Cambridge, Harvard University Press, 1965: 200.
94. Kinsley: 175.
95. As the woman in the dominant position in sexual union empowers Chinnamastā, she in turn empowers her female attendants. A new epithet for Chinnamastā can be 'empowerer of women'.
96. Nathan and Seely: 65.
97. Ibid:46.
98. See Hiltebeitel, A., "Draupadī's Hair" in *Autour De La Deesse Hindou, Collection Purusārtha* no.5, 1981:179-214 (especially 208). Though Draupadī is not naked, the intention to undress her completely is an integral part of the *Mahābhārata*. Also Draupadī's hair was dishevelled because she was menstruating but the pulling of her hair was a forced dishevelment.
99. Hiltebeitel:207.
100. I thank Hemendra Chakravarty for this explanation. Also see Danielou, *Hindu Polytheism*:273.
101. Trungpa:239. Kazi Dawa Samdup states that loose hair "unties the knot which keeps all *dharmas* together so that they do not appear as what they are" and

nudity represents "freedom from the obscurations of defilements of the mind (*kleśa*)(p.20)". Tucci states that, "She is naked with dishevelled hair because she has been set free from the illusions that hide the essence of things (p.24)"

102. Ibid.
103. In some meditations the word for knife is interpreted as 'scissors', so some illustrations depict her as holding a pair of long scissors.
104. See Laufer, Berthold, "Use of Human Skulls and Bones in Tibet", *Field Museum of Natural History*, Chicago, 1923:9-24.
105. These are the three bodies of a Buddha—Nirmāṇkāya as the body of emanation, Sambhogakāya as the body of enjoyment, and Dharmakāya as the body of ultimate truth.
106. The eightfold path consists of right views, right resolve, right speech, right conduct, right livelihood, right effort, right mindfulness, and right concentration.

106a. See *Trikāyavajrayoginī Stuti*, p.74.

107. In Meisezahl's *Geist und Ikonographie des Vajrayana-Buddhismus*, plate one (p.83) is a *maṇḍala* of Chinnamuṇḍa Vajravārāhī with the three goddesses decapitated. I have not found a *sādhana* that describes the three goddesses with severed heads.
108. Misra: 232.
109. Dyczkowski:108.

Conclusion

Throughout this study I tried to answer certain questions about Chinnamastā. What is her origin? Who is she? What does she symbolize? What teaching does she embody? To answer these questions I have studied her legends, rituals, and iconography from both a Hindu and Buddhist perspective. Certain themes are reiterated in both the traditions; other aspects are elaborated more in one tradition only. Both the traditions are concerned with the yogic/tantric method as a symbol of personal sublimation. Many of her legends exemplify the yogic/Tantric technique of severing the head temporarily. As has been examined Chinnamastā's various legends, rituals and iconography, demonstrate that that Chinnamastā is pre-eminently a Tantric goddess. Since she is a Tantric goddess, there are certain generalities that can be deduced concerning her symbolism, and the similarities and differences between Hindu and Buddhist Tantra. Although the origin of Tantra is embedded in Hinduism and Buddhism, interest in the field of Tantra's origin and the relationship between Hindu and Buddhist Tantric adepts is relatively recent. Tantra, as an esoteric teaching, was originally an oral tradition which later became written. Relying primarily on textual sources, it becomes problematic to compare two different types of texts to determine Chinnamastā's origin. The Buddhist textual sources are *sādhanas* with transmission lineages and the Hindu texts are specifically literary ones, such as the *Upapurāṇas*.

In both the traditions Chinnamastā is considered a wisdom goddess, a goddess who has the wisdom necessary for liberation. According to Buddhist Tantric symbolism the female symbolizes transcendental wisdom (*prajñā*) and the inanimate aspect in comparison to the male symbolism of compassion and active method. In Buddhism she is a form of Vajravārāhī/Vajrayoginī, a goddess exemplifying *prajñā* and is connected with more female Mahāsiddhās than male Mahāsiddhas. This is reiterated in the Buddhist legends of Chinnamuṇḍā; swords of wisdom emerge from practitioners' mouths before they enact severing their heads. In Hindu Tantra this symbolism is reversed in that the female represents activity (*śakti*) and the male represents inactivity. Moreover the vivid imagery of 'swords of wisdom' is absent in the Hindu legends. Still, Chinnamastā is clearly a wisdom goddess by her association with Durgā as one of the ten great knowledge goddesses (*daśa mahāvidyās*). One may speculate that the reason for a lack of evidence in Hinduism for explaining why Chinnamastā is a wisdom goddess is that she was borrowed from Buddhism which stresses goddesses as wisdom-holders rather than as *śaktis*.

In this comparative study, the commonality between Hindu and Buddhist Tantric beliefs is evident. An important concept accepted by both Tantric traditions is the system of subtle winds, channels, and *cakras* in the human body. Each agree that there are two primary subtle winds, *prāṇa* and *apāna*, which ascend and descend respectively in the two subtle channels which intertwine with the central subtle channel. At the places of conjunction is a *cakra* which acts as a knot. As long as the two side channels remain thus intertwined, the subtle winds cannot enter the central channel or ascend and descend it freely. An ordinary person is unable to 'untie the knots' and as long as the two subtle winds do not course in the central channel without constriction, one experiences a separation from others. This sense of separation or apparent dichotomy appears to be absolute until the two subtle winds enter the central subtle channel. For an ordinary person the converging of the winds occurs at the time of death. A yogin or Tantric practitioner tries to simulate the death experience in order to realize the relativity of all dualities and to be free from the snares of cyclic existence.

Chinnamastā's legends reiterate the theme of cutting through this apparent duality. Most legends focus on the salient act of her severing temporarily her head. No legend indicates a suicide or a loss of control; quite the contrary, all legends portray her as an adept in the yogic/Tantric technique of 'untying the knots'. Were she not an adept yogin, blood could not ascend and flow freely from her severed head; she would have died and certainly could not have replaced her head. Chinnamastā thus embodies the realization of severing duality. This liberative knowledge is the *raison d'etre* of Tantra. Since this is the essence of Tantra, any deity who teaches this technique is a Tantric deity. Many *sādhanas* of various deities do instruct the practitioner in methods of transcending dualism; however, few deities exemplify this technique in their iconography. Chinnamastā and her two attendants is the most notable example. Her iconography intentionally overwhelms the viewer. The paradox of her living form with head in hand arrests our rational thought and forestalls a facile or hasty interpretation. It purposely creates uncertainty. It also obscures because one who does not know her *sādhanas* cannot understand that her decapitation is temporary. Without knowledge of this key factor, one can never penetrate the apparent paradox.

Since Tantra is fraught with dangerous methods which could make a person insane without the guidance of an adept teacher, it constantly veils its instructions.

Chinnamastā's iconography communicates this concern. To an ordinary viewer, Chinnamastā is decapitated and to some, she is dead. For a Tantric practitioner, however, her iconography is a supreme example of the interaction of the subtle winds and channels. Her two attendants are the two side subtle channels and Chinnamastā is the central subtle channel. The knots are untied and the winds appearing as blood ascend the unconstricted subtle channels. The triad represents the three subtle channels at the navel *cakra* which is their abode—the pivotal point for liberation. This magnified depiction of something invisible to ordinary perception is this extraordinary vision which is aweful and fascinating. One is privy to an experience reserved normally for yogins or Tantric adepts. Chinnamastā reveals the Tantric technique of liberation without words; her iconography is her code. Those who can decipher it can be freed from cyclic existence. For this reason, Chinnamastā is a paramount Tantric deity in both Buddhism and Hinduism.

Though Buddhist and Hindu Tantra share some common elements, other explanations and emphases differ within the two traditions. The Hindu tradition does not have the same system of classification as the Buddhist tradition. The Buddhist Chinnamuṇḍā *sādhanas* are part of the Anuttarayoga Mother Tantra which stresses bliss and the realization of voidnēss of inherent existence in order to experience the supreme state of reality. In the Chinnamuṇḍā *sādhanas* a practitioner must vividly imagine him/herself as Chinnamuṇḍā. A Buddhist practitioner who has Chinnamuṇḍā as his/her chosen deity (*iṣṭadevatā*) should arise in the morning as Chinnamuṇḍā. Moreover if one practises the uncommon preliminaries, one imagines one's body, speech, and mind as inseparable and as 'of one taste' with the body, speech, and mind of the guru. In this way, one experiences great bliss. The Dalai Lama states and explains the 'dissolution process of entirety' which is a visualization of one's entire body melting into light and completely dissolving. One then visualizes oneself as the enjoyment body (*sambhogakāya*) and subsequently as Chinnamuṇḍā generating the pride of the emanation body. (Although he discusses this in the context of Yamānataka practice, not Chinnamuṇḍā practice, both are Anuttarayoga Tantric practices and the same principles apply.) This powerful and continuous visualization process aids a practitioner in understanding Chinnamuṇḍā's symbolism of liminal transcendence. The separateness of life and death or any seemingly mutually exclusive concepts are understood as relative rather than absolute dichotomies.

When comparing the Chinnamastā/Chinnamuṇḍā *sādhanas*, one finds that in both the traditions they consist of three main sections: preliminaries, actual meditation, and offerings.

In both, preliminaries include homage to one's guru and chosen deity, purification and consecration of one's body. The Hindu practice has an extensive purification and consecration compared to the Buddhist practice; however, only the Buddhist practice includes taking refuge in the Three Jewels, generating *bodhicitta*, and cultivating the four immeasurables always coupled with the insight of voidness of inherent existence. The actual meditation of both involves the worship of Chinnamastā/ Chinnamuṇḍā. The Hindu practitioner visualizes Chinnamastā in front of him/her, while the Buddhist practitioner visualizes him/herself as Chinnamuṇḍā. The offering sections of both are similar, but only the Buddhist practice concludes with a dedication of merit. Thus we note both striking similarities as well as significant differences between the two Tantric traditions. Chinnamastā is a paramount Tantric goddess who inspires awe and fascination and gives us a focus for the comparative study of two transformative traditions.

APPENDIX 1

The Thousand Names of the Goddess

Śrī Devī speaks:

Tell, Deva Mahādeva, you are the best among who knows the *Śāstras*. Please do, O Jagannātha, tell me, O Dear One. For the benefit of all the beings, you have told all the praises, *kavacas*, etc. of Pracaṇḍacaṇḍikā Devī. Now be merciful to a devoted worshipper, please reveal to me , O Lord of Gods, these auspicious 1000 names of Chinnamastā.

Śrī Śiva speaks:

Listen, Devī, I shall tell you about Chinnā, so pleasing to the mind. Diligently, guard this which is beneficial to oneself; even under threat of death, do not reveal it anywhere. Listen to this, O Mahesāni, I shall tell you everything. Even without ritual worship, without meditation, without recitation, one can attain *siddhis*. Even without meditation, O Devī, without *bhūtaśuddhi*, only by reciting, one will obtain *siddhis*, that is the truth, O lovely faced woman. Previously in the company of all the gods at the peak of Mount Kailāsa, I told them when they asked, whatever I told them, I shall tell you. Listen, O lovely faced woman.

This is the praise of the thousand names of Śrī Pracaṇḍa caṇḍikā. The *ṛṣi* is Bhairava, verse is *Samrāṭ chandaḥ*, the goddess Pracaṇḍa caṇḍikā, and the accomplishments are the four goals of *dharma, artha, kāma*, and *mokṣa*.

Names 1-100

1. Pracaṇḍacaṇḍikā (powerfully fierce one), 2. Caṇḍā (fierce one), 3. Caṇḍadevyavināśinī (indestructible fierce goddess) / 4. Cāmuṇḍā (name of the emaciated goddess)[1] and 5. Sucaṇḍā (very fierce one) and 6. Capalā (electrifying one),[2] 7. Cārudehinī (incarnation of belovedness) / 8. Lalajjihvā (one with the lolling tongue), 9. Caladraktā (one with quivering blood), 10. Carūcandranibhānanā (who has the appearance of the lovely moon / 11. Cakorākṣī (whose eyes are like the *cakora* bird),[3] 12. Caṇḍanādā (who has a fierce roar), 13. Cañcalā (who trembles)[4] and 14. Manonmadā (who gratifies the mind)/ 15. Cetanā (who thinks), 16. Citisaṃsthā (who remains in thought) and 17. Citkalā (part of Brahman),[5] 18. Jñānarūpiṇī

(who embodies wisdom) / 19. Mahābhayaṅkarīdevī (very frightening goddess), 20. Varadābhayadhārṇī (supportress of the bestowing of fearlessness) / 21. Bhayāḍhyā (possessing fear), 22. Bhayarūpā (has a fearful form), 23. Bhavabandhavimocinī (releaser of the fetters of existence) / 24. Bhavānī (goddess of Being) and 25. Bhuvaneśī (goddess of the earth) and 26. Bhavasaṃsāratāriṇī (who crosses over cyclic existence) / 27. Bhavābdhirbhavamokṣā (releaser from the ocean of existence) and 28. Bhavabandhavidyotinī (knower of the fetters of existence) / 29. Bhāgīrathī,[6] 30. Bhagasthā (abiding in the *bhaga*, i.e., the womb), and 31. Bhāgyabhogyapradāyinī (who bestows fortune and pleasure)/ 32. Kamalā (lotus-like one), 33. Kāmadā (who fulfils wishes), 34. Durgā,[7] 35. Durgabandhavimocinī (the releaser of the difficult fetters of existence) / 36. Durdarśanā (difficult one to perceive), 37. Durgarūpā (difficult form) [to behold]), 38. Durjñeyā (difficult to know), 39. Durganāśinī (destroyer of the difficult)/ 40. Dīnaduḥkhaharā (destroyer of afflicted sorrows) and 41. Nityānityaśokavināśinī (destroyer of the imperishable and perishable sorrows) / 42. Nityānandamayī Devī Nityaṃ (the goddess who eternally possesses imperishable bliss), 43. Kalyāṇakāriṇī (the doer of beneficial [works]) / 44. Sarvārthasādhanakarī (doer of the spiritual practice which attains all goals), 45. Sarvasiddhisvarūpiṇī (embodiment of accomplishing all) / 46. Sarvakṣobhaṇaśaktiḥ (power of all agitation) and 47. Sarvavidrāviṇīparā (supreme one for defeating) / 48. Sarvarañjanaśaktiḥ (power over all exciting passion), 49. Sarvonmādasvarūpiṇī (embodiment of all craziness) / 50. Sarvajñāsiddhidātrī (giver of supramundane success of omniscience) and 51. Siddhividyāsvarūpiṇī (embodiment of the science of supramundane attainments) / 52. Sakalā (she who is whole), 53. Niṣkalā (one without parts), 54. Siddhā (she who has succeeded), 55. Kalātītā (one beyond parts), 56. Kalāmayī (embodies the arts) / 57. Kulajñā (one who knows the clan),[8] 58. Kularūpā (whose form is the clan) and 59. Cakṣurānandadāyinī (giver of the blissful eye) / 60. Kulīnā (Kula practitioner),[9] 61. Sāmarūpā (who has the same form) and 62. Kāmarūpā (takes on any desired form), 63. Manoharā (fascinating to the mind)/ 64. Kamalasthā (one in the lotus), 65. Kañjamukhī (who has a lotus face), 66. Kuñjareśvaragāminī (who rides on the lord of elephants) / 67. Kularūpā (whose form is of the clan),[10] 68. Koṭarākṣī (having eyes like the hollow of a tree)), 69. Kamalaiśvaryadāyinī (confers lordliness of Kamalā)[11] / 70. Kuntī,[12] 71. Kakudinī (one with a hump), 72. Kulā (Kula goddess), 73. Kurukullā,[13] 74. Karālikā[14] / 75. Kāmeśvarī (goddess of love or desire), 76. Kāmamātā (the mother of god Kāma), 77. Kāmatāpavimocinī (liberator from the pain of desire) / 78. Kāmarūpā (can take any desired form),[15] 79. Kāmasattvā (who has desire as her sentience), 80. Kāmakautukakāriṇī (who creates the eagerness of desire) / 81. Kāruṇyahṛdayā (compassionate heart), 82. Krīṃ Krīṃ Mantrarūpā (one who embodies the mantra krīṃ krīṃ)[16] and 83. Koṭarā (the nude goddess) / 84. Kaumodakī (who is (like) Viṣṇu's mace (*Kaumodakī*), 85. Kumudinī (she who is at a place abounding in lotuses), 86. Kaivalyā (identical with the final emancipation),[17] 87. Kulavāsinī (dweller of the Kula) / 88. Keśavī (abundant-haired one), 89. Keśavārādhyā (honoured by Viṣṇu), 90. Keśī Daityaniṣūdinī (who killed the demon Keśī), 91. Kleśahā (the destroyer of defilements), 92. Kleśarahitā (who is free from pains), 93. Kleśasaṅghavināśinī (destroyer of the group of defilements) / 94. Karālī (formidable one) and 95. Karālāsyā (gaping-mouthed one), 96. Karālāsuranāśinī (destroyer of the formidable demigod, Karālāsura) / 97. Karālacarmāsidharā (one who holds the knife and sheath of Karālāsura), 98. Karālakulanāśinī (destroyer of the Karālāsura's clan) / 99. Kaṅkinī (heron-like one), 100. Kaṅkaniratā (devoted to the heron)[18]

Names 101-200

101. Kapālavaradhāriṇī (holding the best skull) / 102. Khaḍgahastā (sword in hand), 103. Trinetrā (the three-eyed one), and 104. Khaṇḍamuṇḍāsidhāriṇī (holding a severed head and a sword) / 105. Khalahā (killer of wicked people), 106. Khalahantrī (destroyer of wicked people) and 107. Kṣaratī (streaming forth), 108. Khagatīsadā (goes through the sky always)[19] / 109. Gaṅgā (the goddess Gaṅgā), 110. Gautamapūjyā (worshipped by Ṛṣi Gautama), and 111. Gaurī,[20] 112. Gandharvavāsinī (dwells among the celestial musicians) / 113. Gandharvā, 114. Gagnaradhyā (worshipped as a sky form), 115. Gaṇā,[21] 116. Gandharvasevitā (worshipped by the celestial musicians) / 117. Gaṇatkāragaṇā Devī (the goddess' troop who acts through the troop),[22] 118. Nirguṇā (without attributes) and 119. Guṇātmikā (with attributes) / 120. Guṇatā (endowed with attributes), 121. Guṇadātrī (the giver of 'qualities') and 122. Guṇagauravadāyinī (bestower of the importance of qualities) / 123. Gaṇeśamātā (mother of Gaṇeśa), 124. Gambhīrā (profound one), 125. Gaganā (sky-form one), 126. Jyotikāriṇī (illuminator) / 127. Gaurāṅgī (white-coloured one), 128. Gayāgamyā (one who goes to Gayā),[23] 129. Gautamasthānavāsinī (who dwells in the place of Ṛṣi Gautama) / 130. Gadādharapriyā (dear to Viṣṇu),[24] 131. Jñeyā (who has insight), 132. Jñāgamyā (who attains knowledge), and 133. Guheśvarī (Goddess of the cave or the hidden one).[25]/ 134. Gāyatrī (identical with the hymn in the Gāyatrī meter), 135. Guṇavatī (who has 'qualities'), 136. Guṇātītā (one beyond 'qualities'), 137. Guṇeśvarī (goddess of 'qualities') / 138. Gaṇeśajananī Devī (the goddess who is the mother of Gaṇeśa), 139.

Gaṇeśavaradāyinī (who grants wishes of Gaṇeśa)/ 140. Gaṇādhyakṣanutā (praised as the leader of the troop),[26] 141. Nityā (eternal one), 142. Gaṇādhyakṣaprapūjitā (worshipped by the lord of the troop)[27]/ 143. Girīśaramaṇī Devī (the goddess who is the wife of Śiva [the lord of the mountain]), 144. Girīśaparivanditā (goddess adored by Śiva) / 145. Gatidā (presenter of the path), 146. Gatihā (who annihilates the path), 147. Gītā (singer of praise), 148. Gautamī , 149. Gurusevitā (who is worshipped by *gurus*) / 150. Gurupūjyā (worshipped by the gurus), 151. Guruyutā (joined to the guru), 152. Gurusevanatatparā (who is entirely devoted to serving the guru)/ 153. Gandhadvārā ([worshipped] with perfumes), and 154. Gandhāḍhyā (who emanates a fragrant smell), 155. Gandhātmā (who embodies a fragrant smell), 156. Gandhakāriṇī (producer of fragrant smells) / 157. Gīrvāṇāpatisampūjyā (whom the lord of mountains and forests worships), 158. Gīrvāṇapatituṣṭidā (who pleases the lord of the mountains and forests)/ 159. Gīrvāṇādhiśaramaṇī (who pleases Śiva), 160. Gīrvāṇādhīsavanditā (one whom Śiva worships), 161. Gīrvāṇādhīśasaṃsevyā (whom Śiva shall serve), 162. Gīrvāṇāḍhīśaharṣadā (who pleases Śiva) / 163. Gānaśaktiḥ (who can sing), 164. Gānagamyā (who will be praised through song), 165. Gānaśaktipradāyinī (who gives power to sing) / 166. Gānavidyā (who has knowledge of singing), 167. Gānasiddhā (through the power of singing becomes a Siddha), 168. Gānasantuṣṭamānasā (who is happy by singing) / 169. Gānātītā (who is beyond singing), 170. Gānagītā (whose qualities will be praised through song), 171. Gānaharṣaprapūrita (filled with gladness through singing) / 172. Gandharvapatisaṃhṛṣṭā (to whom Kubera [lord of the celestial musicians] will rejoice), 173. Gandharvaguṇamaṇḍitā (who rejoices in the qualities of a celestial musician) / 174. Gandharvagaṇasaṃsevyā (whom the celestial musicians serve), 175. Gandharvagaṇamadhyagā (who lives amidst the celestial musicians) / 176. Gandharvagaṇakuśalā (who is beneficial to the celestial musicians), 177. Gandharvagaṇapūjitā (who is worshipped by the celestial musicians) / 178. Gandharvagaṇaniratā (who is loved by the celestial musicians), 179. Gandharvagaṇabhūṣitā (who is surrounded by celestial musicians) / 180. Gharghara (roaring one), 181. Ghorarūpā (frightful in appearance), 182. Ghoraghurghurnādinī (whose fierce roar is frightening) / 183. Gharmavindusamudbhūtā (one born from sweat), 184. Gharmavindusvarūpiṇī (who embodies sweat) / 185. Ghaṇṭaravā (whose sound is like a bell), 186. Ghanaravā (whose sound is like thunder), 187. Ghanarūpā (who has a cloud-like form), 188. Ghanodarī (who has a firm belly) / 189. Ghorasattvā (who embodies fierceness), 190. Ghanadā (gives rain), 191. Ghaṇṭanādavinodinī (who is happy when she hears the sound of the bell) / 192. Ghoracāṇḍālinī (fierce Cāṇḍālinī), 193. Ghorā (fierce one), 194. Ghoracaṇḍavināśinī (destroyer of the fierce demon), 195. Ghoradānavadamanī (controller of the fierce Dānava), 196. Ghoradānavanāśinī (destroyer of the fierce Dānava) / 197. Ghorakarmādirahitā (who is separated from fierce doers, etc.), 198. Ghorakarmaniṣevitā (worshipped by fierce doers) / 199. Ghoratattvamayī Devī (the goddess who embodies a fierce form), 200. Ghoratattvavimocinī (who destroys fierce beings). /

Names 201-300

201. Ghorakarmādirahitā (who is separated from fierce ones), 202. Ghorakarmādipūritā (who is joined with the fierce ones) / 203. Ghorakarmādiniratā (who is involved in fierce acts), 204. Ghorakarmapravarddhinī (who increases fierce actions) / 205. Ghorabhūtapramathinī (who destroys fierce demons) 206. Ghoravetālanāśinī (who kills the fierce 'vampires' [*vetāla*]) / 207. Ghoradavāgnidamanī (who extinguishes fierce forest fires), 208. Ghoraśatruṣūnidinī (who annihilates fierce enemies) / 209. Ghoramantrayutā (who is joined with the fierce *mantra*), and 210. Ghoramantraprapūjitā (who is worshipped with the fierce *mantra*) / 211. Ghoramantramanobhijñā (who knows the minds of others through the fierce *mantra*), 212. Ghoramantraphalapradā (who attains results by [reciting] the fierce *mantra*) / 213. Ghoramantranidhiḥ (whose abode or treasure is the fierce *mantra*), and 214. Ghoramantrakṛtāspadā (who controls the fierce *mantra*) / 215. Ghoramantreśvarī Devī (the goddess of the fierce *mantra*), 216. Ghoramantrārthamānasā (who knows the meaning of the fierce *mantra*) / 217. Ghoramantrārthatattvajñā (who knows the nature of the meaning of the fierce *mantra*), 218. Ghoramantrārthapāragā (who has mastered the meaning of the fierce *mantra*) / 219. Ghoramantrārthavibhavā (who manifests the meaning of the fierce *mantra*), 220. Ghoramantrārthabodhinī (who explains the meaning of the fierce *mantra*) / 221. Ghoramantrārthanicayā (who is the conglomeration of the meaning of the fierce *mantra*), 222. Ghoramantrārthajanabhūḥ (source of the meaning of the fierce *mantra*) / 223. Ghoramantrajaparatā (who is engaged in the recitation of the fierce *mantra*), 224. Ghoramantrajapodyatā (who is ready to recite the fierce *mantra*) / 225. Nakāravaraṇanilayā (lives in the letter *na*), 226. Nakārākṣaramaṇḍitā (who has *na* as an adornment) / 227. Nakārāpararūpa (whose supreme form is the *na*), 228. Nakārākṣararūpiṇī (embodies the *na*) / 229. Citrarūpā (one with variegated form), 230. Citranāḍī (with the variegated subtle channel [*nāḍī*]), 231. Cārukeśī (with the beautiful hair), 232. Cayaprabhā (whose illumination is built up) / 233. Cañcalā (who shakes), 234. Cañcalākārā (creates movement), 235. Cārurūpā (who has a wonderful form) and 236. Caṇḍikā (the fierce one) / 237.

Caturvedamayī (embodies the four Vedas), 238. Caṇḍā (the fierce one), 239. Cāṇḍālagaṇamaṇḍitā (who is adorned by the *cāṇḍālas* [outcastes]) / 240. Cāṇḍālachedinī (destroys wicked ones), 241. Caṇḍatāpanirmūlakāriṇī (eradicates suffering which results from violence) / 242. Caturbhujā (four-armed), 243. Caṇḍarūpā (has a fierce form), 244. Caṇḍamuṇḍavināśinī (who destroyed Caṇḍa and Muṇḍa) / 245. Candrikā (one like moonlight), 246. Candrakīrtiḥ (who is as famous as the moon), 247. Candrakāntisthathā (who is as beautiful as the moon) / 248. Candrāsyā (whose face is like the moon), 249. Candrarūpa (whose form is like the moon), and 250. Candramaulisvarūpiṇī (her own form is the moon crescent)[28] / 251. Candramaulipriyā (adored by Śiva), 252. Candramaulisantuṣṭamānasā (content with Śiva) / 253. Cakorabandhuramaṇī (pleased with the relative of the *cakora*),[29] 254. Cakorabandhupūjitā (worshipped by the relative of the *cakora*) / 255. Cakrarūpā (whose form is the discus), 256. Cakramayī (embodies a discus), 257. Cakrākārasvarūpiṇī (whose own form is like a discus) / 258. Cakrapāṇipriyā (loved by the discus holder, i.e., Viṣṇu), 259. Cakrapāṇiprītipradāyinī (gives love to Viṣṇu) / 260. Cakrapāṇirasābhijñā (who knows Viṣṇu's bliss),[30] 261. Cakrapāṇivarapradā (who bestows the gifts of Viṣṇu) / 262. Cakrapāṇivaronmattā (pleased with Viṣṇu's gifts), 263. Cakrapāṇisvarūpiṇī (whose own form is one who holds a discus) / 264. Cakrapāṇīśvarī Nityam (who is always Viṣṇu's wife), 265. Cakrapāṇinamaskṛtā (to whom Viṣṇu gives homage) / 266. Cakrapāṇisamudbhūtā (arising from Viṣṇu), 267. Cakrapāṇiguṇāspadā (who is at the level of the *guṇas* of Viṣṇu) / 268. Candrāvalī (wears a moon-rosary), 269. Candravatī (who wears a moon ornament), 270. Candrakoṭisamaprabhā (whose brightness is equal to 10,000 moons) / 271. Candanārcitapādābjā (whose lotus feet are adorned with sandalwood), 272. Candanāvitamastakā (whose head is [smeared with] sandalwood) / 273. Cārukīrtiḥ (whose fame is sweet), and 274. Cārunetrā (who has beautiful eyes), 275. Cārucandravibhūṣaṇā (adorned with a beautiful moon) / 276. Cārubhūṣā (one with beautiful ornaments), 277. Cāruveṣā (one with beautiful garments), 278. Cāruveṣapradāyanī (bestower of beautiful garments) / 279. Cārubhūṣābhūṣitāṅgī (adorned with beautiful garments), 280. Caturvaktravarapradā (fulfils the wishes of Brahmā, the four-faced one) / 281. Caturavaktrasamārādhyā (who delights Brahmā) 282. Caturvaktrasamāśritā (united with Brahmā) / 283. Caturvaktrā (four-faced), 284. Caturbāhā (four-armed), 285. Caturthī ([is worshipped] on the fourth day of the month), 286. Caturdaśī ([is worshipped] on the fourteenth day) / 287. Citrā (whose asterim is Citrā),[31] 288. Carmaṇvatī (who lives in the Carman River), 289. Caitrī (associated with Citra), 290. Candrabhāgā (who should be worshipped on the full moon day), 291.

Campakā (who likes to receive campaka flowers)[32] / 292. Caturdaśayamākārā (source of the fourteen Yamas),[33] 293. Caturdaśayamānugā (who is a companion to the fourteen Yamas) / 294. Caturdaśayamaprītā (who is pleased with the fourteen Yamas), 295. Caturdaśayamapriyā (who is dear to the fourteen Yamas) / 296. Chalasthā (she lives in deception),[34] 297. Chidrarūpa (fissured form), and 298. Chadmadā (deceiver),[35] 299. Chadmarājikā (filled with deception), 300. Chinnamastā (who has a severed head).

Names 301-400

301. Chinnā (the severed one), 302. Chinnamuṇḍavidhāriṇī (holding a severed head) / 303. Jayadā (giver of victory), 304. Jayarūpā (embodies victory), and 305. Jayantī (victorious one), 306. Jayamohinī (victorious Mohinī[36]) / 307. Jayā (victory), 308. Jīvansaṃsthā (exists in [every] being), and 309. Jālandharanivāsinī (living in Jālandhara)[37] / 310. Jvālāmukhī (fire-mouthed goddess)[38], 311. Jvāladātrī (bestows fire or light), 312. Jājvalyadahanopamā (resembling the blazing fire of *Ja*) / 313. Jagadvandyā (praised by the universe), 314. Jagatpūjyā (worshipped by the universe), 315. Jagattrāṇaparāyaṇā (entirely devoted to the protection of the universe) / 317. Jagatī (earth), 318. Jagadādhārā (supportress of the all animated ones, i.e., Earth), 319. Janmamṛtyujarāpahā (destroys birth, death and old age) / 320. Jananī (mother of all), 321. Janmabhūmiḥ (the birthplace),[39] 322. Janmadā (creator of birth), 323. Jayaśālinī (resplendent with victory) / 324. Jvararogaharā (cures fevers), 325. Jvālā (blazing one), 326. Jvālāmālāprapūritā (surrounded by flames) / 327. Jambhārātīśvarī (goddess of Jambhara's enemy, i.e., Indra), 328. Jambhārātivaibhavakāriṇī (creates the wealth or glory of Indra) / 329. Jambhārātistutā (praised by Indra), 330. Jambhārātiśatruniṣūdinī (destroys Indra's enemies) / 331. Jayadurgā,[40] 332. Jayārādhyā (worshipped by Jaya), 333. Jayakālī,[41] 334. Jayeśvarī (the goddess of victory) / 335. Jayatārā (brings victory), 336. Jayātītā (beyond winning or losing), 337. Jayaśaṅkaravallabhā (beloved by Śiva)[42] / 338. Jaladā (bestower of rain), 339. Jahnutanayā (Goddess Gaṅgā, daughter of Jahnu), 340. Jaladhitrāsakāriṇī (who creates the fear of the ocean)[43] / 341. Jaladhivyādhidamanī (gets rid of ocean sickness), 342. Jaladhijvaranāśinī (destroys the ocean fever) / 343. Jaṅgameśī (goddess of animated beings), 344. Jāḍyaharā (destroys stupidity), 345. Jāḍyasaṅghanivāriṇī (wards off stupidity) / 346. Jāḍyagrastajanātītā (beyond stupidity), 347. Jāḍyaroganivāriṇī (warding off the disease of stupidity), 348. Janmadātrī (gives birth), 349. Janmahartrī (destroys birth), 350. Jayaghoṣasamanvitā (always with the sound of victory) / 351. Japayogasamāyuktā (conjoined with recitation practice),[44] 352. Japayogavinodinī

(gladdened with recitation practice), 353. Japayogapriyā (pleased by recitation practice), 354. Jāpyā (one who is to be muttered), 355. Japātītā (beyond muttering), 356. Jayasvanā (sound of victory) / 357. Jāyābhāvasthitā (established in the state of a wife), 358. Jāyā (wife), 359. Jāyābhāvaprapūriṇī (filled with the state of a wife) / 360. Japākusumasaṅkāśā (resembles a hibiscus), 361. Japākusumapūjitā (worshipped with the hibiscus) / 362. Japākusumasamprītā (pleased with the hibiscus), 363. Japākusumamaṇḍitā (decorated with a hibiscus) / 364. Japākusumavadbhāsā (her rays are like the colour of the hibiscus), 365. Japākusumarūpiṇī (her form is like the hibiscus) / 366. Jamadagnisvarūpā (her form is Jamadagni),[45] 367. Jānakī,[46] 368. Janakātmajā (Sītā, born from Janaka) / 369. Jhañjhāvātapramuktāṅgī (whose limbs release storms), 370. Jhorajhaṅkāravāsiṇī (dwells in this buzzing-like sound)[47] / 371. Jhaṅkārakāriṇī (makes this buzzing-like sound), 372. Jhaṅjhāvātarūpā (embodies the sound of storms),[48] 373. Jhaṅkarī (makes this buzzing-like sound) / 374. Ñakārānusvarūpiṇī (embodies *ña*)[49] 375. Ṭanaṭaṅkāranādinī (sound of a released arrow) / 376. Ṭaṅkārī (makes the twanging sound), 377. Ṭakuvāṇī (has this sound), 378. Ṭhakārākṣararūpiṇī (embodies *ṭha*) / 379. Ḍiṇḍimā (like the small drum),[50] 380. Ḍimbhā (young child), 381. Ḍiṇḍūḍiṇḍimanādinī (has the sound of this small drum) / 382. Ḍhakkāmayī (embodies the *ḍhakkā* drum)[51], 383. Ḍhilmayī (embodies the sound of the drum), 384. Nṛtyaśabdāvilāsinī (she enjoys the sounds of dance) / 385. Ḍhakkā (big drum), 386. Ḍhakkeśvarī (goddess of the large drum), 387. Ḍhakkaśabdarūpā (embodies the sound of the large drum) / 388. Ḍhakkānādapriyā (pleased with the large drum's sound), 389. Ḍhakkānādasantuṣṭamānasā (enjoys to hear the sound of the large drum) / 390. Ṇakārā (form is *ṇa*),[52] 391. Ṇākṣaramayī (embodies *ṇa* form), 392. Ṇākṣarādisvarūpiṇī (her own form is all 'subtle' sounds) / 393. Tripura (the 3 states of being),[53] 394. Tripuramayī (embodies the three states of being), 395. Triśaktistriguṇātmikā (embodies the three powers and the three 'qualities') / 396. Tāmasī (the 'quality' of inertness or dullness), and 397. Trilokeśī (goddess of three worlds), 398. Tripurā (three cites),[54] 399. Trayīśvarī (goddess of triads) / 400 Trividyā (three knowledge)[55]

Names 401-500

401. Trirūpā (three forms [perhaps Brahmā, Viṣṇu, and Śiva]), 402. Trinetrā (three-eyed), 403. Trirūpiṇī (three forms) / 404. Tāriṇī (protectoress), 405. Taralā (trembling), 406. Tārā,[56] 407. Tārakāriprapūjitā (Kārtikeya, Śiva's son, worships her) / 40. Tārakārisamārādhyā (delighted by Kārtikeya), 409. Tārakārivarapradā (bestows the wishes of Kārtikeya) / 410. Tārakāriprasūstanvī (the slender one who brought forth Kārtikeya, i.e., Pārvatī),

411. Tarūṇī (young one), 412. Taralaprabhā (sparkling shine) / 413. Trirūpā (three-formed), 414. Tripuragā (going to the three cities), 415. Triśūlavaradhāriṇī (holder of the gift of a trident)[57] / 416. Triśūlinī (trident goddess), 417. Tantramayī (embodies Tantra), 418. Tantraśāstraviśāradā (proficient in Tantric treatises) / 419. Tantrarūpā (her form is Tantra), 420. Tapomūrtiḥ (austerities is her form), 421. Tantramantrasvarūpiṇī (her form is Tantra and Mantra) / 422. Taḍittaḍillatākārā (she makes lightning),[58] 423. Tattvajñānapradāyinī (bestows essence knowledge) / 424. Tattvajñāneśvarī Devī (goddess of the essence knowledge), 425. Tattvajñānapramodinī (goddess who bestows the essence knowledge) / 426. Trayīmayī (three-formed), 427. Trayīsevyā (honoured by the three), 428. Trayakṣarī (three-lettered one),[59] 429. Trayakṣareśvarī (goddess of three letters) / 430. Tāpavidhvaṃisinī (destroyer of sufferings), 431 Tāpasāṅghanirmūlakāriṇī (eradicator of much suffering) / 432. Trāsakartrī (terrifying creator), 433. Trāsahartrī (destroyer of terror), 434. Trāsadātrī (terrifying giver), and 435. Trāsahā (killer of terror) / 436. Tithīśā (goddess of the lunar day), 437. Tithirūpā (embodies the lunar day), 438. Tithisthā (established in the lunar day), 439. Tithipūjitā (worshipped on [certain] days) / 440. Tilottamā,[60] and 441. Tiladā (gives seasame), 442. Tilaprītā (pleased with seasame [offerings]), 443. Tileśvarī (goddess of seasame) / 444. Triguṇā (has three distinct powers), 445. Triguṇākārā (makes the three distinct powers), 446. Tripurī (form of the three cities), 447. Tripurātmikā (form of Tripuradevī)[61] / 448. Trikūṭā (goddess of Trikūṭa),[62] 449. Trikūṭākārā (maker of the three peaks), 450. Trikūṭācalamadhyagā (among the three-peaked mountain) / 451. Trijaṭā (three top-knotted),[63] 452. Trinetrā (three-eyed), and 453. Trinetravara-sundarī (the most beautiful of three-eyed one, i.e., Pārvatī)[64] / 454. Tṛtīyā (Śiva's consort, Pārvatī), 455. Trivarṣā (three years old), 456. Trividhā (three kinds), 457. Trimateśvarī (goddess of the three, i.e., Brahmā, Viṣṇu, and Śiva) / 458. Trikoṇasthā (established in the triangle),[65] 459. Trikoṇeśī (goddess of the triangle), 460. Trikoṇayantramadhyagā (amidst the triangle *yantra*)[66] / 461. Trisandhyā (the three meditations or junctions),[67] 462. Trisandhyacaryā (worshipped three times a day), 463. Tripadā (three steps),[68] 464. Tripadāspadā (three feet) / 465. Sthānasthitā (established in holy places), 466. Sthalasthā (situated in a mound),[69] 467. Dhanyasthalanivāsinī (dwells in wealthy areas) / 468. Thakārākṣararūpā (her form is *tha* letter), 469. Sthūlarūpā (has a coarse or corpulent form)[70] / 470. Sthūlahastā (has large arms), 471 Sthūlā (is massive), 472. Sthairyarūpaprakāśinī (manifesting a solid or firm form) / 473. Durgā, 474. Durgārtihantrī (destroyer of difficult affliction), 475. Durgabandhavimocinī (releaser from difficult binds or from jail) / 476. Devī (Goddess), 477. Dānavasaṃhantrī (destroyer of the

demons), 478. Danujeśaniṣūdinī (kills the chief of the demons) / 479. Dārāpatyapradā (gives wives and sons), 480. Nityā, 481. Śaṅkarārddhāṅgadhāriṇī (has the androgynous form of half Śiva and half Pārvatī) / 482. Divyāṅgī (divine-limbed), 483. Devamātā (mother of deities), and 484. Devaduṣṭavināśinī (destroyer of what is wicked to deities), 485. Dīnaduḥkhaharā (destroyer of poverty), 486. Dīnatāpanirmūlakāriṇī (eradicator of suffering [caused by] poverty) / 487. Dīnamātā (mother of the poor), 488. Dīnasevyā (served by the poor), 489. Dīnadambhavināśinī (destroys those who cheat the poor) / 490. Danujadhvaṃsinī (destroys demons), 491. Devī, 492. Devakī (Kṛṣna's mother), 493. Devavallabhā (beloved by the gods), 494. Dānavāripriyā (dear to the enemy of demons),[71] 495. Dīrghā (tall one), 496. Dānavāriprapūjitā (worshipped by the enemy of demons) / 497. Dīrghasvarā (having a long sound), 498. Dīrghatanuḥ (long-bodied, i.e., tall), 499. Dīrghadurgatināśinī (destroys prolonged difficulties) / 500. Dīrghanetrā (has elongated eyes).

Names 501-600

501. Dīrghacakṣuḥ (having elongated eyes)[72], 502. Dīrghakeśī (having long hair), 503. Digambarī (nude one) / 504. Digambaraprīyā (dear to the nude one, i.e., Śiva), 505. Dāntā (controls or restrains [the senses]), 506. Digambarasvarūpiṇī (her own form is nudeness) / 507. Duḥkhahīnā (devoid of sorrow), 508. Duḥkhaharā (destroys suffering), 509. Duḥkhasāgaratārinī (crosses over the ocean of suffering), 510. Duḥkhadāridryaśamanī (quells poverty and sorrow), 511. Duḥkhadāridryakāriṇī (creates sorrow and poverty) / 512. Duḥkhadā (gives suffering), 513. Dussahā (endures the difficult), 514. Duṣṭakhaṇḍanaikasvarūpiṇī (her form is vanquisher of wicked people) / 515. Devavāmā (who is to the left of the god, i.e., consort or wife), 516. Devasevyā (served by the gods), 517. Devaśaktipradāyinī (bestows power to the deities) / 518. Dāminī (lightning), 519. Dāminīprītā (pleased with the sound of thunder),[73] 520. Dāminīśatasundarī (lovely as 100 lightning flashes) / 521. Dāminīśatasaṃsevyā (served with 100 lightning flashes), 522. Dāminīdāmabhūṣitā (adorned with a girdle of lightning), 523. Devatābhāvasantuṣṭā (pleased with divine beings), 524. Devatāśatamadhyagā (surrounded by 100 deities) / 525. Dayārdrā (merciful and harsh), 526. Dayārūpā (has merciful form), 527. Dayādānaparāyaṇā (involved in being merciful) / 528. Dayāśīlā (cultivates mercy), 529. Dayāsārā (essence of mercy), 530. Dayāsāgarasaṃsthitā (established in the ocean of mercy) / 531. Daśavidyātmikā (incarnate of the ten knowledges),[74] 532. Devī, 533. Daśavidyāsvarūpiṇī (embodies the ten knowledges) / 534. Dharaṇī (Earth), 535. Dhanadā (bestows wealth),

536. Dhātṛī (nourisher), 537. Dhanyā (bestower of wealth), 538. Dhanyaparā (giver of wealth), 539 Śiva (peaceful one) / 540. Dharmarūpā (embodies *dharma*), 541. Dhaniṣṭā,[75] 542. Dheyā (nourisher), 543. Dhīragocarā (dwelling with the wise ones) / 544. Dharmarājeśvarī (goddess of Yama), 545. Dharmakarmarūpā (her form is virtuous action),[76] 546. Dhaneśvarī (wealth goddess) / 547. Dhanurvidyā (teaches archery), 548. Dhanurgamyā (is armed with a bow), 549. Dhanurdharavarapradā (gives boon to archers) / 550. Dharmaśīlā (cultivates *dharma*), 551. Dharmalīlā (manifests *dharma*),[77] 552. Dharmakarmavirahitā (not moving in *dharma* and *karma*)[78] / 553. Dharmadā (gives *dharma*), 554 Dharmaniratā (involved with *dharma*), 555. Dharmapākhaṇḍakhaṇḍinī (defeats heretics of *dharma*) / 556. Dharmeśī (lord of *dharma*), 557. Dharmarūpā (her form is *dharma*), and 558. Dharmarājavarapradā (bestows boons to righteous rulers) / 559. Dharmaṇī (virtuous wife), 560. Dharmagehasthā (virtuous householder), 561. Dharmādharmasvarūpiṇī (embodies both *dharma* and not *dharma*) / 562. Dhanadā (gives wealth), 563. Dhanadaprītā (worshipped by the one who gives wealth, i.e., Kubera), 564. Dhanadhānyasamṛddhidā (gives both wealth and grain) / 565. Dhanadhānyasamṛddhisthā (established in the accumulation of wealth and grain), 566. Dhanadhānyavināśinī (destroys wealth and grain) / 567. Dharmaniṣṭhā (devoted to *dharma*), 568. Dharmadhīrā (is steadfast in *dharma*), 569. Dharmamārgaratā sadā (always rejoices in those who follow the path of *dharma*)/ 570. Dharmabījakṛtasthānā (dwells in the seed of *dharma*), 571. Dharmabījasurakṣiṇī (protects well the seed of *dharma*), 572. Dharmabījeśvarī (goddess of the *dharmic* seed), 573. Dharmabījarūpā (embodies the seed of *dharma*), 574. Dharmagā (follows *dharma*) / 575. Dharmabījasamudbhūtā (born from the seed of *dharma*), 576. Dharmabījasamāśritā (is protected by the seed of *dharma*) / 577. Dharādharapratiprāṇā (who is the respective vital breath of Viṣṇu) / 578. Dharādharapatistutī (praised by holder of a mountain, i.e., Kṛṣṇa) / 579. Dharādharendratanujā (born from the king of the mountains (Himālaya), i.e. Pārvatī), 580. Dharādharendravanditā (honoured by king of the mountains) / 581. Dharādharendragehasthā (lives in the Himālaya, i.e., Pārvatī), 582. Dharādharendrapālinī (protected by Pārvatī) / 583. Dharādharendrasarvārtināśinī (Pārvatī destroys all suffering), 584. Dharmapālinī (protectoress of *dharma*) / 585. Navīnā (young), 586. Nirmūlā (pure), 587. Nityā (epithet of Durgā),[79] 588. Nāgarājaprapūjitā (worshipped by the god Himālaya), 589. Nāgeśvarī (goddess of the *nāgas*),[80] 590. Nāgamātā (mother of the *nāgas*), 591. Nāgakanyā (Nāga maiden or young girl), 592. Nagnikā (young girl) / 593. Nirlepā (untained), 594. Nirvikalpā (without discursive thoughts), 595. Nirlobhā (free from avarice), 596. Nirupadravā (free from affliction) / 597. Nirāhārā (fasting), 598. Nirākārā (without form), 599.

Nirañjanasvarūpiṇī (her form is colourless) / 600. Nāginī (wife of a *nāga*).

Names 601-700

601. Nāgavibhavā (lord of *nāgas*), 602. Nāgarājaparistutā (praised by the king of the *nāgas*) / 603. Nāgarājaguṇajñā (knows the 'qualities' of the king of the *nāgas*), 604. Nāgarājasukhapradā (gives happiness to the king of the *nāgas*) / 605. Nāgalokagatānityā (always goes to the Nāga realm), 606. Nāgalokanivāsinī (dwells in the Nāga realm) / 607. Nāgalokeśvarī (goddess of the Nāga realm), 608. Nāgabhaginī (sister of *nāgas*), 609. Nāgapūjitā (worṣhipped by *nāgas*) / 610. Nāgamadhyasthitā (surrounded by *nāgas*), 611. Nāgamohasaṅkṣobhadāyinī (causing pride and delusion in the *nāgas*) / 612. Nṛtyapriyā (pleased with dance), 613. Nṛtyavatī (belongs to dance), 614. Nṛtyagītaparāyaṇā (devoted to song and dance) / 615. Nṛtyeśvarī (goddess of dance or proficient in dance), 616. Nartakī (dancer), 617. Nṛtyarūpa (has a dancing form), 618. Nirāśrayā (has no permanent abode) / 619. Nārayaṇī (Viṣṇu's wife), 620. Narendrasthā (established among the kings); 621. Naramuṇḍāsthimālinī ([wears] a human skull and bone garland), 622. Naramaṃsapriyā Nītyā (always pleased with human flesh), 623. Nararaktapriyā Sadā (always pleased with human blood)) / 624. Nararājeśvarī (goddess of kings), 625. Nārīrūpā (woman's form), 626. Nārīsvarūpiṇī (her own form is a woman's) / 627. Nārīgaṇācitā (worshipped by women), 628. Nārīmadhyagā (amidst women), 629. Nūtanāmbarā (new clothes) / 630. Naramadā (is this river),[81] 631. Nadīrūpā (her form is a river), 632. Nadīsaṅgamasaṃsthitā (lives at the confluence of rivers, i.e., holy place) / 633. Narmadeśvarasamprītā (pleased with the lord of the Narmadā River, Śiva),[82] 634. Narmadeśvararūpiṇī (embodies the lord of Narmadā) / 635. Padmāvatī (dwells in a lotus), 636. Padmamukhī (lotus-like face), 637. Padmakiñjalkavāsinī (dwells in the middle of the lotus) / 638. Paṭṭavastraparīdhānā (wears silken garments), 639. Padmarāgavibhūṣitā (adorned with rubies) / 640. Paramā (supreme), 641. Prītidā Nityā (always gives happiness), 642. Pretāsananivāsinī (lives among corpses) / 643. Paripūrṇarasonmattā (intoxicated by complete nectar), 644. Premvihvalavallabhā (beloved by Śiva) / 645. Pavitrāsavaniḥpūtā (purifier),[83] 646. Preyasī (loved by Śiva), 647. Paramātmakā (embodies the supreme) / 648. Priyavrataparā Nityaṃ (always keeps her vows), 649. Parampremadāyinī (gives supreme love) / 650. Puṣpapriyā (pleased with flowers), 651. Padmakośā ([dwells in] the calyx of the lotus), 652. Padmadharmanivāsinī (dwells in the lotus and *dharma*), 653. Phaṭkāriṇītantrarūpā (incarnate of the Phaṭkāriṇītantra), 654. Pherupheravanādinī (sound of a jackal) / 655. Vaṃśinī (has a clan), 656. Veśarūpā (her form is any clothes), 657. Bagalākāmarūpiṇī (her form is the love of a crane) / 658. Vāgmayī

(endowed with speech), 659. Vasudhā (the earth), 660. Dhṛṣyā (overpowers), 661. Vāgbhavākhyā (utterance of speech), 662. Varānarā (best people) / 663. Buddhidā (bestower of intelligence), 664. Buddhirūpā (embodies intelligence), 665. Vidyā (knowledge), 666. Vādasvarūpiṇī (embodies elucidation) / 667. Bālā (youth), 668. Vṛddhamayīrūpā (increases in size), 669. Vāṇī (Speech), 670. Vākyanivāsinī (dwells in speech) / 671. Varuṇā (a river), 672. Vāgvatī (another name for Saraswatī), 673. Vīrā (heroine), 674. Vīrabhūṣaṇabhūṣitā (surrounded by heros) / 675. Vīrabhadrārcitapadā (Vīrabhadra worships at her feet),[84] 676. Vīrabhadrāprasūḥ (mother of Vīrabhadra) / 677. Vedamārgaratā (pleased with Vedic way), 678. Vedamantrarūpā (embodies the Vedic *mantra*), 679. Vaṣaṭprīyā (pleased with the word of oblation)[85] / 680. Vīṇāvādyasamāyuktā (conjoined with the sound of the *vīṇa*),[86] 681. Vīṇāvādyaparāyaṇā (devoted to the sound of the *vīṇa*), 682. Vīṇāravā (sound of the *vīṇā*), 683. Vīṇaśabdarūpā (embodies the sound of the *vīṇā*), 684. Vaiṣṇavī (Viṣṇu's wife) / 685. Vaiṣṇavācāranitratā (pleased with the Vaiṣṇava practices), 686. Vaiṣṇavācāratatparā (protects the Vaiṣṇava practices), 687. Viṣṇusevyā (served by Viṣṇu), 688. Viṣṇupatnī (Viṣṇu's wife), 689. Viṣṇurupā (has Viṣṇu's colour and form), 690. Varānanā (beautiful) / 691. Viśveṣvarī (goddess of all), 692. Viśvamātā (mother of all), 693. Viśvanirmāṇakāriṇī (creator of all emanations) / 694. Viśvarūpā (embodies all), 695. Viśveśī (lord of all), 696. Viśvasaṃhārakāriṇī (destroyer of the universe) / 697. Bhairavī (fierce one), 698. Bhairvārādhyā (honoured by Bhairava [a form of Śiva]), 699. Bhūtabhairavasevitā (served by the fierce beings [*bhūta*])/ 700. Bhaiaveśi (lord of fierce ones).

Names 701-800

701. Bhīmā (formidable), 702. Bhairaveśvaratuṣṭidā (gives contentment to Śiva) / 703. Bhairavādhisaramaṇī (pleased with Śiva), 704. Bhairavādhīśapālinī (protectoress of the fierce chief, Śiva) / 705. Bhīmeśvarī (lord of formidable ones), 706. Bhimeśī (leader of formidable ones), 707. Bhīmā (formidable), 708. Bhīmavarapradā (fulfills wishes of Bhima), 709. Bhīmapūjitapādābjā (Bhīma worships at her lotus-like feet), 710. Bhīmabhairavapālanī (protects with ferocity and strength), 711. Bhīmāsuradhvaṃsakarī (destroys Bhīmāsura), 712. Bhīmaduṣṭavināśinī (destroys the formidable wicked ones) / 713. Bhuvanā (the universe), 714. Bhuvanārādhyā (honoured by those on earth), 715. Bhavānī (another name for Pārvatī), 716. Bhūtadā Sadā (always gives children) / 717. Bhayadā (gives fear), 718. Bhayahantrī (remover of fear), 719. Abhayābhayarūpiṇī (embodies both fear and fearlessness) / 720. Bhīmanādāvihvalā (unperturbed by formidable sounds), 721. Bhayabhītivināśinī (destroys being afraid), 722. Mattā

(intoxicated), 723. Pramattarūpā (embodies complete joy), 724. Madonmattasvarūpiṇī (her form is intoxicated with delight) / 725. Mānyā (praised), 726. Manojñā (charming), 727. Mānā (respectful), 728. Maṅgalā (auspiciousness), 729. Manoharā (fascinating) / 730. Mānanīyā (respected), 731. Mahāpūjyā (greatly worshippable), 732. Mahāmahiṣamardinī (slayer of the great buffalo), 733. Mātaṅgī (one of the Daśamahāvidyā) 734. Māyāvāsinī (dwells in Māyā)[87] / 735. Mādvī (wine), 736. Madhumayī (embodies honey), 737. Mudrā,[88] 738. Mudrikā (tantric consort), 739. Mantrarūpiṇī (embodies *mantras*) / 740. Mahāviśveśvarī (goddess of Mahāviśva), 741. Dūtī (female messenger), 742. Maulicandraprakāśinī (who is the light of the moon crescent) / 743. Yaśaḥsvarūpiṇīdevī (goddess incarnate of fame), 744. Yogamārgapradāyinī (bestows the yogic path) / 745. Yoginī (practices yoga), 746. Yogagamyā (follower of yoga), 747. Yāmyeśī (lord of the southern direction or of Yama), 748. Yogarūpiṇī (yogic-form) / 749. Yajñāṅgī (form of the sacrifice [*yajña*]), and 750. Yogamayī (embodies yoga), 751. Japarūpā (form of repetition [*japa*]), 752. Japātmikā (her form is repetition [of sacred names]) / 753. Yugākhyā (named aeon), 754. Yugāntā (termination of aeon), 755. Yonimaṇḍalavāsinī (dwells in the *yonimaṇḍala*) / 756. Ayonijā (not born from a womb),[89] 757. Yoganidrā (yogic sleep), 758. Yogānandapradāyinī (gives bliss through yoga) / 759. Rāmā (joyful one),[90] 760. Ratipriyā Nityaṃ (always dear to Rati), 761. Ratirāgavivṛddhinī (lit., increased sensuality, i.e., involved in the realm of desire) / 762. Ramaṇi (pleasant), 763. Rāsasambhūtā (born from the *rāsa*),[91] 764. Ramyā (beautiful), 765. Rāsapriyā (likes Rāsalīlā), 766. Rasā (essence)[92] / 767. Raṇotkaṇṭhā (battle cry), 768. Raṇasthā (battlefield), 769. Varāraṅgapradāyinī (bestower of the best colour) / 770. Revatī (wife of Balarāma, Kṛṣṇa's brother),[93] 771. Raṇajetrī (victorious in war), 772. Rasodbhūtā (born from *rasa*), 773. Raṇotsvā (fighting festival [is dedicated to her]) / 774. Latā (creeper), 775. Lāvaṇyarūpā (beautiful form), and 776. Lavaṇābhisvarūpiṇī (her form is [as vast as] the salty ocean) / 777. Lavaṅgakusumārādhyā (worshipped with the clove flower), 778. Lolajihvā (quivering tongue), 779. Lelihā (licking lips) / 780. Vaśinī (who subdues), 781. Vanasaṃsthā (lives in the forest), 782. Vanupuṣpaprīyā (pleased with forest flowers), 783. Varā (the best) / 784. Prāṇeśvarī (goddess of vital breath), 785. Buddhirūpā (embodies intelligence), 786. Buddhidātrī (bestows intelligence), 787. Buddhyātmikā (scholar) / 788. Śamanī (night), 789. Śvetavarṇā (white coloured), 790. Śāṅkarī (wife of Śiva), 791. Śivabhāṣiṇī (utters auspicious words) / 792. Śāmyarūpā (who has a conciliating form), 793. Śaktirūpā (power is her form), 794. Śaktibindunivāsinī (dwells in the point of power)[94] / 795. Sarveśvarī (omnipresent goddess), 796. Sarvadātrī (giver of everything), 797. Sarvamātā (mother of all), 798. Śarvarī (Night) / 799. Śāmbhavī (a kind of hand gesture), 800. Siddhidā (giver of *siddhis* [supernatural powers]).

Names 801-900

801. Siddhā (accomplished in *siddhis*), 802. Suṣumṇāsvarabhāṣiṇī (understanding the sound of the *suṣumṇā nāḍī*)[95] / 803. Sahasradalamadhyasthā (established in the 1000-petalled lotus, i.e., the Sahasrāracakra),[96] 804. Sahasradalavarttinī (abiding in the 1000-petalled lotus) / 805. Harapriyā (dear to Śiva), 806. Haradhyeyā (Śiva meditates [on her]), 807. Huṃkārabījarūpiṇī (her form is *Hūṁ*) / 808. Laṅkeśvarī (goddess of Laṅka), 809. Taralā (trembling), 810. Lomamāṁsaprapūjitā (she is worshipped with leaves and flesh) / 811. Kṣemyā (lucky), 812. Kṣemakarī (creates peace), 813. Kṣāmā (Earth), 814. Kṣīrabindusvarūpiṇī (embodies drops of *amṛta*) / 815. Kṣiptacittapradā (makes one absent-minded), 816. Nityā, 817. Kṣaumavastravilāsinī (a playful woman with silken garments) / 818. Chinnā (severed one), 819. Chinnarūpā (has a severed form), 820. Kṣūdhā (food or hunger), 821. Kṣautkārarūpiṇī (her form is *Kṣaut*) / 822. Sarvavarṇamayīdevī (goddess who embodies all the letters), 823. Sarvasampatpradāyinī (bestows all wealth or success) / 824. Sarvasampatpradātrī (donor of all accomplishments), and 825. Sampadāpadabhūṣitā (adorned by the rich and the poor) / 826. Sattvarūpā (the 'quality' of *sattva* is her form),[97] and 827. Sarvārthā ([gives] all goals), 828. Sarvadevaprapūjitā (worshipped by all deities) / 829. Sarveśvarī (goddess of all), 830. Sarvamātā (mother of all), 831. Sarvajñā (omniscient), 832. Surasātmikā,[98] 833. Sindhuḥ ([lives] in Sindhu river), 834. Mandākinī ([lives] in the Mandākinī river), 835. Gaṅgānadī ([lives] in the Ganges), 836. Sāgararūpiṇī (embodies the oceans) / 837. Sukeśī (beautiful hair), 838. Muktakeśī (loose hair), and 839. Ḍākinī (name of Chinnamastā's attendant), 840. Varavarṇinī (name of a goddess) / 841. Jñānadā (confers wisdom), 842. Jñānagaganā (knowledge as vast as the sky), 843. Somamaṇḍalavāsinī (dwells on the moon disc) / 844. Ākāśanilayānityā (always lives in the intermediate space [*ākāśa*]), 845. Paramākāśarūpinī (her form is the space in the heart)[99] / 846. Annapūrṇā full of food), 847. Mahānityā,[100] 848. Mahādevarasodbhavā (Māhadeva's pleasure), 849. Maṅgalā (fortunate), 850. Kālikā (name of the tenth avatar of Viṣṇu), 851. Caṇḍā (fierce one), 852. Caṇḍanādātibhīṣaṇā (very fierce sound) / 853. Caṇḍāsurasyā (of Asura Caṇḍa), 854. Mardinī (destroyer), 855. Cāmuṇḍā (name for the goddess who destroyed Asura Caṇḍa and Muṇḍa),[101] 856. Capalātmikā (embodies lightning) / 857. Caṇḍī (fierce one), 858. Cāmarakeśī (shaggy hair) and 859. Calatkuṇḍaladhāriṇī (wears dangling ear rings) / 860. Muṇḍamālādharānityā (always wears a skull

rosary), 861. Khaṇḍamuṇḍavilāsinī (woman with a severed head) / 862. Khaḍgahastā (sword in hand), 863. Muṇḍahastā (skull in hand), 864. Varahastā (boon-giving hand gesture), 865. Varapradā (gives boons) / 866. Asicamaradharā Nityā (always holds knife and shield), 867. Pāśaṅkuśadharā (holds noose and goad), 868. Parā (greatest) / 869. Śūlahastā (trident in hand), 870. Śivahastā (auspicious hand), 871. Ghaṇṭānādavilāsinī (woman who has the sound of the bell) / 872. Dhanurbāṇadharā (holds the bow and arrow), 873. Ādityā (sun), 874. Nāgahastā (snake in hand), 875. Nagātmajā (born from the mountain) / 876. Mahiṣāsurahantrī (destroyer of Mahiṣāsura),[102] 877. Raktabījavināśinī (also destroyer of Raktabīja),[103] 878. Raktarūpā (red colour), 879. Raktagātrā (red or bloody body), 880. Raktahastā (red-coloured hand), 881. Bhayapradā (gives fear) / 882. Asitā (black colour), and 883. Dharmadharā (has virtue), (has virtue), 884. Pāśāṅkuśadharā (holds the noose and the goad), 885. Parā (supreme) / 886. Dhanurbāṇadharā Nityā (always holds the bow and arrow), 887. Dhūmralocananāśinī (destroys the demon Dhūmralocana)[104]/ 888. Parasthā (lives in the supreme, i.e., Brahman), 889. Devatāmūrti ([dwells] in divine images), 890. Śarvāṇī (Pārvatī or Durgā, wife of Śiva), 891. Śāradā parā (Brahmā's wife, Sarasvatī) / 892. Nānāvarṇavibhūṣāṅgī (decorated with various colors or with the four classes), 893. Nānārāgasamāpinī (fulfills whatever you desire), 894. Paśūvastraparidhānā (wears an animal skin), 895. Puṣpāyudhadharā (holds a flower weapon [as the god of love, Kāmadeva]), 896. Parā (supreme) / 897. Muktarañjatamālāḍhyā (wears a pearl necklace), 898. Muktahāravilāsinī (a woman who delights in her pearl necklace) / 899. Svarṇakuṇḍalabhūṣa (adorned with gold earrings), 900. Svarṇasiṃhāsanasthitā (sits on a golden lion throne).

Names 901-1000

901. Sundarāṅgī (beautiful limbed one), 902. Suvarṇabhā (golden one), 903. Śāmbhavī (Pārvatī, Śiva's wife), 904. Śakaṭātmikā (a cart is her form) / 905. Sarvalokeśavidyā (knowledge of all the worlds), 906. Mohasammohakāriṇī (creates delusion) / 907. Śreyasī (best), 908. Sṛṣṭirūpā (creation is her form), 909. Chinnachadmamayī (embodies the stopping of deception), 910. Chalā (deceit) / 911. Chinnamuṇḍadharā Nityā (always holds a severed head), 912. Nityānandavidhāyinī (always causes bliss) / 913. Nandā,[105] 914. Pūrṇā, and 915. Riktā, 916. Tithayaḥ Pūrṇaṣoḍaśī[106] / 917. Kuhūḥ (full moon), 918. Saṅkrāntirūpā (changing from one constellation to another), 919. Pañcaparvavilāsinī (woman of the five lunar days (*tithi*), 920. Pañcabāṇadharānitya (who has obligation to hold the five arrows [like Kāmadeva]), / 921. Pañcamaprītidā Parā (who is the supreme giver of the fifth joy) / 922. Pañcapatrāmabhilāṣā (five kinds of leaves [she likes]

for worship), 923. Pañcāmṛtavilāsinī (woman of the five nectars)[107] / 924. Pāñcālī (daughter of Pañcāla, i.e. Draupadī),[108] 925. Pañcamī Devī (Draupadī),[109] 926. Pañcaraktaprasāriṇī (who makes the five bloods flow), 927. Pañcabāṇadharā Nityā (always holds the five arrows), 928. Nityadātrī (gives forever), 929. Dayāparā (always compassionate) / 930. Palalādiprīya Nityā (always pleased with meat, etc.),[110] 931. Paśugamyā,[111] 932. Pareśitā (highest wishes [realized]) / 933. Parā (supreme),[112] 934. Pararahasyā (very secret), and 935. Paramapremavihvalā (supreme love to sentient beings) / 936. Kulīnā (the best class), 937. Keśimārgasthā (standing in the path of the demon Keśin),[113] 938. Kulamārgaprakāśinī (illuminates the *kula* path) / 939. Kulākulasvarūpā (her form is the union of Śiva and Devī),[114] and 940. Kulārṇavamayī (embodies all classes), 941. Kulā (she who is the clan) / 942. Rukmā (radiant), 943. Kālarūpā (form of time, or Yamarāja), 944. Kālakampanakāriṇī (instills fear in Yamarāja) / 945. Vilāsarūpiṇī (her form is of pleasure),[115] 946. Bhadrā (good or helpful), 947. Kulākulanamaskṛtā (Śiva and Śakti pay honour to her) / 948. Kuberavittadhātrī (bestows the wealth of Kubera [god of wealth]), and 949. Kumārajanani Parā (the supreme mother of Skanda, Śiva's son)[116] / 950. Kumārirūpasaṃsthā (established in a young girl's form), and 951. Kumārīpūjanāmbikā (the Mother [Chinnamastā] is worshipped through a virgin) / 952. Kuraṅganayanā Devī (goddess with the deer-like eyes), 953. Dineśāsyāparājitā (face like the sun) / 954. Kuṇḍalī (decorated with earrings or bracelets), 955. Kadalīsenā ([to her] armies are like banana trees), 956. Kumārgarahitā (free from evil ways), 957. Varā (best) / 958. Anantarūpā (infinite forms), 959. Anantasthā (established in infinity), 960. Ānandasindhuvāsinī (lives in the blissful Sindhu River) / 961. Ilāsvarūpiṇī Devī (goddess with Ilā as her form),[117] 962. Iībhedabhayaṅkarī (creates the dualism of *i* and *ī*) / 963. Iḍānāḍī (name of subtle channel), 964. Piṅgalānāḍī (name of subtle channel), 965. Ikārakṣararūpiṇī (has the form of letter *ī*) / 966. Umā (another name for Śiva's wife), 967. Utpattirūpā (form of origin), 968. Uccabhāvavināśinī (destroys egoism) / 969. Ṛg Vedā, 970. Nirārādhyā (worshipped without [form]), 971. Yajurvedaprapūjitā (worshipped with the Yajur Veda) / 972. Sāmavedenā (with the Sāma Veda), 973. Saṅgīta (with praises), 974. Atharvavedabhāṣiṇī ([gives] understanding through the Atharva Veda) / 975. Ṛkārarūpiṇī (embodies the vowel *ṛ*). 976. Ṛkṣā (the north or a bear), 977. Nirakṣarasvarūpiṇī (no letters are her form) / 978. Ahidurgasamācārā (who acts as difficult as a snake), 979. Ikārāṇasvarūpiṇī (the vowel *i* is her form) / 980. Auṁkārā (AUṀ), 981. Praṇavasthā (established in AUṀ), 982. Auṁkārādisvarūpiṇī (Auṁ, etc. is her form) / 983. Anulomavilomasthā (established in both the natural order and unnatural order), 984. Thakāravarṇasambhavā (born from *tha*) / 985. Pañcāśadvarṃabījāḍhyā (eminent by the fiftieth letter), 986. Pañcāsanmuṇḍamālikā (wears a fifty skull necklace), 987. Pratyekādaśasaṅkhyā (counted for each eleventh day), 988. Ṣoḍaśī (name of one of the Mahāvidyās), 989. Chinnamastakā, 990. Ṣaḍaṅgayuvatīpūjyā (six *mantras* used when a young girl is worshipped), 991. Ṣaḍaṅgarūpavarjitā (abandoned the form of six limbs) / 992. Ṣaḍvaktrasaṃśritānityā (always the six-faced one, i.e. Skanda, seeks refuge in her),[118] 993. Viśveśī (goddess of all), 994. Ṣaḍgadālayā (six parts used for herbal medicine)[119] / 995. Mālāmantramayī (embodies many syllables),[120] 996. Mantrajapamātā (mother of those who recite the *mantra*), 997. Madālasā (intoxicated) / 998. Sarvaviśveśvarī (goddess of the entire universe), 999. Śaktiḥ (power), 1000. Sarvānanda-pradāyinī (gives all kinds of joy) /

Here are the thousand names of Śri Chinnamastā. Her practitioners will achieve happiness by performing the worship as directed. Certainly this *should be kept secret.* Anyone who worships the goddess in the following way: for six months at midnight a devotee with loose hair recites (*mantras*) and performs the worship with the repetition of the thousand names; (this devotee) will attain knowledge and *siddhis* (supernatural abilities). The goddess controls everyone and creates delusion. She seizes the power of the gods and defeats enemies. Enemies become servants, evil is destroyed, and death is destroyed by reciting and knowing (the 1000 names). By praising with purity all *siddhis* on earth (will be obtained). This secret should not be revealed to others. With certainty after wearing amulets great *siddhis* will be obtained. The great Goddess has no knowledge (*vidyās*) better than this.[121] If one recites this once, all good *siddhis* will appear. Listen to the results by adoring and reciting on Tuesday or Friday, the eighth day of waning moon, change in constellation, or on full moon. After reciting the 108 (names), reciting the thousand names with devotion and after praising the great Goddess, all sins will be eliminated, one will be freed from all sins, and one will obtain control of all the *siddhis*. If for three months on the eighth day at midnight at the crossroads, a clean person offers from one's left side *bali* with the recitation of the thousand names, one becomes unconquerable, beautiful, strong, and brave. If one worships a virgin with the recitation of the *mantras*, one will obtain all the *siddhis*. I have told you, Devi, all the *siddhis* you can obtain. After reciting the praises of the great goddess, you will be released from all sins. All gods do obeisance to the Goddess. Do not tell this to anyone. You should keep this secret and protect this from ones who cannot understand. This is the entire powerful reason for praising and reciting. Who reads this book of Chinnamastā's praise will become wealthy as Kubera (god of wealth), kings will respect one, everyone will seek one's help, and will receive all *siddhis.* This is the conversation between Śiva and Parvatī about the essence of the entire Tantra; the praises of Śrī Chinnamastā's thousand names has been completed.

This is the classification of the one thousand names of Chinnamastā according to the nine *rasas*.

(1) **Erotic:** 7, 10, 11, 32, 48, 56, 63, 65, 73, 147, 153-56, 168, 171, 185, 188, 231, 235, 245, 247-54, 258-59, 262, 268-69, 274-77, 279, 337, 357, 360, 363, 380, 384, 411, 453, 495, 498, 500, 502, 515, 520, 522, 585, 592, 612, 614-17, 625-26, 629, 636, 638-39, 655-58, 661-62, 667, 690, 702, 726, 761-65, 774-75, 817, 837, 848, 859, 878, 895, 897-99, 901-2, 952, and 954.

(2) **Comic:** 49.

(3) **Pathetic:** none.

(4) **Furious:** 1-3, 5, 8-9, 12, 19, 22, 74, 94-95, 107, 180-82, 186, 189, 192-93, 199, 203-4, 236, 238, 369, 434, 566, 621-23, 697, 701, 707, 717, 778-80, 851-54, 857, 866-67, 874, 880-82, 884, and 944.

(5) **Heroic:** 34, 47, 68, 84, 88, 90, 96-98, 102, 104-6, 117, 194-96, 200, 202, 205-8, 240-41, 243-44, 255-56, 263, 302, 304-5, 375-76, 435, 440, 470-74, 477-78, 489-90, 514, 547-48, 660, 673-75, 710-12, 721, 732, 767-68, 771, 773, 855, 862-63, 872, 876-77, 886-87, 937, and 955.

(6) **Terrible:** 13, 21, 184, 405, 654, and 809.

(7) **Odious:** 4, 45, 51, 54, 58-59, 60, 64, 71, 72, 83, 87, 101, 167, 218, 223-24, 233, 239, 297, 300, 301, 370-72, 417-21, 503-6, 597, 635, 637, 642-43, 648, 653, 722-24, 735-38, 745-46, 748-50, 781, 801-4, 818-19, 838-40, 858, 860-61, 879, 894, 931, 936, 950-51, 961-65, 986, and 997.

(8) **Marvellous:** 6, 14, 17, 20, 23-31, 33, 35-42, 46, 50, 52, 53, 55, 59, 61-62, 66-67, 69-70, 75-80, 82, 86, 89, 91, 93, 103, 108-16, 118-23, 125-27, 130, 133-44, 146, 149-52, 157-62, 164-65, 169-70, 172-79, 183, 187, 190-91, 197-98, 201, 209-17, 219-22, 225-30, 232, 234, 237, 242, 246, 257, 261, 264-67, 270-73, 280-96, 298-99, 303, 306, 308-15, 317-22, 324-29, 332, 334, 335, 338-55, 361-62, 364-68, 374, 377-79, 381-83, 385-410, 412-17, 422-33, 436-39, 441-52, 454-69, 479-88, 492-94, 496-97, 499, 507-13, 523-25, 531-38, 541-46, 552-53, 556-65, 572-73, 577-84, 587-91, 598-611, 618-20, 624, 627-28, 630-34, 640-41, 644-47, 649-52, 659, 663, 665-66, 668-72, 676, 680-89, 691-96, 698-700, 703-6, 708-9, 716, 718-20, 725, 727-31, 733-34, 739-44, 747, 751-60, 769-70, 776-77, 782-84, 786, 788, 790, 792-800, 805-8, 810-11, 813-16, 820-36, 841-47, 849-50, 856, 864-65, 868-71, 873-75, 883, 885, 889-93, 896, 900, 903-30, 932-35, 938-43, 945-49, 953, 956-60, 966-85, 987-996, and 998-1000.

(9) **Peaceful:** 15, 16, 18, 44, 81, 85, 92, 124, 131-32, 145, 526-30, 539, 540, 550-51, 554-55, 567-71, 574-76, 586, 593-96, 664, 677-79, 785, 787, 789, 791, 812, 888.

In the classification according to *rasas*, the thousand names were divided into 87 for erotic, 1 for comic, none for pathetic, 50 for furious, 68 for heroic, 5 for terrible, 86 for odious, 699 for marvellous and 4 were not classified.

If one compares the one hundred and eight names classification with the thousand names, both groups of names have approximately two-thirds of the names under the marvellous category.[122] This category of marvellous (*adbhuta*) exemplifies the divine and I agree with Rudolf Otto that the word *adbhuta* could be translated as 'numinous' or 'awesome'.[123] This category of marvellous represents Chinnamasta accurately: indeed she is the Awesome Goddess.[124]

REFERENCES

1. Cāmuṇḍā is a terrific form of the Indian goddess, Durgā.
2. Also an epithet for Lakṣmī.
3. This *cakora* bird feeds on moonbeams.
4. This is also an attribute for Lakṣmī.
5. In *Lalitāsahasranāma* :286 #728, it states that *cit* (is) Brahman which is existence, knowledge and bliss; *kalā* (is) part.
6. This is a name for the goddess Gaṅgā.
7. A common name for a goddess (lit., of difficult access).
8. This word *kula* has many connotations, such as family race, group but it can also be referring to a type of Tantric worship known as *kula*. A practitioner of a goddess cult (*śākta*) worships according to the right or left hand method. The one who worship according to the left hand are known as Kulas Also in the *Lalitāsahasranāma*:87 (citing from *Cidagaganacandrikā*) "*Kula* is the measurer, the thing to be measured and the measuring."
9. Woodroffe, *Great Liberation*: 192 ft.8 states: Kulā according to Tantra, means Śaktī, Akula means Śiva, and the union of Kula with Akula is called Kaula. Hence the Devī is called Kaulinī or Kulinā.
10. Ibid.
11. In the text it is *Kamalaiśvara* (*ai* [read: *e*]).
12. Mother of the Pāṇḍavas in the *Mahābhārata*.
13. Kurukullā is a name of a Buddhist goddess that is associated with passion. Also this name could be 'Kurukulā' (frequently a consonant is doubled) which refers to the family of the Kurus, cousins to the Pāṇḍavas.
14. A fierce form of Goddess Durgā.
15. Also indicates one of the major seats of the goddess in Kāmarūpa, Assam.
16. Woodroffe, *Great Liberation* :185 states : ka=Kālī, ra=Brahma, ī=Mahāmāya. The half circle of the *candrabindu* is the Universal Mother and the point is the Destroyer of misery.
17. This is a technical term, *kaivalya*, which expresses the state of final emancipation.
18. This epithet is curious and perhaps that Chinnamastā's vehicle is an heron.
19. This word *sadā* (always) could be taken with each name or the last one.
20. This name is a frequent name for Pārvatī, Śiva's consort; also it means white

or pale yellow in colour.

21. This word, *gaṇa*, usually refers to Śiva's troop of helpers.
22. *Ganat* is read as *gaṇat*.
23. There are three Hindu holy places which expediate one's wishes—Varanasi, Gaya and Prayag (present-day Allahabad).
24. Gadādhara literally means the one holding a club; this is a common epithet of Viṣṇu.
25. This is a common name for a Tantric goddess; it means the hidden one. Also she is the goddess for sailors.
26. The word, *gaṇa*, means troop in the generic sense, but it can be referring to specifically Śiva's troop of helpers.
27. Probably in this case the lord of the Gaṇas is Śiva.
28. This moon crescent can be referring to Śiva's head adornment thereby indicating either the goddess' supremacy or her intimacy with Śiva.
29. *Cakora* is a bird which feeds on moonbeams.
30. This word, *rasa*, is very difficult to translate because of its many connotations. The word, *rasa*, means essence, pith, taste, etc. Thus when one knows Viṣṇu's essence, one experiences bliss.
31. This indicates that under the asterism, Citra, it is the best time to worship her.
32. The literal translation is only, *campaka*, a sweet smelling small white flower. However this verse discusses the worshipping of Chinnamastā, one assumes that this *campaka* flower is offered to Chinnamastā during worship.
33. See Amara, *Nāmaliṅgānusāsanam*:7 (for the 14 Yamas).
34. This word, *chala*, signifies deceit, deception, guise, etc. This name can be interpreted as creating illusion, *Māyā*.
35. See preceding reference.
36. Mohinī (lit., is a fascinating woman) but this might refer to the form assumed by Viṣṇu to prevent the *asuras* from obtaining their share of the nectar of immortality.
37. Jālandhara is a special site for the goddess—one of the major *pīthas*.
38. In Himachal Pradesh, India, there is a famous temple dedicated to the goddess with a fire-mouth; it is known as Jvālāmukhī Temple.
39. This name signifies that Chinnamastā is the origin of creation
40. A name of the goddess Durgā.
41. A name of the goddess Kālī.
42. Jayaśaṅkara is a name for Śiva.
43. The ocean symbolized by the terrifying waters represents cyclic existence.
44. *Japa* is a technical word for reciting certain words, such as *mantras* or the names of the deity.
45. This name is interesting because Chinnamastā is associated with Reṇukā who is the wife of Jamadagni. One might expect the Reṇukā's name instead of her husband's.
46. A name for the goddess Sītā.
47. This sound is a particular meditative state. See Wayman, *Buddhist Insight*:394 fn.8 which discusses King Śibi's spiritual attainments.
48. Ibid. The first level of yogic success is the buzzing of the bees and the fifth one (highest state) is the sound of the roar of thunder.
49. This signifies that she is very subtle because this *ña* cannot be used by itself.
50. This *ḍiṇḍima* is a small drum used in making announcements.
51. This *ḍhakkā* drum is a large or double-barreled drum.
52. One of these subtle sounds which cannot be used alone.

53. In the *Tripurā Rahasya*:5 Goddess Tripurā symbolizes the three sates: the waking (*jāgrat*), dream (*svapna*), and deep sleep (*suṣupti*) states.
54. This word *tripura* has numerous connotations. This name can refer to the three cities of the demons. These are the cities of gold, silver, and iron built for the demons by Māyā but destroyed by Śiva at the request of the gods.
55. Perhaps it is referring to the three Vedas.
56. A name of a goddess, one of the Mahāvidyās.
57. This might refer to the episode in the *Devīmāhātmya*.
58. This indicates her swiftness and being quick to help her practitioners.
59. These three letters refer to her seed syllable (*bīja*) which is *hrī*.
60.. A name of a Brahman woman who became a heavenly nymph (*apsarā*) because she bathed at an improper season. The reason she was born as *an apsarā* was to destroy the demons Sunda and Upasunda. See Dowson, J.; *A Classical Dictionary of Hindu Mythology*:319.
61. *Devīmāhātmya*:240 states Goddess Tripurā is comprised of three *guṇas* each of which is a *pura*, and, Tripurasundarī becomes manifest as Mahāsaraśvatī (equal to *dhyāna*), Mahākālī (equal to *kriyā*), and Mahālakṣmī (equal to *artha*).
62. In this one and the following names (*u* [read: *ū*]. This Trikūṭa is a mythical mountain in Sri Lanka where the city of Lanka, the capital of the demon Rāvaṇa, is supposed to be situated. See Dowson, A *Classical Dictionary of Hindu Mythology*:320. Moreover in the *Lalitāsahasranāma*:86 it mentions three *kūṭas*: *vāgbhavakūṭa*, *madyakūṭa* or *kāmarājakūṭa*, and 1,175 *saktīkūṭa*.
63. Another meaning is that this name refers to a demoness (*rākṣasī*) who befriended Sītā during her captivity in Sri Lanka. See Dowson:320.
64. This three-eyed one can refer to Śiva and the most beautiful as his wife Pārvatī.
65. This is the 'triangle' in the navel *cakra*.
66. This means that Chinnamastā is in the middle of the triangle which indicates that she is in the *bindu*, the centre of creation.
67. See *Lalitāsahasranāma*: 212 cites from *Reṇukā Pr.* "Iḍā is *Kālī*, Piṅgalā is Lakṣmī, Suṣumṇā is Ekavīrā, thus the Sandhyā is threefold.
68. There is the legend of Viṣṇu taking three steps and covering the whole universe.
69. This name may have other meanings, Vraj Vallabha Dwivedi interpreted it as the goddess found in 108 Vaiṣṇava holy places. Also Sircar:96&92 states that Sthala is another name for Nīla which could refer to the Puri Temple in Orissa or the Nīla Mountains in the Kāmarūpa (Assam).
70. Goddesses usually have three major forms: (1) gross (sthūla), (2) subtle (*sūkṣma*), and (3) beyond (form) (*para*).
71. Also could be dear to the gods (enemies of the demon Danu).
72. Since these phrases follow each other, 'elongated eyes' may refer to a meditative yogic gaze.
73. Perhaps this is the fifth yogic state.
74. This refers to the ten great knowledge goddesses.
75. This is one of the 27 asterisms and one should perform rituals (*pūjā*) on this day for Chinnamastā.
76. This word *dharma* is a protean word which can be translated as law, virtue, duty, nature, essential quality, resemblance, etc. In the following names which have *dharma*, I shall usually translate it as duty or virtuous actions or simply not translate it so that all these meanings could be inserted.
77. The Goddess frequently is described as playing (*līlā*); in this name one could understand that she is manifesting correct action or dutiful action (*dharma*) for the sake of sentient beings.

78. The Goddess, unlike humans, is unaffected by one's dutiful actions and by cause and effect.
79. See *Lalitāsahasranāma*: 195. Also this name refers to performing ritual worship on a daily (*nitya*) basis.
80. The word *nāga* means the black cobra or the serpent-like beings who inhabit the waters, especially wells and springs, and the netherworld.
81. See Dowson:221 for personification of the river.
82. This Narmada river is a well-known holy place; moreover from this river are found natural *Śivaliṅgams*. (VVD)
83. This is a purifying liquor used in rituals, hence she has the same quality of purifying things.
84. See Dowson: 358. This Vīrabhadra was a powerful son or emanation created from Śiva's mouth.
85. 'Vasaṭ' is an exclamation used in making oblations to a deity. For the philosophical explanation of this word, see *Devīmāhātmya*:13.
86. Vīṇā is an Indian lute which is held by the goddess of knowledge and learning, Sarasvatī.
87. The word *māyā* can be understood in the philosophical sense as illusion of the world, in the mythological sense as the demon who built the three cities (*tripura*), or in the worldly sense as art.
88. This word, *mudrā*, has several connotations, such as a consort or parched grain in certain Tantric rituals or a hand gesture.
89. *Lalitāsahasranāma*:339 states *ayoniḥ* means without origin or having no abode, i.e., unlimited.
90. Also a name for goddess Lakṣmī.
91. This word *rāsa* may refer to sound, speech, or Kṛṣṇa's dance with the cowherdesses (*rāsalīlā*).
92. *Rasa* is a protean word in Sanskrit which has meanings, such as essence, pith, mood, taste, etc.
93. Also one of the 27 asterisms or constellations.
94. This *śaktībindu* can refer to the specific place in the centre of the *yoni* found at the navel *cakra*.
95. In the *Maitri Upaniṣad* 6.22, ". . . By closing the ears with the thumbs they hear the sound of the space in the heart. There is a sevenfold comparison of it, like rivers . . . . They disappear (become merged) in the supreme, the non-sound, the unmanifest Brahman."
96. In *The Serpent Power* by J. Woodroofe, he states, ". . . is the Lotus of a thousand petals. This lotus, lustrous and whiter than the full Moon, has its head turned downward . . . . Its body is luminous with the letters beginning with A, and it is the absolute bliss (p.419).
97. The *Sattva* is one of the three *guṇas* (qualities); the *sattva guṇa* symbolizes clarity, purity, illumination, etc.
98. See Dowson:310 for this deity who lives in the sea in the Hanuman story.
99. See *Maitrī Upaniṣad* 7.2. ". . . Verily the nature of the *ākāśa* within the space of the heart is the same as the syllable *AUṀ*."
100. There are sixteen *nityas* (holy places) in the middle of these is the great *nitya* (*mahānitya*) (VVD).
101. See *Devīmāhātmya*:101 (7.25).
102. Ibid:59-63 (3.20-41).
103. Ibid:109-13 (8.39-8.62).
104. Ibid:93 (6.5-9).

105. This and the next two names are days when worship should be done or not be done. It is a cycle of three times per half month. There are five but only three are mentioned : (1) Nandā, (2) Bhadrā, (3) Jāyā, (4) Riktā, and (5) Pūrṇā. One should do worship on Nandā, Jāyā, and Pūrṇā and not on Bhadrā and Riktā.
106. Also one should do worship on the sixteenth day (*tithī pūrnaṣoḍaśī*).
107. In worship one offers to deities the five nectars which are: milk, curd, ghee, honey, and sweets.
108. See Dowson:94.
109. Ibid., Draupadī was the wife of the five Pāṇḍava brothers.
110. This meat, etc. refers to the Tantric practice of the five *m's* which are *madya, māṃsa, matsya, mudrā*, and *maithuna*. See Bose and Haldar, *Tantras*, 1981:131ff.
111. There are three different kinds of Tantric practitioners: *paśu, vīra*, and *divya*. See Gupta, *Hindu Tantrism*, 1979 :72ff.
112. See *Lalitāsahasranāma* (1962):79-80. Parā equals Ultimate . . . also implies, that since all *śabda* denotes names, Parā is *avyakta* or undifferentiated power that creates all names.
113. See Dowson:156 Keśī is a demon who fought with Indra.
114. See *Lalitāsahasranāma*:89.
115. See *Lalitāsahasranāma*:76 states that "The Universe is of her pleasure, or she at her pleasure either opens the way to self-realization or closes the way to the same in the devotee.
116. See Dowson:152. Kumāra, Skanda, or Kārtikeya is said to be born from Śiva without a woman.
117. This refers to the subtle channel, Iḍā, the instructress of Manu, or the goddess who presides over the earth. See Dowson: 122-23.
118. See Dowson:152 (Kārtikeya).
119. These parts include the leaves, roots, stems. etc. (VVD).
120. This refers to a garland of various *mantras* which must have the total of least 100 syllables. (VVD)
121. *Vidyā* can mean knowledge but in this case it refers to *mantras* of goddesses which are called *vidyās*.
122. Since both the groups of names have *adbhuta rasa* as the predominate category, one can understand the statement made by Śiva to Pārvatī: "Without doubt one will attain the same results by reciting the one hundred and eight names as by reciting the thousand names."
123. Otto, R., *The Idea of the Holy*: 129 note 1.
124. I disagree with Radhakamal Mukerjee who categorizes Chinnamastā under the terrible *rasa*. (*Cosmic Art of India*, Bombay, Allied Publishers, 1965:167-68.)

Plate one. The Dasámahāvidyās poster bought in Varanasi

Plate two. Chinnamastā with her two attendants poster bought at Kālīghāt, Calcutta

Plate three. Chinnamuṇḍā and two attendants, 14 century Nepalese-Tibetan painting (detail) permission from owner (Mary Slusser)

Small Chinnamastā Shrine near Changu Narayan, Kathmandu Valley, Nepal

In the Durgā Temple Complex in Ram Nagar, U.P.

At Entrance of Cintapūrṇī Temple, H.P.

At Entrance of Cintapūrṇī Temple, H.P.

APPENDIX 2

Chinnamastā Temples in Nothern India and the Kathmandu Valley

Temples dedicated to Hindu Chinnamastā are rare and I have not found any temple dedicated to Buddhist Chinnamuṇḍā. Though one finds paintings to the Daśa Mahāvidyās at various temples, such as Jvālāmukhī and Kangra Temples in Himachal Pradesh, Dakṣewara Mahādeva Temple in Kankhal near Haridvar and the Sithala Temple in Haridvar, and the Sankat Mochan Temple in Varanasi; temples solely dedicated to Chinnamastā are few. I am unaware of any temples dedicated to Chinnamastā in south India and the ones I found are in Himachal Pradesh, Uttara Pradesh, Bihar, Bengal and Assam in India and in the Kathmandu Valley, Nepal.

HIMACHAL PRADESH

In H. P. one of the most important temples of Chinnamastā is located in Cintapūrṇī about halfway between Kangra and Hoshiarpur in District Una. The temple is known as the Cintapūrṇī Temple (lit. fulfilling one's thoughts or wishes) but the carved marble entrance plate reads Chinnamastakā Mandir. As you climb the steps to the main courtyard, the entrance is flanked by two large folk style paintings of Chinnamastā's two attendants and above the entrance is a painted Chinnamastā. Above the main sanctuary is a carved relief of a decapitated Kālī; however the main image in the sanctuary is an aniconic stone, a *piṇḍī*. According to the ritual priests this *piṇḍī* changes form but during the day it is covered with a red cloth. The courtyard and the surrounding areas, including the curio shops, have no images of Chinnamastā or her attendants. I wanted to purchase a print of Chinnamastā but was told that only prints of Durgā were available. Householders should imagine Chinnamastā as Mother Durgā· only *sadhus* could imagine Chinnamastā in her severed-head form. For a brief description see Erndl, Kathleen, *Victory to the Mother.* 50-53.

UTTARA PRADESH

In a beautiful Durgā Temple complex in Ram Nagar near Varanasi one small chapel dedicated to Chinnamastā is located in a corner of this complex. The chapel has an inner circumambulation walk around the main image of Chinnamastā and her two attendants which are made of carved white alabaster with painted black eyes and red rubber tubing symbolizing the spurting bloodstreams. Though I visited this temple five times and never saw anyone worshipping, it was maintained with small food and flower offerings. See Kinsley, David, *Hindu Goddesses*: 177.

BIHAR

By the Rajrappa Falls in the Ramgarh District, Bihar is a popular temple dedicated to Chinnamastā. Though unable to visit this temple, I was told on numerous occasions that this is one of the most important Chinnamastā temples. K. N. Sahay in *Hindu Shrines of Chotanagpur* describes the temple:

> The shrine situated on the banks of the Damodar River, at the confluence of the Damodar and Vairanandi Rivers. The deity known as Chinnamastakā Devī is represented by a stone image of a beheaded female with a head in her left hand and a sword in her right hand (p. 13).

He continues to explain that during a battle with an Asura (demon) the Goddess' body was cut into 12 pieces. The shrine is located where the Goddess' head fell. Also it is said that any person with some desire to be fulfilled comes to the temple and evokes a sacred vow to offer as a sacrifice when their desire is fulfilled. It is interesting to note the similarities with the Cintapūrṇī Temple in H. P. where supposedly the Goddess' forehead fell and that she will fulfill one's wishes.

BENGAL

Since I visited Bengal very briefly, I was unable to visit any Chinnamastā temples; however, I was assured that Chinnamastā is a popular goddess in Bengal. When I visited the Kālīghāt Temple in Calcutta, I was hoping to find a shrine of Chinnamastā. I only found the Daśa Mahāvidyās depicted on the golden embossed door in front of the main Kālī image. I found numerous "penny-posters" of Chinnamastā for sale and also the British Museum has an ink drawing of Chinnamastā made during the early 1900's which was purchased at the Kālīghāt Temple. In *The Temples of Bankura District* David McCutcheon mentions that in the Shyama Rai

Temple built in 1643 in Visnupur there is an image of Chinnamastā (he does not describe this image) (p. 8).

ASSAM

At the famous Kamakhya Temple in Assam, there are shrines dedicated to the Daśa Mahāvidyās. Chinnamastā's temple is built against a rock wall and the cleft in the rock is considered to be the main *mūrti* of the temple.

KATHMANDU VALLEY IN NEPAL
CHANGU NARAYAN

In the Nepalese government publication, *Kathmandu Valley*, it mentions that there is a thirteenth century image of Chinnamastā in the Śaptamātṛkā Temple in Changu Narayan (Vol. 1:156). Not being allowed to enter since I am not a Hindu, I asked someone to describe the image. He said that the image is covered with a red cloth but where the head is severed, it is worn by devotees touching the spot. He could not tell if she was holding a head due to the covering and did not see any attendants.

Also near Changu Narayan at the edge of a cliff near cultivated fields is a shrine dedicated to Chinnamastā. This is a small nameless nondescript hut with three red painted stones. I was told that the large center stone was Chinnamastā and the two smaller flanking stones were her attendants. This shrine was being used because the stones were smeared with red powder and had fresh flowers and offerings at their bases.

PATAN

In contrast to the lonely nameless shrine near Changu Narayan, the Chinnamastā open shrine in Momari Galli, Patan is accessible to all. According to *Kathmandu Valley*, the shrine was built in 1732 when King Jayavisnu Malla arranged a parcel of land for its *guthi*. It is described as follows:

> This open shrine is built against a tile wall. The carved *torana* is surrounded by dragons. The sanctum contains images of Chinnamastā in different postures and an eight petalled lotus *maṇḍala*. (Vol. 2:160)

When I visited this active shrine on several occasions, there was usually a person presenting an offering of flowers and a token amount of food.

Bibliography

Sanskrit and Hindi Sources

Āgamavāgīśa, Kṛṣṇānanda, trans. Ramadatta Sukla; *Hindi Tantrasāra*, Prayag, Kalyan Mandir Prakasan, 1981.

Bṛhaddharma Purāṇam, Shastri, Haraprasad, ed., Varanasi, Krishnadas Academy, 1974.

Cakrasamvara Tantra, Kazi Dawa-Samdup, ed., New Delhi, Aditya Prakashan, 1987 (rpt.).

Devānandasiṃha, compiled; *Śākta Pramoda*, Bombay, Śrī Venkaṭeśvara Sṭīm Press, 1984.

Dhīḥ: A Review of Rare Buddhist Texts, Vol. 1, Sarnath, 1986 (*Lakṣmīsādhana*, no. 22; *Chinnamastāsādhana*, no. 23; *Trikāyavajrayoginī*, no. 25).

Kalyāṇa *Śākti Aṅka*, Chandigarh, Śrī Gītā Press, 1982 (rpt.).

Kalyāṇa Śiva Aṅka, Gorakhpur, Śrī Gītā Press, 1937.

Kaviraj, Gopinath, *Tāntrika Sāhitya*, Lucknow, Rajarsi Purusottam Das Tandan Hindi Bhavan, 1972.

Mahābhāgavata Purāṇa, Bombay, Gujurati Press, 1913.

Mahāraja, Swami, *Śrī Chinnamastā Nityārcana*, Prayag, 1979.

Mahidhara, *Mantramahodadhi*, Vol. 1&2, Delhi, Śrī Sat Guru Publications, 1981.

Misra, Janardana, *Bhāratiya Pratikavidyā*, Patna, 1959.

Prāṇatoṣiṇī Tantra, Calcutta, Basumati Sahitya Mandir, 1928.

Rākeśa Viṣṇudatta, *Daśa Mahāvidyā Mimāṃsā*, Kanakhala, Śrī Mahānirvāṇī Pancāyatī Akhāḍā, 1984.

Sādhanamālā, Bhattacharyya, Benyotosh, ed., Gaekwad's Oriental Series, Vol. II, no. 41, Baroda, Oriental Institute, 1928.

Śaktisaṃgama Tantra, Bhattacharyya, Benyotosh, ed., Vol. 1, no. 61 *Kālīkhaṇḍa*; Vol. II, no. 91 *Tārākhaṇḍa* (see section 23 for "Chinnamastā kramo nāma") Vol. III, no. 104 *Sundarīkhaṇḍa*, Gaekwad's Oriental Series, Baroda, Oriental Institute, 1932, 1941, 1947 (respectively).

Śaktisaṃgama Tantra, Dwivedi, V.V., ed., *Chinnamastākhaṇḍa*, Vol. 4 Baroda, Gaekwad's Oriental Series, No. 166, 1979.

Sukla, Ramadatta, *Mantrakośa*, Allahabad, Kalyan Mandir Prakasan, 1986.

Sanskrit Sources in the Nepalese Archives

(The following are from the Nepalese Archives in Kathmandu. I have included the manuscript, the microfilm reel and folio numbers.)

Chinnamastā Hṛdaya Stotra, no mss. number, H241/4, four leaves (similar to *Śākta Pramoda*).

Chinnamastā Kavaca from *Bhairava Tantra*, no mss. number, H241/7, five leaves (similar to *Śākta Pramoda*).

Chinnamastā Kavaca Saṃgraha, no. 3.246 mss. (Tantra: Stotra 229), A630/43, sixteen leaves.

Chinnamastā Sādhana, Siddhācarya Virūpākṣa, no. 278 mss., D26/2, sixty-three leaves in Newari script.

Chinnamastā Sahasranāma Stotra from *Śrī Rudrayamala*, no. 1.1356 (Stotra), A979/19, sixteen leaves in Newari script (similar to *Śākta Pramoda*).

Śrī Chinnamastā Sahasranāma Stotram from the *Visvasāratantra*, no mss. number, H241/10, eighteen leaves (similar to *Śākta Pramoda*).

Chinnamastā Stotra, no mss. number, H241/8, three leaves, (similar to *Śākta Pramoda*).

Pracaṇḍacaṇḍikā Stotra, no mss. number, E536/9, three leaves (not about Chinnamastā).

Tibetan Sources

'Jam dbyangs brtsei dbang po and 'Jam dbyangs Blo gter dbang po, *sGrub thabs kun btus*, Vol. 4, Dehradun, G.T.K. Lodoy, N. Gyaltsen, and N. Lungtok, 1970.

———, *rGyud sde kun btus*, Vol.23, Delhi, N. Lungtok and N. Gyaltsen, 1971.

Tāranātha, *Yidam rgya mtsho'i sgrub thabs rin chen 'byung gnas*, Vol.1, New Delhi, Chopel Legdan, 1974.

bsTan 'gyur (Derge edition), *rGyud 'grel*, Vol.23 *Vajrayoginī sādhana* by Lakṣmīnkarā (no. 32); *Chinnamuṇḍā vajravārāhī sādhana* by Lha mo dpal gyi blo gros (no. 39); *Chinnamuṇḍā sādhana nāma* by Mahācarya Birwapa (no. 40); Vol. 43, *Nandyvarta Traya Mukhagama Nāma* by Mekhala and Kanakhala; Vol. 52 *Chinnamuṇḍā sādhana* by Śrīmatīdevī (no. 2262), *Chinnamuṇḍā sādhana* by Virūpa (no. 2263); Vol. 82 *Chinnamuṇḍā Vajrayoginī* by Paṇḍita Śariputra.

gTer dBag gLing pa, collected; *sGrub thabs 'dod 'jo bum bzang*, Vol.1, New Delhi, 1972.

rTse Le sNa tshogs rang grol, *Collected Works*, Vol.5, New Delhi, 1974.

Secondary Sources

Abhinavagupta, Singh, J., trans., *A Trident of Wisdom*, Albany, SUNY Press, 1989.

Agrawala, Vasudeva S., *The Glorification of the Great Goddess*, Varanasi, India, All-India Kashiraj Trust, 1963.

Aquilar, H., *The Sacrifice in the Ṛg Veda*, Delhi, Bharatiya Vidya Prakashan, 1976.

An Alphabetical List of the Feasts and Holidays of the Hindus and Muhammadans, Imperial Record Dept., Calcutta, Superintendent Government Printing, 1914.

Amipa, S.G., *The Opening of the Lotus: Developing Clarity and Kindness*, London, Wisdom Publications, 1987.

Aziz, B. and Kapstein, M., ed.; *Soundings in Tibetan Civilization*, Delhi, Manohar Publications, 1985.

Banerji, S.C., *Tantra in Bengal: A Study in its Origin, Development, and Influence*, Calcutta, Naya Prokash, 1978.

Barua, H., and Baneja, J.D., *The Fairs and Festivals of Assam*, Gauhati, Assam, B.N. Dutt Barua, 1956.

Beane, Wendell, C., *Myth, Cult, and Symbols in Śākta Hinduism*, Leiden, E.J. Brill, 1977.

Bharati, Agehananda, *The Tantric Tradition*, New Delhi, B.I. Publications, 1983.

Bhattacharyya, Benoytosh, *An Introduction to Buddhist Esotericism*, Varanasi, Chowkhamba Sanskrit Series, 1964.

———, *The Indian Buddhist Iconography*, Calcutta, Firma K.L. Mukhopadhya, 1963.

Bhattacharyya, N.N., *History of the Śākta Religion*, New Delhi, Munshiram Manoharalal, 1974.

Bleeker, C.J., ed., *Initiation: Studies in the History of Religions*, Vol.10, Leiden, E.J. Brill, 1965.

Bose, D.N., and Haldar, H., *Tantras: Their Philosophy and Occult Secrets*, Calcutta, Firma KLM Private Ltd., 1981.

Briggs, George, *Gorakhanāth and Kāṇphaṭa Yogis*, Delhi, Motilal Banarsidass, 1982 (rpt.).

Chakravarti, Chintaharan, *The Tantras: Studies on their Religion and Literature*, Calcutta, Punthi Pustak, 1972.

Chakravorty, Hemandra Nath, trans., *The Narada Purāṇa* (Part III), Delhi, Motilal Banarsidass, 1982.

Chaterjee, Rama, *Religion in Bengal*, Calcutta, Punthi Pustak, 1985

Coburn, Thomas B., *Devī Māhātmya: The Crystallization of the Goddess Tradition*, Delhi, Motilal Banarsidass, 1984.

Courtright, Paul, *Gaṇeśa: Lord of Obstacles, Lord of Beginnings*, Oxford, Oxford University Press, 1985.

Danielou, Alain, *Hindu Polytheism*, Bolligen Series 73, New York, Bolligen Foundation, 1964.

Diehl, Carl Gustav, *Instrument and Purpose: Studies on Rites and Rituals in South India*, Lund, CWK Gleerup, 1956.

Dimitt, Cornelia and van Buitenen, J.A.B., ed. and trans.; *Classical Hindu Mythology: A Reader in Sanskrit Purāṇas*, Philadelphia, Temple University Press, 1978.

Dimock, E.C., *The Place of the Hidden Moon: Erotic Mysticism in the Vaiṣṇava Sahajiyā Cult of Bengal*, Chicago, University of Chicago Press, 1966.

Dowman, Keith, *Masters of the Mahāmudrā*, Albany, SUNY Press, 1985

Dowson, John, *A Classical Dictionary of Hindu Mythology*, New Delhi, Oriental Reprint, 1973.

Dyczkowski, Mark, *The Doctrine of Vibration: an Analysis of the Doctrines and Practices of Kashmir Śaivism*, Albany, SUNY Press, 1987.

Ghosh, Mạnomohan, *The Naṭyaśāstra*, Vol.1, Calcutta, Manisha, 1967.

Gnoli, R., *The Aesthetic Experience According to Abhinavagupta*, Varanasi, Chowkhamba Sanskrit Studies, Vol.42, 1968.

Gonda, Jan, *Medieval Religious Literature*, (A History of Indian Literature, Vol.II), Wiesbaden, Otto Harrassowitz, 1975.

———, *Notes on Names and the Name of God in Ancient India*, Amsterdam, North Holland Publishing Co., 1970.

Goswami, B.K., *The Bhakti Cult in Ancient India*, Varanasi, Chowkhamba Sanskrit Series, Vol. 52, 1965.

Gupta, Sanjukta, Dirk Jan Hoens, and Teun Gondriaan, *Hindu Tantrism*, Leiden, E.J. Brill, 1979.

Gyatso, Geshe Kelsang, *Clear Light of Bliss*, London, Wisdom Publications, 1982.

Gyatso, Tenzin (14th Dalai Lama), *The Union of Bliss and Emptiness*, Ithaca, Snow Lion Press, 1988.

———; Tsong-kha-pa, ed. and trans. by J. Hopkins; *Tantra in Tibet: The Great Exposition of Secret Mantra*, London, George Allen and Unwin, 1977.

———, Tsong-kha-pa, ed. and trans. by J. Hopkins, *Yoga of Tibet*, London, George Allen and Unwin, 1981.

Hale, Wash, *Asura in Early Vedic Religion*, Delhi, Motilal Banarsidass, 1986.

Hawley, John and Wulff, Donna, ed., *The Divine Consorts: Radha and the*

Goddesses in India, Boston, Beacon Press, 1982.

Hazra, Rajendra, *Studies in the Upapurāṇas*, Vol.2, Calcutta, Sanskrit College, 1979.

Hubert, Henri and Mauss, M., *Sacrifice: its Name and Function*, Chicago, University of Chicago Press, 1964.

Hulin, Michel, *Le Principe de l'Ego dans la Pensee Indienne Classique la Notion d'Ahamkara*, Paris, Publications de Institut de Civilisation Indienne, Series 8, Vol.44, 1978.

Ingalls, Daniel H.H., trans., *An Anthology of Sanskrit Poetry*, Harvard Oriental Series 44, Cambridge, Harvard University Press, 1965.

Khanna, Madhu, *Yantra: The Tantric Symbol of Cosmic Unity*, London, Thames and Hudson Ltd., 1979.

Kinsley, David, *Hindu Goddesses: Visions of the Divine Feminine in the Hindu Religious Tradition*, Berkeley, University of California Press, 1986.

Kumar, Pushpendra, *Śakti Cult in Ancient India*, Varanasi, Bharatiya Publishing House, 1974.

Kvaerne, P., *An Anthology of Buddhist Tantric Songs*, Bangkok, White Orchid Press, 1986.

Layle, P.G., *Studies in Devī Bhagavata*, Bombay, Popular Prakashan, 1973.

Lessing, F.D. and Wayman, A., *Introduction to the Buddhist Tantric Systems*, Delhi, Motilal Banarsidass, 1983.

Levi, Sylvain, *La Doctrine du Sacrifice dans les Brahmanas*, Paris, Presses Universitaires de France, 1966.

Lhundrub, N.K., *The Beautiful Ornament of the Three Visions*, Singapore, Golden Vase Publications, 1987.

Masson J.L. and Patwardhan, M.V., *Aesthetic Rapture: the Rasadhayaya of the Natyaśāstra*, Vol. 1&2, Poona, Deccan College, 1970.

———, *Śāntarasa and Abhinavagupta's Philosophy of Aesthetics*, Poona, Bhandarkar Oriental Research Institute, 1969.

Meisezahl, R.O., *Geist und Ikongraphie des Vajrayana Buddhimus*, VGH Wissenschaftsverlag, Sankt Augustin, 1980.

Mishra, Hari Ram, *The Theory of Rasa in Sanskrit Drama*, Chatarpur, India, Vindyachal Prakashan, 1964.

Murthy, Chaganti S., trans., *Śrī Lalitātriśatī Bhāṣya*, Madras, Ganesh and Co., 1973.

O'Flaherty, Wendy Doniger, *Women, Androgynes, and Other Mythical Beasts*, Chicago, University of Chicago Press, 1980.

Obeyesekere, G., *The Cult of the Goddess Pattini*, Chicago, University of Chicago Press, 1984.

Otto, R., *The Idea of the Holy*, New York, Oxford Press, 1958.

Pal, P., *The Hindu Religion and Iconology*, Los Angeles, Vichitra Press, 1981.

———, *Nepal/Where the Gods are Young*, New York, Asia Society, 1975.

Pandey, Kanti, *Abhinavagupta*, Varanasi, Chowkhamba Sanskrit Series, 1963.

Ramachandran, T.P., *The Indian Philosophy of Beauty*, Part 1&2, Madras, University of Madras, 1979.

Rao, Appa, *A Monograph on Bharata's Natya Śastra*, Hyderabad, India, Natya Mala Publishers, 1967.

Rao, S.K., *Tibetan Tantrik Tradition*, Delhi, Arnold Heinemann, 1977.

Renou, Louis, *Etudes sur le Vocabulaire du Ṛg Veda*, 1st Series, Pondicherry, Institut Francais d'Indologie, 1958.

Roerich, George, trans., *The Blue Annals*, Delhi, Motilal Banarsidass, 1979.

Sastry, R. Ananthakrishna, trans., *Lalitāsahasranāman with Bhāskarāya's Commentary*, Madras, Adyar Library, 1976 (rpt.).

———, trans., *Visnusahasranām with the Bhasya of Śrī Śankaracārya*, Madras, Adyar Library, 1980.

Shankaranarayanan, S., *The Ten Great Cosmic Powers*, Pondicherry, Dipti Publications, 1975.

Sharpa Tulku and Michael Perrott, *A Manual of Ritual Fire Offerings*, Dharamsala, Library of Tibetan Works and Archives, 1987.

Sinha, Jadunath, *Shakta Monism: The Cult of Shakti*, Calcutta, Sinha Publishing House, 1966.

Sircar, D.C., *The Śātka Pīṭhas*, Delhi, Motilal Banarsidass, 1981.

Slusser, M., *Nepal Mandala: A Cultural Study of the Kathmandu Valley*, Princeton, Princeton University Press, 1982.

Snellgrove, D., *Indo-Tibetan Buddhism*, London, Serindia Publications, 1987.

Suryanarayanamurthy, C., *Śrī Lalitā Sahasranāman*, Madras, Ganesh and Co., 1962.

Thite, Ganesh U., *Sacrifice in the Brahmana Texts*, Poona, University of Poona, 1975.

Tiwari, Jagdish, *Goddess Cults in Ancient India*, Delhi, Sundeep Prakashan, 1985.

Tsong-kha-pa, ed. and trans. by J. Hopkins, *Tantra in Tibet: The Great Exposition of Secret Mantra*, London, George Allen and Unwin, 1977.

———, *Yoga of Tibet*, London, George Allen and Unwin, 1981.

Vidyarnava, S.C., *The Daily Practice of the Hindus*, New Delhi, Oriental Books Reprint, 1979.

Wayman, Alex, *Buddhist Insight*, Delhi, Motilal Banarsidass, 1984.

———, *The Buddhist Tantras*, New York, Samuel Weiser, 1973.

Woodroffe, J., *Principles of Tantra*, Madras, Ganesh and Co., 1986.

Articles

Basu, A., "Diksa", *Studies in the History of Religions*, Vol.10, Leiden, E.J. Brill, 1965 : 81-86.

Benard, E., "The Living Among the Dead: A Comparison of Buddhist and Christian Relics", *Tibet Journal*, Vol.XIII, No. 3, Autumn 1988 : 33-48.

———, "Ma Chig Lab Dron", *Chos Yang*, No. 3, 1990 : 43-51.

Biardeau, Madeleine, "Narasimha, Mythe et Culte", *Purusartha*, Paris, 1975 : 31-48.

Charpentier, Jarl, "The Meaning and Etymology of Puja", *The Indian Antiquary*, Vol.65, May 1927 : 93-99 and July 1927 : 130-36.

Chemburkar, Jaya, "Sriradhikanamasahasram", *Annals of the Bhandankar Oriental Research Institute*, Poona, Vol.57, 1976 : 107-16.

Coomaraswamy, A.K., "Atmayajna: Self-Sacrifice", *Harvard Journal of Asiatic Studies*, Vol.6, 1941-42 : 358-98.

Eliade, M., "Cosmical Homology and Yoga", *Journal of the Indian Society of Oriental Art*, Vol. 5, 1937 : 188-203.

Hiltebeitel, Alf, "Draupadi's Hair", *Autour de la Deesse Hindoue, Purusartha*, no.5, Paris, 1981 : 179-214.

Mallmann, M.T., "Introduction a l'Iconographie du Tantrisme Bouddhique", *Bibliotheque des Centre Recerches sur l'Asie Centrale et la Haute Asie*, Vol.1, Paris, 1975.

Padoux, A., "On Mantras and Mantric Practices in the Agni Purana", *Purana*, Vol. 20, no.1, Jan. 1978 : 57-65.

Thurman, Robert, "Tsong-kha-pa's Intégration of Sutra and Tantra", Aziz and Kapstein, ed., *Soundings in Tibetan Civilization*, Delhi, Manohar Publications, 1985 : 372-82.

Trungpa, C., "Sacred Outlook: the Vajrayogini Shrine and Practice", Klimburg-Salter, D.E., *The Silk Route and the Diamond Path*, Los Angeles, UCLA Art Council, 1982 : 227-41.

Index

Note: In Tibetan words if one letter is capitalized look under that letter. For example, dGa 'rab rdo rje'—look under "G".